ANARCHISM & THE MEXICAN WORKING CLASS, 1860-1931

John M. Hart

ANARCHISM & THE MEXICAN WORKING CLASS, 1860-1931

University of Texas Press, Austin & London

The publication of this book was assisted by a grant from the Andrew W. Mellon Foundation.

Library of Congress Cataloging in Publication Data

Hart, John Mason, 1935–
    Anarchism and the Mexican working class,
1860–1931.
    Bibliography: p.
    Includes index.
    1. Anarchism and anarchists—Mexico—History.
2. Labor and laboring classes—Mexico—History.
I. Title.
HX851.H37   335'.83'0972   77-16210
ISBN 0-292-70331-7

"History has two sacred dimensions:
not to record falsely and not to fear the truth."
                              —Clavijero, 1754

"People! No more governments, down
with tyrannies, on to social guarantees!"
                    —Plotino C. Rhodakanaty, 1861

"We know more about the cave man
than we know about the origins of
socialism in Mexico."
                       —Luis Chávez Orozco, 1936

Contents

Preface

This is a historical study of the Mexican anarchist movement and its crucial impact upon the Mexican working class between 1860 and 1931. It is not a history of the Mexican working class per se. That task of synthesis awaits the completion of numerous monographs treating regional and topical aspects of Mexican working-class history.

This study explores anarchism as an important factor in the development of the Mexican urban working-class and agrarian movements. It does not contend that anarchism, at any time, was the only ideology present within the Mexican working-class movement or that it commanded the ideological allegiance of a majority of either the urban or the rural workers. In explaining the history and defeat of anarchism it does not attempt to deny other forms of socialism or Marxism their rightful places in working-class history. It does destroy some old myths, but the fact that the nineteenth-century leaders, Plotino Rhodakanaty, Santiago Villanueva, Francisco Zalacosta, and José María González; the twentieth-century revolutionary precursor, Ricardo Flores Magón; the Casa del Obrero founders, Amadeo Ferrés, Juan Francisco Moncaleano, and Rafael Quintero; and the majority of the Centro Sindicalista Libertario, leaders of the General Confederation of Workers, were anarchists who emphatically denied government does not detract from the richness of the socialist-Marxist tradition in Mexico.

The anarchist tradition is an extremely complex one. It involves various social classes, including intellectuals, artisans, and ordinary workers; changing social conditions; and political and revolutionary events which reshaped ideologies and thinking. During the nineteenth century the anarchists could be distinguished from their various working-class, socialist, and trade unionist counterparts by their singular opposition to government. In the early twentieth century the lines were even clearer because of hardening anarchosyndicalist, anarchist-communist, trade unionist, and Marxist doctrines. While acknowledging both my sympathy for libertarian ideals and my impatience with often self-defeating and otherwise unrealistic tactics and goals, I have made a sincere attempt to explain events and to achieve unattainable objectivity. It may not be possible, with all the emotion surrounding the topic, but I hope that this is a dispassionate assessment of the Mexican anarchists and their rightful place in Mexican working-class history.

I want to express my appreciation to the many colleagues and friends without whose help and advice this study would not have been possible. At the very inception of the project Dieter Koniecki of Mexico City selflessly made available extensive historical data obtainable only through private sources. Rudolph de Jong, Director of the International Institute of Social History in Amsterdam, went beyond the call of duty in receiving me and then helping in the quest for many important documents. Stanley Payne and Fred Bowser both lent early encouragement and the inspiration to continue. James Wilkie made important suggestions regarding the twentieth century and George T. Morgan, Thomas Howard, and Laurens B. Perry lent considerable editorial advice. Special gratitude is reserved for Ingeniero Ernesto Sánchez Paulín, who out of generosity and faith gave me six priceless photographs and access to thousands of crumbling rare anarchist newspapers dating from the early twentieth century. The University of North Dakota Faculty Research Committee assisted in the completion of this study with grants during the summers of 1971 and 1972. The University of Houston Faculty Research Committee provided a similar grant for the summer of 1974.

The editorial staff of *The Americas* was most cooperative in making available for publication in this volume material which originally appeared in the October 1972 and January 1974 issues of that fine journal. I owe a special thanks to the many Mexican scholars who have furthered the study of Mexico's working-class movements: among them are José Valadés, Luis Chávez Orozco, Manuel Díaz Ramírez, Rosendo Salazar, Luis Araiza, and Jacinto Huitrón. The pioneering work of Fernando Pérez Córdoba in his unpublished *licenciado* thesis provided countless leads. Finally, many thanks to Lisa for her manuscript assistance and to Mary for her unflagging support and patient forebearance.

John M. Hart

ANARCHISM &
THE MEXICAN
WORKING CLASS,
1860-1931

1. The Origins of Mexican Anarchism

European Influences

The Mexican anarchist, or libertarian socialist, movement, which took root and grew during the fifty years prior to the Mexican Revolution of 1910, emanated from Mexico's own unique developmental process and from European influences. Representing but one of several responses to a half century of profound industrial, social, and political change, anarchism as both a doctrine and a movement suffers from popular misunderstanding. Despite its consistent denial of state authority, the simplistic conception of anarchism as violent opposition to all forms of government and as unrestrained individualism is totally inadequate for understanding the role of this ideology in the turbulent history of Mexico's urban and rural working-class movements and for measuring its impact upon that nation's development. First developed in Europe, anarchist theory underwent substantial and often conflicting modifications prior to its importation into Mexico where further fragmentation of an already inconsistent body of thought occurred.

The precursors of anarchist ideology flourished during the eighteenth-century Enlightenment. The French *philosophes* in particular, by providing western society with an optimistic belief in progress—in the perfectibility of man and his social institutions—based upon human reason, created a climate of opinion conducive to the emergence of anarchist thought. Jean Jacques Rousseau, one of the Enlightenment's most creative thinkers, contributed additional impetus in the form of an examination of the relationship of man to society and the state. His observation that "man was born free and is everywhere in chains" became one of the fundamental tenets of the anarchist movement, which sought to break the chains by reorganizing the economy and the polity in order to eliminate the oppressive power of the state.

The initial stages of specific anarchist ideology—the "Holy Idea," as its more devoted adherents referred to it—can be traced to two fanatical proponents of individualism in the late eighteenth and early nineteenth centuries: Max Stirner (pseudonym used by Kaspar Schmidt) in Germany and William Godwin in England. Stirner envisioned a "union of egoists" composed of independent supermen untrammeled by legal fetters; Godwin, more importantly for the future course of anarchism, refined and developed Rousseau's contentions. Godwin traced the sources of human travail to bad government and inadequate institutions; he insisted that human reason, developed by means of education, could solve man's problems. Such refinement of man's comprehension would enable him to control his passions, seek equality and the simple life, and dispense with government. Later anarchists drew upon and refined these ideas of individualism and placed them within the social context of the Industrial Revolution.

Anarchism attracted its first sizable urban and rural working-class support in response to the concept of the mutualist association advanced by Pierre Joseph Proudhon, a product of the small-town culture and peasant agricultural economy of southern France. Proudhon carried the convictions and values of the French village artisan and farmer with him to Paris where he reacted against the severe conditions of working-class life in the industrializing cities of France. Many French intellectuals shared Proudhon's negative response to the growing cities. The appearance of his first critical essays protesting the emerging capitalist-industrial culture and proposing political-economic alternatives to the government-supported capitalist social order coincided with the formation of entire communities in the countryside by expatriate intellectuals who extolled the peasant way of life. In the world of fine arts the Barbizon school of painters became famous during this period for its idealized portrayals of healthy, hard-working, clean-living peasants in a "natural" human order. Many of these artists and their writer counterparts adopted peasant attire, married *campesina* women, and worked part-time in the fields sowing, ploughing, and harvesting. Later nineteenth-century writers, such as Tolstoy and Kropotkin, sought psychological relief in much the same manner. To many early nineteenth-century French intellectuals and artists the mode of living and seemingly equalitarian way of life in the peasant village and farm, unlike that of the city, placed man in the midst of nature and in concert with both his fellow man and his environment. The individualistic-communitarian values expressed by Proudhon and those who adopted and developed his ideology found enthusiastic pockets of support among the transplanted former peasants who formed the world's emergent nineteenth-century urban proletariat, and peasants in many parts of the world would agree with its principles. Emergent anarchism in the 1830's and 1840's was very much an intellectualization and defense of traditional countryside values and mores.

Proudhon applied the libertarian principles of Godwin and Rousseau to Fourier's earlier idea of regimented-authoritarian socialist utopian communities, or phalansteries. His modification of Fourier's theories resulted in a vision of an agricultural and small-shop industrial society based upon voluntary communes and workers' cooperatives bound together by contracts of exchange and mutual credit. Proudhon's system also provided for individual retention of the neces-

sary products of labor and for equitable distribution of all surpluses.
A people's bank would provide economic assistance and development.
Proudhon viewed associations as essential replacements of rule by the
capitalists, whose power grew daily. He in effect hoped to preserve the
values and perfect the way of life of the traditional society of preindustrial France. He opposed private property because it was the cor-
nerstone of French capitalism, and he deemed the state's support of
the new capitalistic organization of society the cause of increased governmental intervention in and regulation of individual lives. The individual, Proudhon insisted, represented the basic component of the
community, and social and political control belonged in the village or
working-class unit of society. But one did not challenge the intrusion
of government into the life of the individual by advocating political
reform alone. For Proudhon the ultimate defense of individual liberty
required that social and economic reform must precede political ad-
justments. Proudhon favored change without violence—a communism
which defended the sanctity of the community against the encroachments of capitalism and, by restricting large-scale capitalism or private property, removed the increasing threat of the state to individual
liberty. His communal solution initially attracted elements of the artisan and agrarian population of France with their long-standing heritage of mutual aid, but after the middle of the nineteenth century, as
the Industrial Revolution progressed, Proudhon's mutualism became
increasingly unrealistic in a vastly more complex European society.

During their earliest stages, nineteenth-century working-class ideas
for social change were moralistic in tone and utopian in character,
but, during the latter half of the century, these beliefs were elaborated
into relatively hard doctrines and carried to the "masses" by organizers. Mutualism, as an initial stage in the development of working-
class anarchism, became obsolete with the growth of industry and a
massive urban proletariat during the nineteenth century. Anarchism
was a by-product of the Industrial Revolution, and its development
paralleled that of the bourgeoisie and urban working class. The tensions wrought upon the working classes by the changing milieu of industrial society encouraged modifications in existing doctrines and
the formulation of new social and political conceptions.

Anarchism's appeal to the European working class increased significantly during the 1860's and 1870's as a result of the ideology and
activities of the movement's leading revolutionary of the time, Mikhail
Bakunin. A Russian revolutionary exile for most of his life, Bakunin
developed effective techniques for the spread of the anarchist movement and its theory throughout much of Europe. Unlike Proudhon,
Bakunin favored direct, violent, revolutionary action. His message was
best received in those societies where the working class suffered the
worst hardships, especially Spain and Italy. As the leader of the anti-

Marxist dissenters in the First International Workingmen's Association, Bakunin formed a counterorganization called the International Alliance for Social Democracy with branches in individual countries where he expected eventually to organize communes and cooperatives into federations on a regional basis. When sufficiently well organized, the regional organizations would develop and coordinate economic and trade activities through periodically convened congresses. As opponents of the nation-state the anarchists expected the regional bodies to affiliate in the common interest without regard to national boundaries because they believed economic, cultural, and natural barriers to be the decisive factors in sociopolitical reorganization. In anticipation of government repression Bakunin also encouraged the formation of secret, conspiratorial societies to disseminate political propaganda and carry on organizing efforts despite such opposition.

The most significant changes in economic focus between Proudhon and Bakunin are found in the sheer magnitude of working-class units as seen by the latter. As the Industrial Revolution progressed and its accompanying process of urbanization continued, the anarchist movement reacted to the changing needs of the times with Bakuninist collectivism. This form of anarchism paralleled Proudhon's; yet, important differences existed. Bakunin envisioned and accepted larger groups of workers than did Proudhon and sought self-sufficient cooperatives intended for production and consumption in both urban and rural sections. Actually, collectivism represented the beginnings of a separate communal socioeconomic existence within the still-capitalist economy. While this order, as a way of life in the traditional countryside, repelled the new bourgeoisie, it seemed even more threatening to them when Bakuninists began to organize the urban working class. In part, collectivism owed its success to the artisans who adopted it in the 1860's and 1870's as a defensive response to their declining status as the Industrial Revolution reached its most brutal and exploitative stage.

Bakunin and the collectivists made other important modifications of Proudhon's thought. They altered his concept of small-scale individual possession with the idea of ownership by the voluntary collective, a modification which enhanced anarchism's appeal to the broader spectrum of the working class. But the right of the individual to enjoy his own productivity, or its equivalent, still belonged to each worker. Thus, the collectivists maintained the dominant thread which runs through all varieties of anarchist thought—individual liberty. The major tactical shift between Proudhonism and Bakuninism lay in the adoption of revolutionary activism and the messianic propagation of anarchist doctrines wherever its disciples wandered.

Peter Kropotkin and his communist anarchists, who came to the fore during the last quarter of the nineteenth century, differed with the old teacher Bakunin and the collectivists on one major point. The Bakuninist system obligated the individual worker to perform a certain amount of work for which he received remuneration in direct proportion to his contribution of labor. Kropotkin and the communist anarchists regarded this stress on performance, rather than need, as a violation of the spirit of true cooperation and as another form of wage slavery. Kropotkin thus expressed a philosophical dimension of anarchism which found general acceptance within the movement and resulted in the rejection of the Bakuninist wage concept. He maintained that "love, sympathy and self-sacrifice" played an important part in the development of human morality, but solidarity—"the force of mutual aid"—provided the real basis for the success of human society. The well-being of the individual depended upon "a sense of justice" and equality for all—on this foundation humankind would progress.[1]

The communist anarchists took the position that a system of wages based upon the quantity and quality of production drew a distinction between inferior and superior labor and between what is mine and what is yours; in other words, it created a form of private property, and that, they felt, meant placing the rights of one individual above those of another. The communist anarchists therefore regarded this aspect of the collectivist system to be incompatible with the ideals of pure anarchism. The collectivist system also inferred the establishment of some form of authority within the collectives to measure individual performance and accordingly supervise the distribution of goods and services. Instead, Kropotkin proposed the principle of need in place of the wage system: "from each according to his means, to each according to his needs."[2]

An accomplished naturalist, Kropotkin stressed man as a social animal:

> . . . the vast majority of species live in societies, and they find in association the best arms for the struggle for life, understood . . . as a struggle against all natural conditions unfavorable to the species. The animal species, in which individual struggle has been reduced to its narrowest limits, and the practice of Mutual Aid has attained the greatest development, are invariably the most numerous, the most prosperous, and the most open to further progress. In man, the clan, tribe, village, guild, federation of villages, the city, are all examples of the need for association. The state, however, based on loose aggregations of individuals does not answer this need in individuals.[3]

Man prospered in free and voluntary cooperation with others. Contrary to T. H. Huxley and the contemporary Social Darwinists, Kropotkin held that spontaneous cooperation among animals, and therefore

man, was far more important for survival than fierce competition.[4]
This generalized type of argument, typical of the nineteenth-century
intellect, provided the anarchists with an essential refutation of the
Social Darwinist elitist ideological onslaught. It also supplied anarchists with badly needed scientific-intellectual support for their optimistic view of human nature and their belief in the need for a future
collectivist society.

Equally important, Kropotkin gave anarchism a theory of history.
He identified human and technological progress with the practices of
mutual aid and association:

> The Greek City and the Medieval City gave man freedom. . . .
> They were a combination of Mutual Aid as it was practiced with-
> in the guild or the Greek clan with a large initiative left to the
> individual.[5]

> . . . Consider the astounding rapidity of progress from the
> twelfth to fifteenth centuries in weaving, working of metals, ar-
> chitecture, and navigation; and the scientific progress of the
> fifteenth century. . . .
> For industrial progress, as for any other conquest of nature,
> mutual aid and close intercourse are . . . much more advanta-
> geous than mutual struggle.[6]

He also anticipated the impact of anarchist revolutionary ideology
in economically distressed and culturally traditional societies. He
agreed with Bakunin that the anarchists would find "their supporters
among the humble, in the lowest, downtrodden layers of society,
where the mutual aid principle is the necessary foundation of every-
day life."[7]

Libertarian socialism reached its most mature industrial form with
anarchosyndicalism, which appeared in Europe during the last years
of the nineteenth century. This phase of development reflected a still
further reaction by the anarchist movement to an increasingly urban
and industrialized society. Anarchosyndicalists organized tremendous
numbers of factory workers into syndicates which advocated commun-
alized worker ownership of the factories based upon the principles developed by their mutualist, collectivist, and communist anarchist predecessors. The weapons used in the struggle for social revolution by
this new form of anarchist organization included the general strike,
the boycott, and sabotage. Because of its viable base of support and
wide range of effective tactics, anarchosyndicalism attracted many of
the diverse factions within the anarchist movement and synthesized
them. Even Tolstoyist pacifists found its relatively nonviolent charac-
teristics compatible with their own beliefs.[8] Anarchosyndicalism pri-

marily voiced a libertarian socialist response to the modern urban industrial complex, but it did not fail to consider the rural population.

Anarchosyndicalism, through its avant-garde twentieth-century Spanish ideologues, provided the most comprehensive description of the anarchist society yet seen:

> There is only one regime that can give the workers liberty, well-being and happiness: it is Libertarian Communism.
>
> Libertarian Communism is the organization of society without a State and without private property.
>
> It is unnecessary to invent anything or to create any new social organization to achieve it.
>
> The centers of organization around which the economic life of tomorrow will be coordinated exist in present-day society: they are the syndicate and the free municipality.
>
> Workers in factories and other enterprises . . . group together spontaneously in the syndicates.
>
> With the same spontaneity the inhabitants of the same locality join together in the municipality, an assembly known from the origins of mankind. In the municipality they have an open road to the solution, on a local basis, of all the problems of communal living.
>
> These two organizations, federative and democratic, will have sovereignty over their own decisions, without being subjected to the tutelage of any higher organs.
>
> Nonetheless they will be led to confederate for the purpose of common economic activities and, by forming federations of industry, to set up organs of liaison and communication.
>
> In this way the syndicate and the municipality will take collective possession of everything that now belongs to the sphere of private property; they will regulate . . . economic life in every locality, although they will have men in charge of their own actions: that is to say, liberty.
>
> Libertarian Communism thus makes compatible the satisfaction of economic necessities and respect for our aspirations to liberty.
>
> Because of the love of liberty the libertarians repudiate the communism of the convent, the barracks, the ant hill or the herd as in Russia.
>
> Under Libertarian Communism, egoism is unknown; it is replaced by the broadest social love.[9]

While many variations of anarchist thought existed, they shared one important characteristic: a unique anti-intellectualism. Starkly visible in the written work of Bakunin and the Polish ideologue Jan

Waclaw Machajski, as well as in the essays of Mexican José María González, anarchist anti-intellectualism stemmed logically from the general antiauthority, antielitist position taken by the libertarian socialists. This strident anti-intellectualism often manifested hostility toward university degrees and professional licensing. Within the socialist movement, the anarchists feared that the government envisaged by orthodox socialists would result in the ascendancy of a new bureaucratic elite composed of former déclassé Marxist and university-educated intelligentsia. Thus, the anarchists' concern for a self-governing classless society, their contempt for the upper strata of society which they considered utterly corrupt, and their rivalry with Marxist groups (generally led by intellectuals) combined into a strong and persistent antagonism toward intellectual elites.

The most important consequence of anarchist anti-intellectualism lay in its special appeal to the working class in those countries where laborers found themselves most frustrated by the parliamentarianism of social democracy at the end of the nineteenth century. The workers expressed special disgust with the intellectual and nonworker leadership of social democracy, which seemed to compromise every important issue. As a result, anarchosyndicalism prospered in the societies of Spain, Portugal, Italy, and France.[10] But Latin America also suffered the same ills; and Spain's former colony, Mexico, experienced a powerful and sustained history of anarchist activity.

Another, and fatal, consequence of anarchist thought in which anti-elite intellectualism played an important role stemmed from the anarchists' failure to create a viable means to provide for the security of their society during the revolutionary period of change from capitalism to the anarchist utopia. It is true that anarchists saw the early communes, based upon the traditional peasant community and later urban labor syndicates, as the basis for this transition, but they failed to agree upon a durable thesis both in Europe and in Mexico as to how the commune or syndicate would survive the critical period of violence associated with the revolution. Anarchists unrealistically chose to rely upon workers' militia and village defense units, both of which repeatedly demonstrated an inability to conduct campaigns successfully against disciplined and coordinated armies, because they could not accept any suggestion which advanced the idea of an army organized in the usual elitist-authoritarian manner.

The militias, while not leaving the communes and syndicates completely defenseless, could not sustain military discipline, logistics, or, as a result, a successful offense. As a result, after each defeat the counter-revolutionary forces had time to withdraw, reorganize, and strike again until they achieved success. This unresolved dilemma plagued the agrarian-peasant insurrectionists of nineteenth-century Mexico, the Makhno-led peasants of the Russian Revolution, the southern *campesinos* during the Mexican Revolution, and the anarchist militias in old Aragón and Catalonia during the Spanish Civil War.[11]

The historical patterns of Mexican anarchism in working-class history roughly paralleled the evolution of the movement in Europe and reflected a synthesis of the impact of social change in Mexico and the continuing intrusion of European anarchists, especially Spaniards, and their ideas.

The European and Mexican urban and rural working classes had a long history of preideological preindustrial protest. The historical urban crowds of Paris and the Mexico City *tumultos* of 1624 and 1692 exhibited a single-minded desire on the part of the lower classes to redress a particular set of grievances. These early manifestations of working-class unrest became quite serious at times and toppled governments, not just in Paris during the French Revolution, and in Barcelona, Spain, but in Mexico City during the Mexican Viceroyalty as well. The progressive development of the Industrial Revolution and the introduction of nineteenth-century revolutionary ideologies, such as anarchism and communism, channeled deepening urban working-class grievances and hostility into the formation of organized workers' groups. As the nineteenth century wore on, the social problems of the urban working class intensified and resulted in anarcho- and revolutionary syndicalism. The modern early twentieth-century industrial workers' syndicates of Mexico City flowed not only from contemporary conditions and events but also from long-standing social patterns.

The Mexican peasantry, like the European, had long contested, by both passive and violent means, political interference and economic control of the locality by outsiders. In the past such resistance meant "peasant wars," such as those of sixteenth-century Germany and Mexico's indigenous uprisings against the Aztec and Spanish empires. In Mexico a long-standing tradition of social banditry preceded the modern leader of violent peasant resistance, the agrarian revolutionary. The social bandit of Río Frío, Chihuahua, or eastern Morelos personified elements of peasant culture and reinforced the village economy by expropriating wealth from outsiders and expending it in the peasant community. He represented the most persistent violent form of peasant resistance to the hegemony of the European-oriented urban cultural-economic complex over the indigenous hinterlands. The symbiotic economic relationship between bandit and village and his consistent adherence to *campesino* values were essential for the continuance of his local support and, thus, to his survival. The long-standing socioeconomic grievances of the peasantry were consistently manifested in social banditry. The introduction and adoption of nineteenth-century revolutionary ideologies into the Mexican countryside provided agrarian resistance with a rationale and transformed bandits into revolutionaries. The social bandit was the preideological precursor of the Mexican agrarian revolutionary. Anarchism, a doctrine consistent with peasant values, helped to transform Mexican *campesino* resistance into militant Mexican agrarianism.

Domestic Influences

The Mexican Industrial Revolution transformed traditional socioeconomic patterns and intensified social stresses which developed during the three centuries when Mexico existed as a colony of Spain and which persisted after independence. During the late formative colonial period, a conservative elite composed of the Church, the military, the great landowners, and Spanish merchants and government officers dominated Mexican society. Leaderless and seemingly without hope at the time of the independence struggle in 1810, the poverty-ridden *campesinos* of the countryside, many of whom lived in communal villages, and the lower working classes of the cities joined the armies led by the first leader of the Mexican independence movement, Miguel Hidalgo. Confronted by an incipient popular social revolution, the conservative Mexican-born Creole elite, seeking to maintain its favored position within the colonial social order, sided with the Spaniards until the threat from below subsided. When the Creoles finally supported independence from Spain, they sought to create a sovereign nation under their leadership. The antagonistic positions taken during the independence struggle by revolutionary *campesinos* and conservative Creoles anticipated the pattern of rivalries that would plague Mexico until the revolution of 1910.

The chaos of the decade-long struggle for independence left Mexico with political instability, fiscal bankruptcy, economic stagnation, dire poverty, and social antagonisms—conditions that the nation could not quickly overcome. The revolution achieved national independence, but it did not dislodge the dominant conservative elite of colonial Mexico. The conservatives' power remained intact, and, against all opposition, they tenaciously defended the sources of that power: the traditional, corporatelike Spanish institutions inherited from the past. For sixty-five years after the beginning of the independence struggle, the nation suffered from political instability, widespread corruption in government, economic decline, and miserable living conditions for the lower classes in the cities and the countryside.

But nineteenth-century Mexico underwent dramatic and sudden changes. After three centuries of relative order and stability under Spanish governance, the liberalism of the Enlightenment and the heresies of the *philosophes* reached Mexico. Also, an indigenous liberal movement led by lawyers and other professionals whose main economic tenets echoed the laissez-faire economics and free trade of Adam Smith exacerbated growing social tensions. Had the conservatives confronted only these developments, they might have survived; but the added threat posed to them by the beginnings of the Industrial Revolution in Mexico hopelessly undermined their position. Soon, a new class of factory owners, *nuevos ricos*, flaunted their vastly increased wealth in Mexico City and demanded concomitant political power. With the development of the factory system during the period following independence, this new urban-based group slowly increased in both numbers and economic strength. Allying with the conservative elite, they provided further reason for their rising antagonists, the urban working class, along with the increasingly large middle and professional strata of urban society, to increasingly identify with liberalism. As the latter two groups' power and influence grew and the needs of the growing urban areas became increasingly apparent, the unresponsive government of the old, weakening conservative alliance became more and more obsolete. The result was a challenge the traditional elite could not forestall.

Even before the prominence of new industry the liberals viewed the old system as an anachronism which desperately needed modernization. The leading liberal spokesman of the 1830's, José María Luis Mora, frequently noted the exorbitant expenditures in the national budget for an incompetent army which kept the nation in constant bankruptcy. Mora, like the other liberals, saw the costs of the military and the large tax-free and relatively unproductive landholdings of the Church held in perpetuity through mortmain as the major economic problems confronting Mexico. Mora and his colleagues also resented the *hacendado*'s ability to escape taxation, and they opposed the government's policy of low tariffs which facilitated the acquisition of European-produced consumer gooods for the upper-class conservatives and at the same time discouraged the development of national industry. When the liberals took power by force of arms in 1854, they inaugurated a reform program, known appropriately enough as La Reforma, which attacked the traditional privileges of the Church, the landed oligarchy without threatening its holdings, and the military. The liberals in their flaming rhetoric promised liberty, justice, and hope for all; and they opened the door to new forces for change.

A program to bring the army, Church, and nation under one set of laws held first place on the liberal agenda of reform. The Ley Juárez, which became law in November 1855, overhauled the judicial system by restricting the special courts and privileges enjoyed by the military and clergy and subordinated them to the secular, civil authority. But the Ley Lerdo of June 1856 had even more far reaching consequences. It ordered the Church and all other corporate bodies to divest themselves of their landholdings. The law's definition of corporate bodies included the traditional rural village governments, or *munici-pios*, whose communal holdings must now be divided. Some liberals failed to foresee the consequences of this provision. While the majority anticipated a transfer of agricultural holdings into nonindig-enous and therefore more productive lands, an idealistic minority hoped that individuals in the local *municipios* would maintain possession of the affected communal lands; but those who anticipated such retention expressed incredible naïvete, because sufficient wealth and strength never existed in the majority of the *comunidades* to contest large-estate claimants without state protection. As a result, during the last half of the nineteenth century persons other than villagers obtained the great majority of tracts.

Typical of nineteenth-century liberals, the Reforma government sought to encourage private enterprise and small, private agricultural holdings. Despite delays in the Ley Lerdo's fulfillment, brought on by chaotic civil wars, the Reforma and, especially, the succeeding governments of Presidents Sebastián Lerdo de Tejada and Porfirio Díaz saw this process of village land seizures carried out to an extreme. Thus, communal holdings that had survived the Aztec Empire, the Spanish conquest, the entire Spanish colonial period, and the early years of independence fell sacrifice to the demands of agricultural impresarios espousing liberal economic theory based upon the doctrine of laissez faire. The battles for national political power between 1854 and 1867 basically constituted a confrontation between the old conservative oligarchy—the military, clergy, mercantile elite, and some of the great landowners—and the liberals of the Mora tradition and their urban supporters, including the professional and artisan classes. In spite of the seeming victory by the liberals, the losers did not forfeit all. The clergy lost much of its economic and political preeminence, but the military and *hacendados* survived the Reforma and throughout the rest of the century possessed much of the same power and prestige in society that they previously had enjoyed.

The defeat of the old guard did, however ironically, open up the society for the *nuevo rico*, or urban bourgeoisie. During the brief tenure of the French-dominated empire administered by Maximilian, liberals and conservatives shared a favorable impression of European methods and industry. When the liberals returned to power in 1867 they pursued economic developmentalism with increasing fervor and encouraged the formerly conservative urban industrialists and monied elements, as well as foreign capitalists, to invest in and develop key sectors of the economy. Enjoying the advantages of newly won political power concomitant with its wealth, this group of entrepreneurs purchased a considerable portion of the agricultural property made available by the Ley Lerdo. This process ultimately resulted in the partial economic consolidation of some of the new urban industrialists, the traditional great landholders, and the politically dominant liberals into a reconstituted elite amalgam which ruled Mexico until the revolution of 1910. During the reign of Porfirio Díaz this new landed elite was known as the younger Creoles. Despite differences between 1876 and 1910, these two groups, urban and rural, entered into a period of relatively harmonious co-existence known as the *paz porfiriana*. Characterized as an equilibrium of urban capital and rural *hacendado* interests, the *paz* also meant suppression of political dissidents.

The legalized seizure of rural lands that began in the 1850's and continued until 1910 contributed greatly to the intensification of a series of agrarian uprisings that began in the 1850's and did not terminate until the death of Emiliano Zapata in 1919. During this period anarchist theory, carried to the countryside by libertarian socialist organizers from Mexico City, came to play an important part in the developing struggle.

During the forty-five years that preceded the Mexican Revolution the anarchists, who were the first urban *agraristas*, helped to contribute a body of doctrine to the previously poorly understood Mexican agrarian movement. In this way they hoped to change the nature of Mexican agrarianism from profound but relatively inarticulate uprisings into a movement reinforced by a coherent peasant view of the world to come. Resistance provoked by oppression and the lack of basic necessities articulated a program designed to preserve traditional patterns of peasant life. The anarchist *agraristas* specifically demanded local autonomy from centralized government; seizure and redistribution of agricultural properties by the *municipios libres*, or free village governments; and an end to the political corruption of national and local government officials. Their success in becoming a part of the Mexican agrarian movement stemmed from the compatibility of their program with the values, traditions, and aspirations of the sedentary-indigenous people. This agrarian heritage consisted of individual identification with the local village; a sense of egalitarianism; an abiding distrust of outsiders, such as absentee landlords, labor recruiters, tax collectors, military conscriptors, and government officials; and a persistent suspicion of politics in general. The *campesino* population had long struggled to preserve a peasant order that included village control of the land and self-government. A long record of *campesino* insurrections in support of these aspirations, aided by anarchist and other radical ideologies after the 1860's, challenged the very existence of the prevailing political and economic system and led to the agrarian upheaval of 1910.

At the same time that the agrarian movement acquired ideological dimensions, the Mexican urban labor movement evolved during the late 1860's through the revolutionary period of 1910–1917 from mutualism to cooperativism to revolutionary anarchosyndicalism. Mexican working-class organizations, influenced by forceful and militant anarchist organizers, stressed deplorable working conditions in the factories, decried miserable living conditions in the cities, and aspired to a better life. Thus, the anarchists facilitated labor's view of what the ideal society should be and in what manner the working class should organize in order to achieve it.

The rise of the bourgeoisie and the factory system of commodity production in the second half of the nineteenth century spawned an unprecedented number of urban workers. This new proletariat consisted of former farm workers who migrated to the city in search of the opportunities and social mobility that its expanding economy seemed to offer. They failed, however, to realize their hopes; new forms of futility confronted them in the seamy, unsalubrious *vecindades*—slums devoid of such basic services as adequate streets, lighting, water, transportation, sanitation, and health facilities.[12] Such oppressive urban social conditions contributed to the rapid spread of revolutionary ideas and organizations.

The working hours for those fortunate enough to find full-time employment—men, women, and children—ranged from twelve to eighteen hours per day. Impossible working conditions and subsistence wages added to discontent. An open letter of protest written by the participants in one of Mexico's first large urban labor strikes vividly portrayed the situation:

> . . . there are workers who receive a weekly salary of sixteen cents, and this cannot be denied. The work day extends from 5:15 A.M. to 6:45 P.M. in the summer . . . in the winter from 6:00 A.M. to 6:00 P.M., . . . the foremen only concede five minutes daily to the workers in order for them to eat.
>
> The conditions within the factories in Puebla are not much better; working men receive a salary of 2½ to 3½ reales daily, while working women receive from ½ to 1½ reales. The work day spans eighteen hours with two fifteen-minute lunch breaks.[13]

During the fifty years before the revolution, the *vecindades* and factories increasingly became seedbeds of revolutionary ideas broadcast by ideologues and organizers expounding the European doctrines of Fourier, Proudhon, Bakunin, Kropotkin, and, to a lesser extent, Marx. The Mexican anarchists, a distinct group of social revolutionaries, are often incorrectly discussed in the context of subsequent Marxian socialism.[14] Although they called themselves "socialist," their anarchist ideology distinguished them from the post-Russian revolutionary Marxist movement. The "socialism" that they adhered to at first was the Proudhonist-Bakuninist version, exported first to Spain and then to Latin America. Later, in the early twentieth century, they adopted the communist anarchism of Peter Kropotkin and eventually espoused anarchosyndicalism. In Mexico and Latin America, anarchism far exceeded Marxism in importance until after the success of the Russian Revolution.

The organizers of the nineteenth- and early twentieth-century Mexican labor and socialist movements were sometimes students, common laborers, or intellectuals but usually artisans. Students who became involved in labor-organizing activities also had artisan backgrounds. The artisan class, with its tradition of the Spanish guild and the protected marketplace, traced its ancestry to the Roman conquest of Iberia. In Mexico, these handicraftsmen prospered until factories began to produce shoes, clothing, and bread. Unable to compete, they often descended to the status of factory workers, victims of progress. But they continued to be literate carriers of the Spanish guild tradition with its emphasis on mutual aid and fierce individualism. Apparently, a great majority of both the artisans and the urban labor force, in the name of progress and needed change, initially supported the liberals' program. But the guild tradition of the artisans and the communal heritage of the *campesinos* were ill-suited to prepare this new urban working class for the situation which confronted it in the slums. Because Mexico's prevailing social, economic, and political conditions could not meet their expectations, an eventual clash between the urban workers and the urban industrialists supported by the government was probably unavoidable. During the resultant conflict, a considerable portion of the Mexican working-class movement, led by the artisans, developed an anarchist ideological stance.

The nineteenth-century Mexican urban labor movement maintained direct contact with the Jura branch of the divided, European-based First International Workingmen's Association and at one stage openly affiliated with it. During the late 1890's and the first decade of the twentieth century, new anarchist leadership emerged which once again led working-class opposition to the *ancien régime*, helped to foment the labor strikes which immediately preceded the revolution, and organized urban labor during the seven years of revolutionary tumult. The anarchists' record in organizing urban labor and in supporting agrarian reform unquestionably establishes them as precursors of the Mexican Revolution of 1910. During the revolution, aided once again by European influences, anarchism in the form of an internationally affiliated anarchosyndicalist union, the Casa del Obrero Mundial, made its appearance in Mexico. It played a significant role in the outcome of that struggle.

Anarchist sentiment received added impetus in the closing decades of the nineteenth century as a result of the considerable influx of Spanish immigrants into Mexico. Between 1887 and 1900 the number of Spaniards living there with émigré status increased from 9,553 to

16,258.[15] Spain at that time had the largest anarchist movement in the world, and some of these utopian revolutionaries naturally fled to Mexico. In the first years of the twentieth century the Spanish government's policy of coercively exiling them ensured their flight and the Barcelona anarchists' wish to organize Spanish America, including the Mexican working class, assured Mexico as one of their choices for exile.

2. The Proselytizer

Plotino Rhodakanaty, immigrant, scholar, crusader, and political activist, the first advocate of anarchist doctrine and founder of the first anarchist working-class organizing group in Mexico, wielded a profound influence on the emerging urban working-class and agrarian movements of the 1860's, 1870's, and 1880's. Born in Athens, Greece, on October 14, 1828, he was taken by his Austrian mother to Vienna shortly after the death of his father, a member of Greek nobility, during the Greek war of independence against the Turks. His mother encouraged him in the study of medicine, but like so many of his liberal-minded, university student contemporaries he became a supporter of Hungarian independence and traveled to Budapest in order to take part in the abortive 1848 uprising. Later that year a somewhat disillusioned Rhodakanaty moved with his family to Berlin, where he once again took up his study of medicine. While living in Berlin he developed a great interest in political philosophy and became an admirer, first, of Hegel and, then, of Fourier and Proudhon.

In 1850 Rhodakanaty made a special trip to Paris in order to meet Proudhon after having been inspired by the latter's book *What Is Property?* Within a few years his family began to experience financial difficulties, and his medical studies started to lag. When his family returned to Vienna in 1857, the discouraged young medical student decided to move to Paris in order to study political philosophy. While there he also found time to study languages and write his first philosophical essay, *De la Naturaleza*, published in Paris in 1860.[1]

While Rhodakanaty lived in Paris he met, among his young socialist friends, a Mexican national who told him about the land decrees passed by the Mexican government, President Ignacio Comonfort's pronouncements on land reform, and his invitation to foreigners to immigrate to Mexico and attempt new independent agricultural colonies. This news enthused Rhodakanaty and he decided that he should go to Mexico in order to ensure that the new agricultural communities would be organized and developed into communes based upon utopian socialist concepts.

Just as Rhodakanaty prepared to depart for Mexico, word arrived announcing the fall of the Comonfort government and the beginning of the turbulent Wars of the Reforma. As a result, he decided to live in Spain in order to develop his ability with the Spanish language. He went to Barcelona, waiting for the violence to subside; when the news of victory for the Juárez government arrived in early 1861, he left

Spain and sailed for Mexico. He arrived in Veracruz late in February, only to discover that the agrarian colonies planned by Comonfort had been long since forgotten. Undaunted, Rhodakanaty observed that the Mexican *campesinos* in their traditional peasant villages already implemented the basic ideals espoused by Fourier and Proudhon, but in his view they continued to be oppressed by the encroachments of *hacendados* and the insensitivity of an unsympathetic government. He decided to organize the *campesinos* and build a system of socialist agrarian colonies on his own initiative.[2]

In an initial attempt to gain adherents, Rhodakanaty published a pamphlet entitled *Cartilla socialista* which explained the principles of a utopian agricultural community along the lines of Fourier. In the pamphlet, Rhodakanaty sought to convince the reader of the desirability of socialism through argumentative rhetoric:

> What is the highest and most reasonable purpose to which the human mind can be dedicated? The achievement of universal brotherhood, between both individuals and peoples, in order to reach mankind's terrestrial destiny. What is the present actual state of mankind? Man is dividing the land everywhere in the interests of industry, classes, parties, nationalities, etc. This situation creates among men, to the detriment of each and every one, hostilities and hate, more or less violent, in place of the harmony that ought to unite them for their common happiness and for the fulfillment of their common destiny. Because of this situation in spite of the marvelous progress made by humanity in the last three centuries, especially in the nations of Europe, humanity is still universally under evil rule.[3]

Rhodakanaty shared the common Proudhonian socialist view of man's inherent goodness, but he believed that private property, the unequal distribution of wealth, and the exploitative nature of the prevailing societal order created moral perversions, corrupted government, and set one man against another.[4] At the time both Marxists and, especially, anarchists so strongly held this view that many assumed that after the success of the revolution jails would no longer be necessary.

Following his failure to recruit the number of adherents sufficient to attempt an agricultural colony, Rhodakanaty tried to obtain a teaching position in the Colegio de San Ildefonso in Mexico City. Unable to gain acceptance by the *colegio*, he instead accepted a post with a local preparatory school. During his tenure as an instructor at the preparatory school he influenced several students who became adherents to "libertarian socialism," and in 1863 they formed a study group which by 1865 called itself El Grupo de Estudiantes Socialistas. The members considered their new organization the Mexican branch of

Bakuninism. The group included the future leaders of Mexican socialism: Francisco Zalacosta, a young zealot who took the lead in future
agrarian struggles; Santiago Villanueva, the organizer of Mexico's
original urban labor movement; and Hermengildo Villavicencio, who
worked with Villanueva in the 1860's but died before the major events
of the 1870's and 1880's took place.[5] They all became artisans after
leaving school and began their organizing activities among Mexico
City's handicraftsmen, who expressed increasing disgruntlement with
the growing factory system of commodity production. The factories
had rendered the artisans economically vulnerable and their traditional guild system of mutual protection impotent. Also, the Mexican
guild heritage, an offshoot of the Spanish and European guild system
that had so profoundly influenced Proudhon, contributed to the Mexico City artisans' ready acceptance of Proudhonian mutualist doctrines.

The students, in one of the first projects they undertook, revived
the defunct Mexican mutualist organization La Sociedad Particular de
Socorros Mutuos, originally formed in 1853 by artisans in the hat-
making industry.[6] Of course the new Sociedad de Socorros Mutuos did
not share the ideological position of its identically named predecessor,
because in 1853 socialist ideology was not yet well received in Mexico.

In 1864, while teaching at the preparatory school, Rhodakanaty
published a pamphlet entitled *Neopanteísmo*.[7] The essay became a
focal point of discussion among the students, and other essays soon
followed which commented on its more provocative points in detail.
Like *Cartilla socialista* it helped to consolidate a loyal group of followers for him.[8] Rhodakanaty's ideas established a basis for the philosophic development of Mexican anarchism. He cherished the idea of
the utopian village phalansteries originated by Fourier, and, like
Proudhon, he adapted it to the idea of mutualist societies and cooperatives coupled with a rejection of the state. He wanted a federalized
political structure, denounced most political activity, and rejected the
dictatorship of the proletariat. His essays followed the pattern of
pseudoscientific jargon typical of nineteenth-century thinkers. Like
Comte, Marx, and Spencer, he sought universal laws. Like Comte and
Spencer, he idealistically wanted to find the "true nature of man." In
his view the "true nature of man" demanded the libertarian socialist
way of life that is now known as anarchism. He wanted to eliminate
the role of the state in domestic economic affairs, reorganize private
property into cooperatives, and abolish politics and political parties.[9]
These steps would lead to a higher social order:

> . . . [I]n the beginning there will be the equitable distribution of
> industrial production and wealth. Then this practice will be
> spread very quickly by the efforts of brothers united by their com-

mon interests. Following this we will march on the social road
which is natural.[10]

He elaborated as follows:

The formula of socialism today is that of the French Revolution
in 1793—liberty, equality, and fraternity, to which we add unity.
Liberty means the development of all professions or crafts, and
of all individual talents without restraint. Liberty means the right
to practice all professions without acquiring formal titles and
licenses or permitting their monopoly by the universities. *Liberty
means* the emancipation and rehabilitation of the woman and
individual freedom from all restrictions.

Equality means equal rights before the law, the equality of
social positions within each nation, equal distribution of wealth,
and equality of conscience before the universal moral order represented by humanity. This is the axiom of common law. Fraternity means solidarity achieved by means of love and philanthropy
between all members of the great human family. No more discord, no more hatred between political parties, no more religious
crusades or persecutions like those we have seen carried out by
groups that claim a place in Heaven, but have represented here
on Earth only ignominy for all of humanity.

Unity is the convergence of all individual interests with those
of the general well being. Unity is the joining together for all
time, by means of the association, of the talents of both labor and
capital.[11]

In his call for man's freedom from all restrictions, Rhodakanaty expressed the most extreme libertarian views of his time. Ironically, one
can also see the seeds of anarchist anti-intellectualism bearing fruit,
even in the work of intellectually oriented Rhodakanaty. His opposition to university control of the professions, formal degrees, and
licensing typified the reactions of a group of men struggling against
what they saw as the restrictive institutions of capitalist society. As
the struggle intensified, the resentment toward intellectuals and the
institutions they represented grew accordingly.[12] Consistent with
Rhodakanaty's argument for liberty in the professions, the anarchist
writers in *El Hijo del Trabajo* defended a quack medicine man named
Julián González against frequent attacks by outsiders for many years.
González advertised his miracle cures in almost every issue of the
newspaper.[13]

Rhodakanaty, consistent with European anarchist ideologues, called
for the dissolution of all national boundaries and a universal brotherhood of man. "The accumulation of enormous amounts of capital will
be necessary and then, as the movement spreads, all the nations on
Earth will unite based upon the spirit of cooperativism, and egoism

will be converted into respect for the common interest."[14] The anarchist organization La Social, created out of the Grupo de Estudiantes Socialistas in 1865 and led by Rhodakanaty, intended to be the vehicle through which these goals would be achieved in Mexico: "La Social has as its program, as we do, world union. It does not recognize nationality. Its three symbols are liberty, equality, and fraternity—the Holy Idea."[15]

Rhodakanaty viewed the political chaos, economic stagnation, and dire poverty in Mexican society as justification for his belief, and Proudhon's, in the failure of government and democracy as formal organized institutions.

> . . . [President] Lerdo lives in fear of that fate which has stalked his predecessors—the revolution. Regardless of their power none of the governments thus far has been able to alleviate the misery and misfortunes of the poor. . . . From this we are able to logically deduce that none of the legally or illegally constituted governments throughout the complete history of Mexico has yet been able to remedy a single problem that has troubled the people. It it because government by its very nature lacks the necessary characteristics essential to produce the desired results. . . . [I]n effect democracy is impotent for creating happiness for the people because of the nature of its organization and the manner of its being.[16]

Seeing the despair among Mexican artisans, urban workers, and *campesinos*, Rhodakanaty observed that democracy will fail "if it is not fertilized by that holy and beloved doctrine, socialism, which emanates from the highest and most exalted principles of philosophy, which assure to the individual human being his sustenance and future by means of the eternal law of labor under whose realm are subject all the beings of nature."[17]

The above reference to the "eternal law of labor" brings under consideration Rhodakanaty's version of the serial mechanism in history first expressed by Fourier and later revised and expanded by Proudhon partly as a response to the Marxian dialectic. Within the serial process of historical change, all beings and modes of behavior are subject to "eternal laws" of development. For example, Proudhon traced the, according to him, "immortal series" of human liberty as a historical process within society as follows: liberty of persons, liberty of work, liberty of conscience, liberty of examination, liberty of voting. The individual, for Proudhon, represented the basic unit, but the evolving society provided the serial order within which each man's personality found function and fulfillment. The individual was an integral unit of society. Just as the internal organ operated as a component of the human body, the individual functioned as an integral part of society.[18]

But regularity went beyond mere individuals and society, he believed, in the existence of universal laws which regulated all celestial bodies and living things in the cosmos. Proudhon's "eternal laws," once discovered and put into practice, according to Rhodakanaty, would emancipate all of humanity because the problems inherent in the search for an equalitarian and just society could then be anticipated and dealt with.[19]

Given the humanist and optimistic confidence held by nineteenth-century socialists in the ability of mankind to ultimately solve its problems, theoretical views like those held by Rhodakanaty were commonly used to justify socialism. However, when taken in a literal sense, especially by conservative Mexican religious writers, who had never read Proudhon or Fourier and who had never heard of the serial principle or Marxian dialectic and who, for traditional reasons, could not accept Comte or Spencer either, Rhodakanaty appeared deranged.[20]

Unlike some of his more sanguinary disciples, such as Zalacosta, Rhodakanaty feared the violence and turmoil of a revolution. Always the thinker and idealist rather than the man of action, he favored the peaceful transition of capitalism into a society based upon the Proudhonist-Bakuninist idea of voluntary organizations grouped into loosely knit federations. These associations would abolish the system of political parties, the wage system, and the varied degrees of wealth within capitalist society and replace them with social and economic equality, free credit, mutual aid, and philanthropy. Rhodakanaty envisioned a new human order evolving which would enjoy the industrial productivity of the old but replace exploitation and misery with brotherly love and cooperation.[21] Consistent with this new order, Rhodakanaty on several occasions expressed his concern for brotherly love and cooperation by calling for the emancipation of women. He carried through on this aspect of thought by recruiting several female members into La Social. These women later served as the first female delegates accepted to the Mexican National Labor Congress.[22] In fact one of them, Carmen Huerta, played a prominent role in the leadership of both organizations.

Rhodakanaty always felt that the individual living within the socialist milieu would do his share without coercion. Therefore, the criteria for the distribution of production would be based upon need rather than the amount of contributed labor. This, of course, preceded the position taken later by Kropotkin.[23] Rhodakanaty believed that, once the system of capitalist political power and exploitation of the individual ended, the worker would contribute to the collective good of his own free will "in the way that was natural." His constant references to the natural cooperativism of man is again Proudhonian in origin and anticipates the later work of Kropotkin. Furthermore, he expected the capitalist to enter into the new cooperative society and freely give up his wealth and privileges in accordance with the dictates of natural law and the instinct for mutual aid which he felt man could not resist indefinitely.[24]

Unlike most other nineteenth-century Mexican socialists, Rhodakanaty revealed in his writings some knowledge of Marxism, indicating both his opposition to it and the fear that it might succeed.[25] In order to increase the effectiveness of his efforts to build an anarchist movement in Mexico, Rhodakanaty favored the creation of Bakuninist-type secret societies to both propagate socialist theory and gain popularity for the theory by advancing a program for the working class based upon immediate issues.[26]

The secret society La Social planned to bring about socialism in Mexico. As Rhodakanaty put it, La Social intended to work toward "undoing the relationship between the state and the economic system, the reorganization of property, the abolition of politics and political parties, the complete destruction of the feudal system, and expedition of the agrarian reform laws. This is socialism and this is what we want."[27] He always saw the cooperative system of artisans' workshops, workers' collectives, and agrarian communes as the moral antithesis of an immoral capitalist society.

Rhodakanaty has been described, with some validity, as a disciple of Fourier.[28] But, as a mid- and late-nineteenth-century socialist, it is clear that Proudhon wielded the greatest influence upon him. His conception of government provides the best example of this influence. He aspired to the Proudhonian ideal of a stateless society while Fourier always assumed the existence of the state. Rhodakanaty obviously admired Fourier, but there can be no doubt as to where Rhodakanaty stood on what role the state should play.[29] He also disagreed with Fourier over the distribution of wealth. Disputing the latter's maxim "to each according to his capital, his labor, and his skill," Rhodakanaty took Proudhon's position that only individual productivity within one's peer group and the individual's personal need should be considered. He viewed roles of individual employment as unequal but saw each of those roles as equally essential to society.[30]

Like Proudhon, Rhodakanaty conceived an elitist role for the intellectual in building socialism and he actively played the part. Adopting the point of view temporarily held by Proudhon in the 1850's, when Rhodakanaty had known him, he wrote: "Those of us privileged by good fortune recognize our mission and obligation . . . [We are] motivated by the love for our wives and children, and by the knowledge provided in the social sciences; . . . [love and knowledge] are combined like the light and other cosmic materials found in the universe at the time of its formation, and they serve us like a talisman."[31] He viewed the intellectual primarily as an elite teacher and disseminator of information for the masses and as a result devoted himself to writing philosophical tracts and newspaper articles usually, but not always, directed toward the readers of the socialist artisan working-class press.

Rhodakanaty's briefly published philosophical journal in 1874, *El Craneoscopio*, contrasted sharply with his usual articles intended for newspapers with an artisan and working-class readership.[32] Rhodakanaty tried to win over his readers to socialism with a history of western philosophy. He also demonstrated a considerable range of knowledge, citing Horace, Pascal, Descartes, Leibnitz, and Herder as authorities whose thought contributed to the development of socialist ideas. Invoking a vision he called "Christian Universalist," Rhodakanaty interpreted the evolution of society and nations as "God's will," God being the "universal laws of the Cosmos." He believed that this process of change, or serial, would result in the creation of a "grand and universal republic on the ruins of the old world."[33] By means of Proudhon's associations, the resulting utopia is by now familiar: no more private property, "women will be emancipated, and ignorance abolished, because everything is subject to the laws of progress. The world is headed toward complete unity under a system of liberty."[34] Hence, while approach to the subject differed in *El Craneoscopio*, the conclusions remained identical. The series of essays in *El Craneoscopio* once more indicate his conviction that the better informed and more cultured elements of society, to which he directed this appeal, had to be approached on a higher intellectual plane than the common workers. Like Bakunin, and for a short time Proudhon, the latter groups' "depravity" and the necessity to stimulate them toward self-improvement remained one of his major concerns.[35] His preoccupation with the challenge of uplifting the workers led him to attempt the foundation of a school, La Escuela de Filosofía Transcendental, to teach "transcendental philosophy to those who sought to gain understanding." The "school" never developed beyond a reading circle.

Rhodakanaty, always the philosopher and intellectual historian, felt that careful reasoning and persuasion alone would convert both worker and capitalist to the socialist cause. Using selected examples he anticipated Kropotkin and argued that man had progressed, not through individual competition in a struggle for survival, but through mutual aid and cooperation. He interpreted intellectual history to prove, consistent with socialist theory, that love, compassion, and goodness filled the hearts of all men. He claimed scientific confirmation in the findings of Spinoza and others that cooperativism worked. He argued that the thought of western philosophers moved toward a libertarian socialist conception of man and society, and that western society would follow those concepts. Rhodakanaty believed that if he could gain acceptance in Mexico for the ideas of these men, as he interpreted them, they would provide the key to a socialist future.[36]

Rhodakanaty, like his European contemporaries, always wrote and spoke vaguely about the details of how his future society, based upon voluntary associations, would function in economic terms. He frequently argued on the basis of moral principle. Stimulated by the dislocation and hardship of the urban lower classes which resulted from the incipient Industrial Revolution, Rhodakanaty saw the solution to the problems of society in the relatively small, decentralized, and antipolitical cooperative societies typical of anarchism in the second half of the nineteenth century. Characteristic of his times, he fitted his scheme into universal laws, similar at least in approach because of their all-encompassing interpretations of human affairs to the Marxist and Positivist thought of the era. Rhodakanaty did not oppose technological progress, but based upon his limited empirical experience with the Industrial Revolution he feared its ultimate effect upon human society unless its development followed another course. He ultimately concluded that man was better adapted to relatively small communities in which mutual aid and human charity would be able to flourish.[37]

Rhodakanaty seemed unprepared to accept the possibility that the Mexican capitalist or working classes would reject the envisaged utopia. As a result, like his anarchist brethren in Europe, he failed to come to grips with the necessity of creating a viable means of survival or self-protection for the cooperative societies of nineteenth-century Mexico both during their early developmental stages or when they might come into direct conflict with existing sociopolitical institutions. The latter stage of development clearly reached fruition during the reign of Porfirio Díaz. This state of mind, combined with his opposition to violent revolution, resulted in his failure to help prepare Mexican anarchism for such contingencies.[38]

After many years of activity, his failure to educate the people and bring about the desired changes undoubtedly led to considerable disillusionment. However, the decline during the 1880's in the zealousness of his essays, the cessation of his revolutionary activities, and his return to Europe in 1886 probably resulted from the repressive measures taken by the Díaz government rather than a sense of despair derived from his own failures.

By the mid-1880's the Díaz regime dissolved the Rhodakanaty-supported National Congress of Mexican Workers, the Congreso Nacional de Obreros Mexicanos, affiliated with the Jura-based anarchist international; sponsored a growing number of government-dominated unions, mutualist societies, and cooperatives; crushed the revolutionary agrarian movement; and closed or forced a change of policy upon all the working-class newspaper staffs for whom Rhodakanaty wrote.

The government took issue with the newspapers' revolutionary propaganda and their attacks upon the state. Many of Rhodakanaty's former associates had been arrested or had fled. Probably as a result of this intimidation, he published his last essay in 1885, a philosophical tract devoid of revolutionary content and safely oriented toward the considerations of the literati, and shortly thereafter, in 1886, he returned to Europe.[39]

3. The Organizers

Within the Mexican anarchist movement which he founded, Rhodakanaty, the passive intellectual and theoretician, saw his ideas advanced from the very beginning of his career by young men less moderate in temperament and more oriented toward action. The Bakuninist organizing group La Social, formed in 1865, served as an early focal point for their activities. Unfortunately, because it operated as a secret organization, little is known about La Social. Apparently its membership during the 1860's, limited to about a dozen, consisted mostly of students. La Social kept the membership list a well-guarded secret, however, and the names of the less prominent members remain unknown. In addition, the complete nature and scope of its activities were not recorded. As a result only the most prominent individuals and some of their projects can be identified.[1]

Although La Social broke up after a few years, not to be re-formed until 1871, some of its original members—Rhodakanaty, Francisco Zalacosta, Santiago Villanueva, and Hermengildo Villavicencio—later played an important part in the creation of the nineteenth-century Mexican agrarian and urban labor movements. Much of the agrarian movement came to rationalize the needs of Mexico's *campesinos* in terms formulated by that staunch defender of the mores of the French peasantry, Proudhon. The urban labor movement, although originally conceived along Proudhonist-mutualist lines, from the very beginning adopted Bakunin's secret society as a tactic of organization.

Born in Durango on March 1, 1844, the son of an officer in the liberal army of Ignacio Comonfort, Francisco Zalacosta followed the victorious liberal forces when they entered Mexico City in 1854. Upon the death of his father during the Wars of the Reforma, in the late 1850's, Zalacosta became the ward of a wealthy Mexico City family. He attended preparatory school in the capital city and shortly before he graduated joined a group of students studying under the direction of Rhodakanaty. Soon Zalacosta participated in theoretical discussions regarding the nature of socialism and its proffered solutions to social ills. Rhodakanaty's essays provided him with the necessary introductory material. Although Zalacosta soon left the preparatory school in order to enter medical school, he was one of Rhodakanaty's most ardent disciples—a discipleship which led him to become one of the original and most active members of La Social.[2]

Santiago Villanueva, born in Mexico City in February 1838, began work in a cabinet shop at a young age in order to aid his poverty-stricken working-class parents. As a teenager he took up woodcarving and apparently mastered that craft. In 1861 Villanueva completed a course in art at the Academy of San Carlos and began attending classes in anatomy at the medical school. During his tenure in the medical school he came into contact with Zalacosta and through him with Rhodakanaty. At that time in his life he must have presented an interesting picture. Rhodakanaty referred to him as a "bohemian-type youth with little self discipline."[3] Rhodakanaty's interpretation of Proudhon and Bakunin attracted Villanueva to anarchism, and he spent the rest of his short life organizing urban workers and propagandizing the doctrine.

Hermengildo Villavicencio, born in the state of México in 1842, also attended medical school where he came into contact with Rhodakanaty by way of Zalacosta. By late 1864 these students and unknown others had formed a small group, and in January 1865 they adopted the name El Club Socialista de Estudiantes. Later that year the group renamed itself La Social, Sección Internacionalista.[4] The name indicated an emotional allegiance, if not a real one, with the Bakuninist faction of the First International Workingmen's Association.

In October 1864, led by Villanueva, the group undertook its first project and reorganized the first Mexican mutualist organization, La Sociedad Particular de Socorros Mutuos. In November of the same year they reinstituted the ten-years defunct mutualist association of tailors known as the Sociedad Mutua del Ramo de Sastrería.[5] The workers who joined these new organizations were inclined toward the more passive type of self-help mutualist groups which did not espouse ideological commitments. The original Mexican mutualist associations, formed in the 1850's, had been little more than attempts to develop group savings plans in order to provide life insurance sufficient to cover burial costs and to provide medical care for those in need. But the zealous students pressed their revolutionary ideas on the workers, a task made easier by the workers' wretched living and working conditions. The students argued for mututalist societies which would demand immediate pay raises and reduced working hours and which as "resistance societies would defend themselves against the attacks of the state and capitalism."[6]

In March 1865 the two newly formed mutualist societies received word from the workers in the textile factories of San Ildefonso in the neighboring town of Tlalnepantla and La Colmena in Mexico City that they wanted to "organize in order to protect their interests."[7] The two mutualist societies elected a delegation to meet with the workers, and Zalacosta and Villanueva were selected. The resultant conferences produced the Sociedad Mutua del Ramo de Hilados y Tejidos del Valle de México and included the workers of the two factories.[8]

On March 15, 1865, the delegation of representatives from the older mutualist organizations joined the newly organized laborers and other employees of the two textile factories in an inauguration dance celebrating the formation of the new mutualist society. The factory owners attended the affair. Either they did not know the intentions of their newly organized employees or they exhibited uncommon intelligence and attended in order to create good will and to avoid a possible cataclysm. The historical circumstances behind the decision by the workers to organize were indeed dreadful. The San Ildefonso plant, though large, depended upon local consumption.[9] The turmoil caused by the French invasion of 1862 and continuing liberal resistance reduced its profits, and in January 1865 the workers in the plant suffered a reduction in their already pitiful pay amounting to one-half real for each approximate yard of material they produced. In addition, about fifty workers lost their jobs in an apparent economy move by the factory management. Moreover, the *tienda de raya* (company store) did not reduce its prices after the reductions in wages and thus commanded the greater part of a worker's pay.[10] Then the owners decided to increase the length of the working day and reset working hours to extend from 5:00 in the morning to 6:45 in the evening for women and 7:45 for men.

On June 10, the employees of the San Ildefonso plant walked off their jobs. The following day their counterparts at La Colmena followed their example.[11] The first strike in Mexican labor history had begun. The workers, perhaps hoping to gain governmental protection, issued a short and pathetic manifesto describing their plight and sent it to the imperial government of Maximilian. The government reacted by creating a *gendarmería imperial* in Mexico City and its environs and sent a directive to the imperial representative in the district ordering him to offer assistance to the proprietor of the San Ildefonso factory.[12]

On June 19, 1865, the government representative, Eulalio Núñez, went to the factory with a contingent of about twenty-five armed men. Upon his arrival, Núñez was confronted by an angry mob and he ordered his men to fire, wounding several strikers. Núñez arrested about twenty-five of the workers and incarcerated them in the jail at Tepeji del Río. Prior to their release, the authorities warned them that if they ever returned to San Ildefonso they would be shot.[13] The first strike in the long struggle of the Mexican labor movement thus ended in an unmitigated defeat.

The background of events in Tlalnepantla is important in understanding the reasons for the developing mass unrest in mid-nineteenth-century Mexico. Throughout the episode the organizing efforts of the anarchists proceeded unimpeded by an imperial government obviously preoccupied with its continuing struggles with the liberals under Benito Juárez. The political instability of Mexico, which bred contempt for government in the long run, permitted in the short run the organizing success of a handful of anarchist activists. Furthermore, it is clear that the workers in the factories of San Ildefonso and La Colmena were responsive to the intrusion of anarchist organizers and were stimulated in their strike efforts because the general economic crisis had affected production and contributed to the intolerable working conditions in the factories. These conditions, typical of the period, would be repeated elsewhere.

In an attempt to recover from their defeat at Tlalnepantla, Villanueva and Villavicencio, following Bakuninist principles, created a new organizing group and called it La Sociedad Artística Industrial. The name derived from an expired mutualist organization originally formed in 1857.[14] The Sociedad became the principal center of anarchist activity and urban labor organizing for extended periods during the late 1860's and the 1870's. Its membership initially was dominated by engravers, painters, and sculptors to whom Villanueva and Villavicencio, following the pattern of their mentor Rhodakanaty, began to teach Proudhonist philosophy.

While his cohorts faced defeat at Tlalnepantla, Rhodakanaty continued to insist upon his long-envisioned communal agricultural colonies, and in January 1865 he began working on that project at Chalco in the southeast corner of the state of México. He explained his ultimate goal as "the undoing of the relationship between the state and the economic system, the reorganization of property, the abolition of politics and political parties, the complete destruction of the feudal system, and the expedition of agrarian reform laws. This is socialism and this is what we want."[15]

Rhodakanaty founded a school for *campesinos* in Chalco which he named La Escuela del Rayo y del Socialismo. This school, as the name implies, was dedicated to the instruction of the *campesinos* in reading, writing, oratory, methods of organizing, and libertarian socialist ideals.[16] The reason for his choice of Chalco is unclear, but progress was encouraging enough so that Zalacosta, apparently attracted by Rhodakanaty's description of the situation, left Mexico City in November 1865 to join his colleague.

The obvious intent of Rhodakanaty's curriculum was to produce literate and socialist *campesinos* capable of effective oratory and possessing knowledge of organizing methods. A student named Julio Chávez López soon attracted the attention of Rhodakanaty, who wrote to Zalacosta about him: ". . . among them there is a young man who works on a hacienda near Texcoco. He has already learned how to deliver a speech with a fair degree of eloquence. He has informed me that he intends to deliver a speech espousing the virtues of socialism very soon.[17] I have told him about you and he has said to me that he will make an attempt to write you.[18] His name is Julio Chávez."[19]

Zalacosta's arrival in Chalco in November 1865 eliminated the immediate need for Chávez López to write to him regarding his plans. For the next two years Rhodakanaty and Zalacosta worked together in the school, recruiting and teaching *campesinos*. Proudhonist agrarian ideology proved to be particularly appealing. The *campesinos*, especially Chávez López, became intent on taking violent steps to redress their grievances and restructure the agrarian order in the Chalco area. Rhodakanaty, who dreaded the implications of violence, left the school in 1867 and returned to Mexico City and his teaching position in the preparatory school. He felt he had accomplished the first stage of his project and turned the school over to Zalacosta, the man of action, for the next step, "because the school is no longer a school, but now is a club *por y para la libertad.*"[20]

Rhodakanaty and Zalacosta profoundly influenced Chávez López. The latter demonstrated his mastery of the anarchist lessons of his mentors when he wrote: ". . . I am communist-socialist. I am socialist because I am the enemy of all governments, and I am communist because my brothers wish to work the lands in common."[21]

Shortly after Rhodakanaty's departure, Chávez López collected a small band of followers and began to raid haciendas in the area between Chalco and Texcoco. Within a couple of months he extended his activities south into Morelos, east to San Martín Texmelucan and west to Tlalpan.[22] The government authorities in the area initially labeled him as a bandit, but they soon realized that his forces constantly grew and that his intentions exceeded those of a mere brigand. In March 1868, Antonio Flores, the prefect of Texcoco, warned the government:

> Julio Chávez and his gang of thugs are creating tremendous problems, as much for the Supreme Government as for state officials. He is recruiting the indigenous class with promises of hacienda lands. His successes are such that, if you do not take opportune, energetic, and violent measures immediately, it will be too late. Of course you are aware that the indigenous people are a vast majority of the population in the countryside. Until recently I was not greatly disturbed, but the rebel forces continue to grow and if they are not dealt with soon their strength will be overwhelming. . . . These rebels started out in Chalco and have recently raided Coatepec, Acuantla, and other places, each time recruiting more individuals of a like mind.[23]

In March 1868 additional government forces arrived in the area under the command of General Rafael Cuéllar. The general had launched an energetic campaign to crush Chávez López earlier in the year before his movement could grow any stronger, but Cuéllar immediately realized that his troop needs exceeded his original estimate. Unable to find his adversary, Cuéllar called for more troops and complained that "the *sublevación*" had become a genuine threat and that it received illegal aid from the villagers. In addition, he observed that the rebels received logistical support from General Miguel Negrete of Puebla, a known advocate of agrarian reform on behalf of the *pueblos* and a long-time opponent of President Juárez.[24] As the struggle continued, Cuéllar determined that the villages provided the basis of Chávez López' strength; he began a controversial scorched-earth military policy in the Chalco-Texcoco region. But the revolt continued. Uprisings in Chalco and Tlalmanalco had to be put down with considerable loss of life.[25]

Constant controversy hampered the government's counterinsurgency efforts. The prefect of Texcoco complained about the revolt's growth and argued that unnecessary abuses and atrocities committed against them by Cuéllar alienated innocent peasants.[26] Complaints of this nature resulted in the dispatch of even more troops to put a quicker end to the revolt and also precipitated a government investigation of Cuéllar's behavior. Judge José María Almarás presided over the inquiry, but he failed to uncover what he considered credible evidence in spite of petitions of complaint drawn up by groups of citizens in Coatepec, Chicoloapan, and Acuantla. These groups, Cuéllar charged, sympathized with Chávez López; he claimed further that Prefect Flores committed atrocities.[27] Charges of corruption also plagued government military operations against the rebels. These allegations charged Cuellar with selling government-owned arms and ammunition to hacienda owners for his own personal profit. Despite eyewitness testimony in support of the charges and a lengthy investigation, no final disposition of the accusations materialized.[28]

Cuéllar, harassed by *campesino* revolutionaries on one side and civilian observers who complained about his tactics on the other, resorted to martial law and mass arrests in those villages where he suspected the populace of aiding Chávez López. He then decided to deport large numbers of the citizenry of Acuantla, Chalco, and Coatepec, and the entire town of Chicoloapan, to Yucatán. Once again Flores objected to Cuéllar's actions and this time the national government temporarily admonished Cuéllar that the detained persons should first be judged in accordance with the law.[29] But the government reversed itself a few days later. President Juárez and Ignacio Mejía, the secretary of war, after examining the reports, determined that Cuéllar had acted correctly: "[The] *jefe político* of Chalco [Cuéllar] has stated that they are guilty . . . they are to be sent to Yucatán."[30]

Flores and other observers continued, however, to appeal, insisting that many of those to be deported had nothing to do with the insurrection. In a final plea, they argued that the investigative reports were invalid because Judge Almarás, who had supported Cuéllar's action, was an outsider who had ignored the citizenry's petitions and "did not understand the depth of trouble and abuse that the people had suffered. Their opposition [to Cuéllar] had gotten the *pueblo* of Chicoloapan into trouble." [31] After a few months' delay, the government carried out the deportation edict and referred further appeals to the government of the state of México. The final decision stated that "in view of new evidence" some of the defendants would receive prison terms only, but "the entire *pueblo* of Chicoloapan, which was in support of Julio López, was deported properly to Yucatán by the Minister of War." [32]

Chávez López survived Cuéllar's campaign during 1868 and discovered growing support for his cause. Early in 1869 he traveled to Puebla where he found agrarian unrest at an acute stage. He began to toy with the idea of a general armed uprising and asked Zalacosta for his reaction: "I have finally arrived here; there is much discontent among the brothers because the generals want to take over their lands. What would you think of it, if we made the socialist revolution?" [33] The reference to the generals', or other outsiders', desire to seize the land, was thereafter, during the remainder of the Reforma epoch and until the revolution of 1910, a continuing theme in the agrarian struggle. However, because of the lack of data, it is not possible to estimate the extent of land seizures during the Reforma. Later, during the early years of the Díaz regime, the agrarian land disputes, debated in the working-class press, in each case originated with the seizure of land from a local community by an outside landgrabber during the Reforma.

Two days before Chávez López launched his all-out effort for a general agrarian uprising, he was somewhere between Chalco and Puebla in the extreme southeastern part of the state of México. He knew of the Juárez government's intent to subdue his movement and realized the poor chances for success, but he remained steadfastly committed to his cause: "We are surrounded by a battalion, [but] it is of no consequence. Long live socialism! Long live liberty!" [34]

The uprising led by Chávez López represents an important turning point in the history of the Mexican agrarian movement. It marked a departure from the prepolitical pillaging and rioting that had typified its predecessors. For the first time, agrarians expressed immediate goals which they derived from an ideological critique of the Mexican government. [35]

The causes of the Chalco dispute were deeply rooted in the past. Long before the arrival of the Spanish in the sixteenth century, the province of Chalco was one of the principal centers of habitation in the central valley of Mexico. Its major town, or *cabecera*, Chalco, on the basis of political importance and population, ranked third behind Tenochtitlan, the Aztec capital, and Texcoco, a principal ally of the Aztecs. After the Spanish intrusion, Texcoco declined rapidly and Chalco soon replaced it as the second-ranking Indian city in the valley. According to tribute statistics, Chalco retained both its size and its political importance, relative to the other pre-Columbian settlements, except Mexico City, throughout the colonial period.[36]

While Chalco retained its relative importance, it, like other indigenous settlements, was decimated by the epidemics of the sixteenth century. Depopulation occurred so rapidly during the latter half of the century that the lands became unoccupied faster than they could be redistributed or absorbed by Spanish seizures. By 1600 much of the land in the Chalco area was abandoned; the indigenous population was simply too small to cultivate the vacant territory. Village agriculture came to be increasingly concentrated in the area contiguous to settlement. Indian town officials under pressure of tribute arrearage and labor levies, or *repartimiento*, either sold or rented property to Spaniards, which, in any event, when vacant, could be acquired by Spaniards from the crown. By the eighteenth century the Chalco area was characterized by Spanish-Creole-owned haciendas that dominated Indian society in the province. The largest, most powerful, and most enduring haciendas established near Chalco during this period were San Juan de Dios and Asunción.[37] The augmentation of Spanish landholdings did not go unnoticed by the Indians, and even in the early colonial period the villagers set about in the courts to defend their acreage.[38] The *pueblos* found it convenient to claim communal village ownership, even when the parcels in question had been privately held, because the titles indicating municipal ownership were easier to establish in the Spanish records, which often listed towns as sovereign but failed to mention the names of individual holders. In this way, as a means of defense, communality in *pueblo* life was exaggerated beyond what it had actually been.[39] This stress on individual village rights laid the basis for the popular later agrarian demand that the *municipio libre*, or politically free and economically independent village, become the fundamental political-social unit of the nation.[40] But, despite their vigilance and energetic self-defense, the villages could not hold off the conquerors. The result in the Chalco–Río Frío, eastern Morelos, and northwestern Puebla area was the early emergence of the most primitive form of agrarian social protest, social banditry. The region teemed with small "bandit armies." This center of banditry later became the locale of organized, ideological agrarian insurrection.

By the close of the colonial epoch the process of land polarization— that is, impoverished villages vis-à-vis the great estates—was quite advanced, and this process continued throughout the nineteenth century.[41] Moreover, the population of the villages continued a comeback that began in the early eighteenth century.[42] By the late nineteenth century the population of Chalco province was estimated by García Cubas at 54,002.[43] Of a population consisting of 3,494 in the *cabecera* of Chalco and its five *pueblos*, "2,460 speak Spanish and Náhuatl."[44] This resurgence of the indigenous population created new pressures upon the *pueblos* and the reduced amount of land that remained available to their inhabitants. The close of the colonial period, however, signaled the introduction of yet another element—the political revolutionary. The fiery rhetoric of the struggle for independence stirred up the *campesino* masses, as the following attracted by Miguel Hidalgo and José María Morelos indicates. The problem of land distribution was now broached in the national political arena for the first time, and it would hereafter play a significant role. In Chalco it was within this milieu of the omnipresent great estate and the increasing impoverished and landless population in the countryside that agrarian turmoil developed.

In 1866, Emperor Maximilian interceded in a dispute between one of Chalco's *pueblos*, Xico, and a local hacienda because the large estate had acquired most of the land in the area and the people of Xico complained that they could not feed themselves after paying traditional crop obligations to the hacienda.[45] A contemporary dispute between the *pueblo* of Coatepec in Chalco province illustrates the conflict that developed in the latter half of the nineteenth century between liberal ideas and the corporate structure of the indigenous countryside. The citizens of Coatepec petitioned the Emperor: ". . . because of the Ley Lerdo we were the first to lose our land. We did not comply with the terms of the law because we did not know how."[46] The villagers claimed landownership records over two centuries old and demanded that the local authorities be removed from control of *pueblo* lands because of "betrayal."[47] The conditions that became the basis of the Chávez López insurrection had been created.

On April 20, 1869, Chávez López issued his manifesto calling the Mexican people to arms in order to establish a new agrarian order and to resist what he described as the oppression of the upper classes and the political tyranny of the central government. The manifesto was an important document in the development of an agrarian ideology, not only because it introduced the European socialist concept of class struggle into the Mexican agrarian movement, but also because it placed the hardships endured by the *campesinos* within a historical context and identified culprits. It called for the revered principle of autonomous village governments to replace the sovereignty of a national government viewed to be the corrupt collaborator of the *hacendados*. This anarchistlike support of the local municipality as the ultimate dispenser of justice in the countryside has been a common thread in many agrarian revolutions. As Eric Wolf observes: "The peasant utopia is the free village, untrammeled by tax collectors, labor recruiters, large landowners, officials. . . . for the peasant, the state is a negative quantity, an evil, to be replaced in short shrift by their own 'homemade' social order. That order, they believe, can run without the state; hence, peasants in rebellion are natural anarchists."[48]

The ideological content of the manifesto was also significant because of the men who collaborated in writing it. Rhodakanaty, a European ideologue, working with a number of social revolutionaries, exerted a profound influence upon the developing ideology of the Mexican agrarian movement. His ideology, which the working-class press publicized during the 1870's, echoed the sentiments of contemporary Spanish Bakuninists who organized large numbers of peasants in Andalusia and Catalonia. The success of this appeal in the Mexican countryside is not surprising, given the similar conditions. The manifesto dramatically expressed the new class-struggle type of ideology emerging from the increasingly desperate Mexican agrarian movement:

> The hour of understanding for men of good heart has arrived; the day has come for the slaves to rise up as one man reclaiming their rights that have been stolen by the powerful few. Brothers! The movement has arrived to restore the countryside, to ask explanations of those who have always demanded them of us; it is the day to impose obligations on those who thought only they had rights. . . . Those that have taken advantage of our physical, moral, and intellectual weakness are called *latifundistas, terratenientes,* or *hacendados.* Those of us who have patiently let them grab what belongs to us are called workers, proletarians, or *peones.* We *peones* have given our lives and interests to the *hacendados* and they have subjected us to the greatest possible abuses; they have established a system of exploitation by which means we are denied the simplest pleasures of life. How does this system of exploitation operate? It is a system that dedicates itself exclusively toward blighting the very existence of the *peón.* Our parents were acquired by the hacienda at the wage of one real per working day. It was not possible to survive on this amount because the stores located on the haciendas sold their goods at greatly inflated prices: much more expensive than the cost of things that month by month and year by year we make by hand. The costs of these store-bought articles created debts that were charged to our parents. How would they be able to settle debts like those when they were earning no more than one miserable real for a day's work? . . .

When we came into this world we were faced with the debts of our parents, which were passed on to us. In this way we became slaves obligated to continue working in the same place, under the same system, with the pretense of paying the now-famous debts. But our wages were never increased, nor was credit ever granted to us and we found ourselves in the same situation as our parents.

And who is it that has cooperated to keep us muted, in humiliation, in ignorance, and in slavery? The Church, especially the Church. . . . Its hypocritical missionaries. . . . The Friars who say everything is in vain. . . . The priests who have deceived us. . . . Let religion reign, but never the Church and even less the priests. . . . If the priests are evil, so are all those men who give orders. What can we say about that which has been given us and called government and which in reality is tyranny? Where is the good government? . . .

The *hacendados* have been the strong men who, relying upon the military that they themselves maintain in order to safeguard their properties, have laid claim to possessions in whatever places they have desired, and they have done so without effective protests. What do we want? . . . We want: the land in order to plant it in peace and harvest it in tranquility; to leave the system of exploitation and give liberty to all in order that they might farm in the place that best accommodates them without having to pay tribute; to give the people the liberty to reunite in whatever manner they consider most convenient, forming large or small agricultural societies which will stand ever vigilant in the common defense, without the need of outsiders who give orders and castigate.

Fellow Mexicans! This is the simple truth with which we will win one way or another in order to bring about the triumph of liberty. We are going to be persecuted, maybe shot full of holes, but this is not important because we carry our dreams with us. What choice do we have with our lives? Death is better than the perpetuation of oppression and misery. As liberals we reject the oppression. As socialists it wounds us. As men we condemn it. Abolition OF THE GOVERNMENT, ABOLITION OF EXPLOITATION!

We want land, we want order, we want liberty. We must emancipate ourselves from all our miseries; we need peace and stability. Finally, what we need is the establishment of a social contract among men based upon mutual respect. Long live socialism! Long live liberty![49]

The anarchists encountered overwhelming obstacles in their attempt to achieve the ideological goals expressed in the manifesto. Cuéllar's

forces surprised and apprehended Chávez López without a fight shortly after he issued his manifesto. However, a few days later, his *campesino* friends attacked and routed the soldiers detaining him. Chávez
López escaped and with his companions went into the nearby hills,
from where they began to successfully enlist increasing numbers of
campesinos. The dire apprehensions of Antonio Flores, prefect of
Texcoco, seemed to be coming true. After sufficient recruits had en-
listed, the insurgents successfully moved against the town and hacienda of San Martín Texmelucan, located on the main road halfway
between Chalco and the city of Puebla. The federal troops they encountered fled, leaving their weapons behind. Chávez López collected
all the money he could find in the town and then, setting a precedent
to be followed in later times, burned the municipal archives.

After reading his manifesto and explaining his ideology, gathering
more followers, and regrouping his army, he next advanced upon the
town of Apizaco in Tlaxcala and once again routed the garrison,
burned the municipal archives, and collected available money and
arms. Reconnoitering and planning strategy, Chávez López understood that his movement needed a widespread base of support in order
to succeed; with this objective in mind, he sent a lieutenant, Anselmo
Gómez, with a contingent of fifty men northward into the state of
Hidalgo, far in advance of the main force, in order to stir up the
countryside. Chávez López followed with the "army" which now numbered about fifteen hundred poorly armed men.[50]

As he advanced, Chávez López continued his attempts to gain the
support of the people in the countryside by reading and explaining
the ideology of his manifesto. He also demonstrated the practical application of the manifesto by seizing haciendas and redistributing the
land to the *campesinos*.[51] In this drive to the north he demonstrated
considerable military skill by evading Cuéllar's main forces. Chávez
López continued to attract new recruits, to burn municipal archives,
and to seize considerable amounts of money, but he failed in his attempts to requisition sufficient arms—a failure which would be his
undoing. The contingent under Anselmo Gómez also enjoyed success
in its recruiting efforts; by June 11, when it captured the town of
Chicontepec in Veracruz, it numbered about 150 men. The government *jefe* in Chicontepec provided an insight into the reaction of the
well-to-do elements of society to Chávez López's ideology and his
motley army when he informed the minister of war that "the bandit
Anselmo Gómez leading 150 men has taken the town and is committing all manner of outrages against private property while proclaim-
ing to the people his refusal to recognize any form of government."[52]

Chávez López, in the meantime, had moved past his own home
town of Texcoco to the relatively large town of Actopan, located
seventeen miles northwest of Pachuca. He established a camp there

and began to prepare an attack, but federal troops surprised and defeated his poorly equipped and trained forces before they could launch their assault on the town. The federal troops took Chávez López prisoner and conducted him to Actopan; then, after ascertaining that his scattered followers no longer constituted a threat, they returned him to Chalco, where the government of Benito Juárez ordered him executed by firing squad in the courtyard of the Escuela del Rayo y del Socialismo on the morning of September 1, 1869. One brief résumé of this episode relates that Chávez López shouted, "Long live socialism!" just as his executioners fired—a believable story in view of his past behavior.[53] The eventual fate of Anselmo Gómez and the contingent of men who invaded the state of Veracruz is unknown.[54]

A significant aspect of the Chávez López movement was the conscious appraisal by the *campesinos* themselves of the ills that beset their society. Previous "agrarian uprisings" had usually been led by relatively well-educated, liberal, and financially well-to-do military leaders who promulgated "plans"; or they were genuine *campesino* insurrections which articulated little and merely resulted in land seizure. With the advent of the Chávez López uprising, the historian encounters for the first time in Mexico a *campesino* movement which called for the reordering of society and advocated the formation of "agricultural societies which will stand ever vigilant in the common defense, without the need of outsiders who give orders and castigate."[55] The agrarian uprisings that originated in the same area during the 1870's and 1880's continued the challenge that Chávez López presented. The call for "agricultural societies," then, presaged the *municipio libre*, which became a regular part of agrarian terminology in the 1870's and such a sacrosanct image by the twentieth century that the "First Chief of the Revolution," Venustiano Carranza, in his address to the Constitutional Convention at Querétaro in 1916, pledged, in an attempt to gain delegate backing for his program, to give the *municipio libre* his full support as the "political" and "economic" basis of free government.[56]

Whether or not Rhodakanaty expected his school in Chalco to become the starting point for a violent agrarian revolution is not clear. But he obviously wanted no part of violence when it occurred. He originally founded the school to prepare the way for the establishment of communal agricultural colonies and he purposely selected a region of both traditional and strong *campesino* resistance to the great estates. When Rhodakanaty noticed the revolutionary Chávez López, he encouraged him. The teacher undoubtedly expected trouble when he left the school because he noted that it had become a group ready to take action in order to achieve "liberty."[57] At the critical stage he placed Zalacosta in charge. Zalacosta, who consistently demonstrated a capacity for violence, ultimately influenced Chávez López and thus helped shape the course of events at Chalco.[58]

Rhodakanaty returned to Mexico City where he once more began working with his former colleagues from La Social. But his role as the central figure in Mexican socialism had passed to Santiago Villanueva and others, who, in his absence began a successful drive to organize the urban workers and to form a central workers' council. Although Rhodakanaty continued to play a prominent role, leadership increasingly passed to younger and more dynamic men.

4. The Anarchists and the Origins of the Urban Labor Movement

The formative urban labor movement during the last third of the nineteenth century developed out of long-standing urban working-class unrest, industrialization, and revolutionary ideology. Because it was a prelude to similar and more famous developments during the violent years of the early twentieth century, analysis of its causes, nature, and significance is essential for understanding an important phase of Mexican history and a critical aspect of the Mexican Revolution. After the imposition of Spanish rule in 1521 preindustrial lower-class unrest consistently existed and sometimes comprised an all-important characteristic of postconquest Mexico City society. The riots, or *tumultos*, of 1624 and 1692 capped urban lower-class crowd anger and carried with them all the classic attributes that made the prerevolutionary preindustrial crowd possible in other societies. In 1624 a crisis within the colonial elite, between the civil authority led by the viceroy and the Church led by the archbishop, caused the viceroy's excommunication and a breakdown in the usually unified Mexico City authority structure. In addition, the populace of Mexico City experienced a critical food shortage, rising food prices, and alleged government corruption in the distribution of food. Following the excommunication, a racial, cultural, and occupational cross section of Mexico City's lower classes attacked and burned the viceroy's palace. The crowd supported the king but shouted its defiance of "bad government."

Unrest continued and flared up again in 1692. Once again food scarcity, rising prices, and alleged government corruption resulted in violence. The triggering event and the breakdown of law enforcement came about when the crowd outside the government granary, the *alhóndiga*, already angry and irritated by long waits and meager food supplies heard that an Indian woman had been whipped to death by one of the authorities. The crowd marched to the palaces of the archbishop and the viceroy, only to be turned away by guards. Finally enraged to the point of violence, a racial, cultural, and occupational cross section of Mexico City's working class once again attacked and laid seige to the viceroy's palace with whatever weapons they could find. This time the crowd's shouting, while still supportive of the king and critical of "bad government," attacked the Spanish economic and social elite: "Death to the *gachupines* who eat all of our maize!" The angry crowd attacked the viceroy's palace, several government buildings, selected places of business, the marketplace, and the Cortés family mansion. Before order could be restored, guards killed scores of persons.

Historian Chester Lyle Gutherie has identified three reasons for urban working-class unrest in preindustrial, preideological Mexico City: "great social inequality, the precarious economic status of the largest part of the population . . . [and] administrative weakness" which allowed the crowds to get out of control. These conditions had not changed by the late nineteenth century, when they were compounded by the creation of a modern urban factory labor force and revolutionary working-class ideologies.[1]

Mexican industrialization, which began during the second half of the nineteenth century, encouraged the parallel appearance of an urban labor movement. Industrialization resulted in a sudden concentration of new workers from the countryside in a few urban areas—especially in the Mexico City area where industrial concentration was particularly heavy with eighty-three factories during the 1860's.[2] Chronic economic and political instability compounded the generally intolerable living conditions suffered by the new city dwellers as did the almost impossible working conditions in the new factories. The working class, virtually in self-defense, began to organize, and the anarchists played an important role in that process from the very beginning.

The background to one of Mexico's first large-scale labor disputes serves to illustrate the socioeconomic origins of the nineteenth-century urban labor movement. A descriptive example can be found in the strike proclamation that appears in Chapter 1 of this study. It cited long working hours, poor wages, insufficient rest periods, and generally unsatisfactory working conditions. It also revealed increasing working-class belligerency and frustration because of the failure of normal political processes to remedy the situation.[3]

The difficult urban-industrial environment profoundly affected the nature of the emerging labor movement. It encouraged a strong radical-revolutionary bent, while corrupt local and unstable national government increased worker belligerency and distrust of formalized political institutions. This distrust of government increased in intensity when anarchist ideologues in the persons of Rhodakanaty's former students and a considerable number of artisan organizers, joined later by Spanish émigrés, added their voices to the labor movement.

In early 1866, while Rhodakanaty and Zalacosta attempted to start their agrarian communal movement at Chalco, Villanueva and Villavicencio reinstituted a mutualist organization which had expired several years earlier. This association, La Sociedad Artística Industrial, became critically important to the developing labor movement and its

ideology during the next few years because of its domination by artisans who declared themselves dedicated to the study and discussion of
the works of Proudhon and Fourier. Beginning in 1866 and during
1867, the Sociedad membership began the radical activity of proselytizing workers in the Mexico City area and recruiting them into "resistance" and mutualist societies. Under Villanueva's leadership,
Mexico entered its first stage of intensive labor organizing.[4]

Following the fall of Maximilian, Epifanio Romero, the founder of
the original Sociedad, returned to Mexico City late in 1867 with other
liberals close to Juárez and attempted to have the organization placed
under the aegis of the government. The Sociedad, under the direction
of Villanueva, attracted the attention and apprehension of the leading
liberals because, in the absence of a central council of workers, it
provided the primary source of labor organization and agitation. When
Villanueva refused to accede to Romero, a power struggle between the
anarchist-led radicals and the liberal-led *moderados* began for control
of the Sociedad. The liberals challenged Villanueva's chairmanship
in a series of debates and organizational elections. In the initial encounters between the rival factions, Villanueva retained control of the
organization.

Following Romero's initial failure to wrest control of the Sociedad
from Villanueva, he and Juan Cano, another supporter of Juárez,
founded the Conservatorio Artístico Industrial as a rival group in the
late summer of 1867. Juárez was named honorary president of the
Conservatorio, and another prominent politician, Francisco Mejía,
honorary vice-president. The Conservatorio subsequently received a
one-thousand-peso donation from one of the president's officers, Colonel Miguel Rodríguez. Opponents of the Conservatorio considered the
cash donation, ostensibly given for the construction of a new school,
evidence of government sponsorship. Their suspicions gained credence
when the liberal-dominated Mexican Congress, in an obvious show of
support for the newly formed Conservatorio, voted it an annual sub-
sidy of 1,200 pesos.[5]

With these successes behind him, Cano, as the new leader of the
moderados, managed to gain enough support to defeat Villanueva in
the December 1867 organizational election and he temporarily gained
control of the Sociedad. The rival societies then united under the
original name of La Sociedad Artística Industrial with Cano as president. Finally, the group received as a personal gift from President
Juárez the old church of San Pedro y San Pablo as a meeting place.[6]
But other factors also played key roles in determining the outcome of
Villanueva's early struggle against the pro-Juárez faction led by Cano.
In January 1868, Villanueva succeeded in organizing the textile factory La Fama Montañesa in Tlalpan, an advance he augmented by the

formation of the Unión Mutua de Tejedores del Distrito del Tlalpan, comprised of new organized workers at the factories of La Fama Montañesa, Contreras, La Abeja, and Tizapán.[7]

On July 8, 1868, the workers at La Fama Montañesa expressed a newly found sense of power and unity when they launched the first successful strike in Mexican history. Their demands consisted mainly of a call for better working conditions and shorter hours for female employees.[8] This victory resulted in enormous prestige for Villanueva and his restoration as president of the Sociedad. Villanueva now had more than enough influence among the lower-class workers and artisans to defeat Cano.

In the aftermath of the successful strike Villanueva directed a flurry of organizing activity. Several new associations espousing Proudhonism appeared during the months of July and August 1868, including La Unión de Tejedores de Miraflores, La Asociación Socialista de Tipógrafos Mexicanos, La Sociedad Mutua del Ramo de Carpintería, and La Unión Mutua de Canteros. In addition workers reorganized the previously defeated and disbanded mutualist societies in the factories of San Ildefonso and La Colmena. Villanueva now found himself surrounded by new associates—all Mexico City artisans who later aided in the advancement of cooperativist doctrines—Benito Castro, Pedro Ordóñez, Agapito Silva, and Ricardo Velatti.[9] All except Silva later became active members of the central anarchist group, La Social.[10]

Villanueva continued his drive to organize the urban working class. He planned for a general labor congress to meet in 1868, but the idea failed because of a lack of funds. He then proposed convening a permanent assembly composed of three delegates from each mutualist society, but the idea again failed for the same reason. Finally, in 1869, he formed a group of radical urban labor militants named the Círculo Proletario and comprised of the above-named cooperativists and Zalacosta, joined by newcomers José María González, Juan de Mata Rivera, Evarista Meza, and Rafael Pérez de León. They coordinated urban labor organizing activities, especially in the textile mills, and disseminated their socialist ideology. Late in 1869 receipt of a newsletter from the First International Workingmen's Association circulated by the Geneva Congress in 1866 rekindled Villanueva's enthusiasm for a central workers' council. The three-year delay before it reached Mexico indicates the isolation from Europe of that country's socialist movement. On January 10, 1870, Villanueva and his associates sent out a call asking for the formation of a "Centro General de los Trabajadores Organizados in order to more effectively defend the interests of labor."

On September 16, 1870, the *centro* met for the first time and called itself the Gran Círculo de Obreros de México. The pro-Villanueva faction immediately established its dominance in the organization, and Zalacosta delivered a speech denouncing the liberals and Cano. The latter, however, refused to be discouraged; he addressed a letter to Juárez in which he expressed his feelings regarding the relationship of the government to the affairs of the Círculo: "My eternal thanks for the demonstrations of generosity which you have shown so many times to my brothers, the artisans. . . . I only hope for just and prudent laws, for peace, for work, the advancement of the arts, the protection of commerce, and the development of agriculture. I salute you in the name of our beloved [artisan] family and conclude with these inspired words—peace, union, protection, and labor."[11] Pledging his support to the president, Cano asked for his reaction to the newly formed Círculo. Juárez replied: "Señor don Juan Cano: Esteemed Sir, It is with pleasure that I reply to your letter of yesterday. I wish to convey to you my belief that the artisans should organize their association in whatever manner they may deem convenient in order to achieve perfection in their respective crafts and skills."[12] Juárez supported his liberal colleagues Romero and Cano and he continued to encourage the artisans to organize in the manner of the Conservatorio. He did not acknowledge in his response the recruitment of common factory workers—a task already undertaken by the Círculo radicals.

In spite of the moderation of Romero and Cano, the Círculo, stimulated by its anarchist faction, continued to advance its program among the common laborers. On March 20, 1871, in an attempt to give the organizing drive better direction, La Social again reconvened. The membership included Rhodakanaty, Zalacosta, Castro, Velatti, and Ordóñez. In a manifesto they declared: ". . . we want the abolition of all systems of government and liberty for all the manual laborers and intellectuals of the universe."[13]

Elected president of the Círculo in early 1871, Villanueva continued the intense campaign to win new adherents. On July 9, 1871, *El Socialista*, the first Mexican newspaper that can be described as socialist, began publication in Mexico City. Several of its writers held membership in La Social and frequently expressed their anarchist ideology. The paper joined the Círculo, became its "official organ," and duly received the customary three delegates. La Social also joined the Círculo and sent Velatti, Ordóñez, and Castro as representatives. Most of the other recently formed mutualist organizations in Mexico City and its environs belonged to the Círculo, which resulted in increased intermingling of anarchists and working men and of their ideas.[14] Individuals who wished to could join the Círculo, provided they were workers and did not belong to any political party. Employers "on good terms with their employees"—usually artisans who had expanded their trade

—could be admitted to associate membership.The Círculo was thus made accessible to almost any sympathizer who cared to join in its activities.[15]

The Círculo's decision not to admit members of political parties expressed a significant anarchist influence: political boycott and the refusal to recognize the legitimacy of governments larger than the local community, or *municipio libre*. This attitude was given double emphasis by the Círculo's insistence that "the struggle for the complete emancipation of the working class has to be conducted by the workers themselves, using as their ultimate weapon the social revolution, which will bring about the socialist world of splendor, justice, and truth."[16] Laborers, while demanding a law guaranteeing the betterment of working conditions, themselves reserved "the right to bring about socialism by means of the social revolution." The Círculo directed its insistence that workers must bear the obligation of improving their lot not only at the laborers but also at parliamentary liberals and their working-class supporters, whom anarchist-oriented radicals regarded as likely traitors.[17]

During 1871 the Círculo's first group of elected officers indicated the strength of Villanueva and the radical contingent: president, Villanueva; vice-president, Romero; first secretary, Mata Rivera; second secretary, Castro; third secretary, Alejandro Herrera; fourth secretary, Pérez de León; and treasurer, Francisco de Paula González.[18] Of these men only Romero represented the progovernment group opposed to Villanueva and what constituted an anarchist-radical coalition. Mata Rivera, a utopian socialist by ideology but no revolutionary, always tried to remain neutral; Castro and Pérez de León actively worked with La Social.[19]

Elsewhere in the country, workers influenced by ideas emanating from Mexico City began forming mutualist "resistance" societies and cooperatives. In San Luis Potosí, the Asociación Potosina de Obreros comprised three new mutualist groups and established contact with the Círculo in Mexico City. In Toluca, workers formed a mutualist society and, on November 8, 1871, affiliated with the Círculo.[20] These events reflected a growing labor movement and acceptance of anarchist ideology in the hinterlands. The mutualist "resistance" societies which affiliated with the Círculo differed from the traditional mutalist societies, which stressed religious beliefs and concerned themselves primarily with workers' loans, burials, and disability compensation. During this period of growth in the early 1870's, the historic red-and-black flag of anarchism, the *roji-negra*, became the official symbol of the Mexican labor movement.

An era in the development of the Mexican labor movement ended with the deaths of President Juárez, on July 18, 1872, and Villanueva, a short time later. The Juárez government had not actively tried to dominate the Círculo; but when Romero replaced Villanueva as president of the Círculo, the situation began to change. The first step took place on September 16, 1872, when the Círculo amended its bylaws to permit the monthly acceptance of 200 pesos from the new president, Sebastián Lerdo de Tejada.[21] By November 1873, the salon of the Sociedad Unionista de Sombrereros, an organization led by Cano and Romero, became the regular meeting place for the group.[22]

At the end of the critical year 1872, the opposing forces within the Círculo stood in clear contrast. One group, greatly influenced by Rhodakanaty, Villanueva, et al., responded to anarchist and revolutionary arguments because of its alienation due to social conditions. Lacking a majority, the anarchists exercised considerable influence upon the rank-and-file membership by constantly pushing for the organization of the working class and questioning the role of the government. The election of La Social members Castro and Pérez de León to the Círculo directorate demonstrated their strength. In addition, Rhodakanaty, Velatti, and Ordóñez continued as prominent spokesmen for the Círculo in *El Socialista*. At the other extreme within the Círculo, the moderates led by Romero and Cano advocated cooperation with the Lerdo regime and a program of remedial parliamentary legislation. The great bulk of the organization's membership, caught between conflicting ideologies, vacillated between Romero's idea of order and progress and the revolutionary militancy of the anarchists and radicals. While electing Romero to the presidency of the Círculo, many members joined *"sociedades de resistencia"* organized by anarchists.

Important strikes occurred during the latter half of 1872. The most serious one began on August 1 in a future trouble spot, the formerly English-owned mine, Real del Monte, near Pachuca in the state of Hidalgo.[23] The English owners, plagued by historic cycles of insolvency and depression in the industry, provoked the strike by announcing a reduction in the workers' salary from two pesos to one peso per day, effective July 15.[24] The Círculo became involved, at least to the extent of offering moral support and sending some contributions to the strikers. The mine workers demanded the reinstitution of their original salary and, in addition, a reduction in working time from eighteen to sixteen hours per day. Although the miners met with severe repression and did not realize their strike objectives, their action set off a wave of protests in the regular press of Mexico City, which demanded that the Lerdo government take vigorous action against the "new and dangerous tactic of striking." Briefly encouraged by their limited success and perhaps by inflammatory articles in *El Socialista*, the miners formed a "resistance society." The government, reinforced by the public outcry against the strikers, reacted by secretly deporting many of the participants to Campeche and Yucatán.[25]

The workers at La Fama Montañesa factory, which still suffered from the economic effects of an unstable and regionally limited market, experienced a similar fate. After a walkout that began on September 9, army troops forced the strikers back to work. At that time the workers apparently could not elicit aid from the Mexico City Gran Círculo or form a permanent organization for "the protection of their interests" vis-à-vis the employers.[26]

During the period 1872–1875, while continuing as a forceful minority within the Gran Círculo principally through the delegates sent by mutualist societies under their control, the anarchists regrouped. Seeking to dominate as many groups as possible, they once again established hegemony in the Sociedad Artística Industrial.[27] They apparently hoped, beyond the obvious desire to continue their activities from within as many of the established and legitimate bases of the labor movement as they possibly could, to utilize the greater resources of the Sociedad Artística in order to push their program further, especially Bakuninist cooperativism. The Sociedad Artística became their base of operations, and they temporarily dissolved La Social.

They founded a newspaper, *El Obrero Internacional*, "the official organ of the Sociedad Artística Industrial," and it became an important part of the campaign to create a viable cooperativist movement. Velatti described the vision: ". . . we poor dreamers for the happiness and material benefit of our brothers do not doubt for a moment that the cooperative system will be better for them than mutualism. It will save them from the charity ward, from misery, from the venomous claw of hunger, and from the greed of capitalism, which today, more than ever before, is the greatest and most fierce enemy of labor."[28]

Moved by the harsh realities of the new urban working class, Mexican anarchist ideology abandoned mutualism for Bakunin's cooperativism, or collectivism. By organizing production and living groups that marketed their goods in common, and bought from similar groups, the cooperativists felt that the working man's interests would be protected against the more powerful elements present in the capitalist society. The anarchists regarded mutualist societies as inadequate because they did not provide a comprehensive program for the transformation of society away from capitalism. They also argued that capitalist "speculators" and their "defenders," the government, remained unchallenged by the mutualists, who made no attempt to ameliorate the differences between the rich and poor, the powerful and weak.

Nineteenth-century Mexican cooperativists adopted a simple and direct approach to the development of their system. It entailed groups of artisans and/or common workers unified for the protection of their products and interests. In 1876, José María González explained the system: "When they have collected enough money they should start cooperative stores stocked with . . . [their products]. The other associations will then produce the goods sold in the stores. In this manner the worker becomes independent of the capitalist, and the value returned to him for his labor is increased."[29] Anarchist ideology conceived cooperativism as a growing movement that would soon embrace everyone. Mexican libertarian socialist labor leaders urged the workers to form a system of equalitarian communities consistent with both contemporary anarchocollectivist theory and many of the workers' recent peasant experience in the free villages. The communities would be economically self-sufficient and capable of existing separately from, while geopolitically still within, a capitalist society governed by a nation-state.[30] They saw the government as the stumbling block in achieving social perfection. González believed that collectivism was a means of eliminating the need for government and the social injustice it defended.

Velatti saw cooperatives as aggressive workers' units fighting capitalism:

> Brothers, the workers of the entire universe are tired of slavery and of being the victims of the limitless ambitions of the capitalists.
>
> They are working to be free and to establish their emancipation from the hated domination that today robs them of the fruits of their labor, from the enemy of the worker—capital.
>
> . . . Our rights as workers do not exist, we are robbed of them and left in misery.
>
> Will you continue to be the object of such exploitation?
>
> Will you submit to the continued imposition of so many outrages?
>
> No! A thousand times no!
>
> . . . Those workers who do not join the new associations are, as a result of their fear or their ambition, making a pact for misery.
>
> The association, in order to succeed, must be based upon the unity of its members.
>
> The association is the primary weapon of the worker against the abuses of the powerful.
>
> . . . In order to gain power you must unite! Now![31]

Throughout the 1870's the anarchists conducted a sustained and vigorous campaign for a collectivist society. They enjoyed at least some success. In 1872, Velatti converted one mutualist group, the Sociedad Progresista de Carpinteros, to cooperativism. At this time the Círculo began a rather sustained attempt to build a system of cooperative workshops. A general effort to organize the mutualist societies into cooperatives began late in 1872. Juan de Mata Rivera, the sympathetic utopian socialist, joined them as one of the leaders in the latter task. He read aloud from Fernando Garrido's *Historia de las asociaciones obreras en Europa* at a general meeting of the Círculo. The book espoused the virtues of collectivism.[32]

During a special holiday meeting of the Círculo on September 16, 1873, Velatti delivered the keynote address and urged the members to adopt cooperativism:

> No more *cofradías* [traditional mutualist societies and guilds]; we are forming consumption cooperatives, which will also have social and international functions. Never doubt it, they will lift us up and cause the growth of [cooperative] workshops, factories, mills, and railroads.

Velatti cleared up any possible misconceptions regarding why he considered cooperation a necessary replacement for capitalism:

> Capital, here we have the terrible enemy of the worker. The ruined ambitions, the tears, and the misery at your doorstep are not enough. Were it not for [the power of] the strike they would reduce salaries that are already too low. All over the valley [of Mexico] we see continuous strikes by workers, in different kinds of factories, who prefer a thousand times the suffering [resulting from the strikes] to that which they have to endure while they continue to increase the wealth of their bosses, who, being despots and tyrants, act like petty kings in order to fill their coffers from the sweat of those who have to work in order to take care of the basic necessities of life.[33]

The anarchists did not recognize the Reforma per se as the beginning of the late-nineteenth-century ascension to power of a newly potent bourgeoisie, whose increased strength flowed from the changing mode of commodity production, that is, the factory system. Rather, they accepted contemporary popular belief and optimistically viewed the Reforma epoch as a progressive period of new hope for artisans and urban and rural workers. However, with the advent of strikes and modern class conflict during the 1860's, the factory owners soon became the primary enemies and took their place alongside the traditional rivals of the militant artisans and workers, the conservative oligarchy, and earned the workers' condemnation as "greedy capitalists."

The anarchists, despite their failure to recognize the ultimate political implications of the Reforma, realistically conceived Mexican society. They verbalized their recognition of the Reforma as the ushering in of a new industrial era. They appreciated the potential of the Industrial Revolution. They complained about underdevelopment and the economic displacement resulting from the new factories. They stressed the need for an agrarian development program to be financed by regional agricultural credit banks in order to increase agricultural production and alleviate the hardships of the *campesinos*. They welcomed an intensified rate of industrialization, but along very different lines than the capitalists. They attacked the poor social conditions and "backward" political institutions in Mexico, which they identified as the Church and the omnipresent and heavy-spending military. They recognized nationalist sentiment as a pride in being Mexican and called upon it in order to face up to the "insolent United States."

The anarchists claimed that the capitalists' system inhumanely placed the heaviest burdens upon the working class. As an alternative they proposed to supplant these methods with a libertarian socialist society based upon cooperatives. The anarchists' campaign for cooperativism included organizing new urban labor associations, continuing activities in previously organized groups, and a steady flow of articles in working-class newspapers, such as *El Hijo del Trabajo, El Obrero Internacional*, and *El Socialista*. Their greatest success came in 1876 when they organized a working-class neighborhood in Mexico City, the Colonia Obrera de Buenavista, into a cooperative called the Asociación Cooperativa de Consumo de Obreros Colonos. José Muñuzuri, a Spanish émigré, a member of La Social, and the editor of *El Hijo del Trabajo*, became president. He commemorated the event in an editorial:

> This group of men have united, using the most powerful weapon of a free people—association. They have said in unison—War on usury and misery! War on the miserable exploitation by a few!
> . . . Only through the union of the working people, of the productive people, those that have always been the sport of the rulers, is happiness possible. No more misery, an end to poor conditions, unity in order to be strong, unity for happiness, unity in order to remedy and correct abuses and to abolish crime.[34]

Continuing adverse working conditions contributed to the growth of the labor movement, anarchism, and radical ideas. By 1874 the Círculo's membership had increased to an estimated eight thousand.[35] It continued to grow, but its moderate leadership left it vulnerable to radical criticism. By 1876 the anarchist members of the Círculo began to make gains against the moderates. They objected to the acceptance of money from the government, to the formation of several "company unions" sponsored by factory owners in conjunction with the Círculo leadership, and to the Círculo's refusal, through decisions of the leadership clique, to support a serious strike at La Fama Montañesa factory. They also strongly attacked *El Socialista* for its increasingly conservative editorial stance.[36]

During the early 1870's, belief in the need for a nationwide labor organization grew, and, at the end of 1875, steps commenced to con-

vene a national workers' congress.[37] The anarchists had long supported this idea, and Villanueva had worked toward it as early as
1869. Mata Rivera, editor of *El Socialista* and friend of Rhodakanaty,
presented the formal proposal for a national workers' congress to the
special junta designated by the Círculo to consider the project.[38] The
junta apparently completed its work successfully, because the Congreso General Obrero de la República Mexicana, with Círculo support,
met for the first time on March 5, 1876, in the salon of the Sociedad
Artística Industrial with thirty-five delegates of the eventual total of
seventy-three present.[39]

The first Congreso spent most of its time with the tedious details
of organizing special committees and electing officers. Although the
Círculo supported the Congreso, no members of its conservative faction won election to the directorate of the congress. José Muñuzuri
enjoyed the distinction of being the only officer elected from the
anarchist-oriented elements.[40] The more radical groups were represented by delegates from several organizations, including the Socie-
ded Artística Industrial.[41] The fact that few delegates from the usually antagonistic radical and moderate factions in Mexico City's
working-class movement held offices in the congress probably resulted
from an initial spirit of cooperation; however, since officers served
one-month terms, both sides were frequently represented later.[42]
The manifesto of the national Congreso contained clauses which indicate the continuing spread of "libertarian socialist" ideology in Mexico.
It contained calls for "social guarantees" and cooperativist enterprises,
"emancipating the workers from the capitalist yoke," and "independence from individual and capitalist interest, in order to put an end
to misery and its accompanying ills."[43] These demands echoed almost word for word the rhetoric used on many previous occasions by
Rhodakanaty, Velatti, and José María González.

La Social reorganized on May 7, 1876. In the inaugural speech
Rhodakanaty explained the need for the society in order to help develop nascent cooperativist ideas, to create an international labor organization, and to fill the need for a "vanguard" revolutionary group.[44]
La Social sent a five-member delegation to join the Congreso, an action
which clearly indicated that La Social planned to influence the national labor organization's policies to the greatest extent possible.[45]

Two women were among the representatives sent by La Social to the
Congreso, and, in an open debate at a general session, the maverick
socialist Mata Rivera opposed their being seated. In his statement he
betrayed a traditional male hostility toward an active role for women
in public affairs. Although he professed the utmost regard for Rhodakanaty and La Social, he charged that admitting female delegates violated precedent. Muñuzuri, as editor of *El Hijo del Trabajo*, now the
official organ of the Círculo, led the debate in support of the women.

Thus, the editor of *El Socialista*, a cooperativist and friend of Rhoda-kanaty but who also had close ties with the moderate Romero faction, opposed the editor of *El Hijo del Trabajo*, the voice of the more militant elements, regarding the seating of female delegates. However, the issues separating them went far beyond this theme. *El Hijo del Trabajo* criticized the moderates in the Círculo directorate and *El Socialista* because of their willingness to take part in national politics and their failure to take a more favorable stance regarding the organization of a cooperativist movement. The debate waxed long and sharp. Mata Rivera, in his self-defense, revealed his feelings about what the role of the Círculo should be when he told the Congreso that the Círculo was "loyal to the principles of Santiago Villanueva, federalist, and opposed to power, regardless of the source." He claimed that he and the Círculo's directorate were not abdicating the defense of the working class but were striving "to abolish the salaried worker." Finally, he concluded: "No more rich and poor, masters and servants, governments and governed, capitalists and workers! We are all men *debajo del mismo cielo y en frente del mismo trabajo justo y digno*." [46]

The assembly supported Muñuzuri, and for the first time in the history of the Mexican labor movement female delegates won seats in the national organization.[47] No doubt passions generated during the rivalries of several years affected the decision of the Congreso as much as did any ethical consideration of women's rights; however, the admission of women had lasting consequences. Thereafter, negotiated labor contracts frequently contained protective clauses on behalf of female and child workers and women soon became important in the affairs of the Congreso. Carmen Huerta became its president in 1879 and again in 1880.[48] Later she organized large numbers of female workers in the Orizaba area. In addition to the gains made by the women, the anarchists had served notice of their widespread support within the Congreso and now constituted a force to be reckoned with.

During 1876 the anarchists continued to gain strength in the congress. Their continuing propaganda effort throughout the country slowly began to affect the balance of power in Mexico City. In addition, by June, only a month after the debate over female delegates, the representation of La Social in the Congreso had been increased with the appearance of Rhodakanaty, Juan B. Villareal, Evarista Meza, and Colín y López.[49] These men represented a formidable contingent in the congress because of their reputations in the labor movement as persuasive agents for their cause.

By 1876 the divisions within the labor movement had become much more complex than the obvious conflict between the moderates and the anarchists. A three-way civil war among elements supporting the national presidential aspirations of Lerdo de Tejada, who sought re-election, Porfirio Díaz, and José María Iglesias revealed the differences. The anarchists opposed working-class participation in the struggle because, they argued, it amounted to no more than a clash between individuals vying for power. They complained that the fighting destroyed the national economy and cost the lives of the workers and *campesinos*, who, they said, did all the fighting with nothing to gain regardless of the outcome.[50]

The leading moderates in the Círculo continued to support Lerdo during the struggle; other members favored Iglesias because of the legal technicalities that legitimized his candidacy.[51] Díaz enjoyed the greatest rank-and-file support because of his outstanding record as an officer in the liberal army of Juárez and because of the rather vague promises regarding social reform that he made to the workers in his plan of Tuxtepec.[52] His failure to fulfill those promises later contributed to the further exasperation of the working class and to increased support for the anarchists.

The situation became more complicated in June 1876 when Lerdo's supporters, including the staff of *El Socialista*, endorsed Lerdo and withdrew from the Círculo because Díaz sympathizers already dominated that group.[53] This event meant the eventual death of the original Círculo. Between 1876 and 1878 other groups of dissenters joined the extreme anarchists in a boycott of the Círculo because of its pro-Díaz sympathies. After their departure, the ranks of the Círculo declined further by the withdrawal of many former Díaz enthusiasts. Initially attracted to the new president by his promises of progressive reforms, they quickly became disillusioned by his delay in reopening *El Hijo del Trabajo* after its shutdown by Lerdo in October 1876.[54] In 1877 and 1878, Díaz followed this offense by allowing the expulsion of some six hundred *campesino* families from the Rancho de San Vicente in the state of San Luis Potosí by armed men from the Hacienda de las Bocas despite vehement and sustained protests from the working-class newspapers in Mexico City.[55] These actions, combined with his failure to make good on his promises to help the workers, resulted in a drastic reduction in the number of Díaz supporters in the labor movement. By 1878 the Círculo was a mere skeleton organization with few, if any, active members.[56]

José María González, an outspoken writer who expressed his anarchist viewpoint in articles that appeared regularly for years in *El Hijo del Trabajo*, led an attack on the Círculo's pro-Díaz leadership by accusing it of accepting gifts, money, and positions from the government. Francisco de Paula González, a vocal cooperativist and Muñuzuri's replacement as editor of *El Hijo del Trabajo*, used his newspaper as the primary propaganda vehicle for the publication of charges against the Círculo. In 1878 both men supported the formation of a rival labor organization, the Zacatecas Gran Círculo de Obreros.[57]

As soon as the new group established itself in Zacatecas, it began to solicit affiliation from other labor groups. It received messages of support from workers' societies located throughout central Mexico. One of its more important endorsements came from the regional strong man in Zacatecas, General Trinidad García de la Cadena, who offered his protection. Another major expression of support for the Zacatecans came from the workers' associations of Tlalpan, San Ildefonso, Contreras, Río Hondo, and La Colmena.[58]

The Zacatecas insurgents next formed a branch in Mexico City, commonly referred to as the Primer Sucursal. The anarchists soon dominated both the Congreso and the new Sucursal and succeeded in the election of La Social members to the two highest offices in each organization. In the Congreso, delegates elected Carmen Huerta president and José María González first secretary. In the new Sucursal, Juan B. Villareal, a Spanish émigré and cooperativist, won the presidency and Félix Riquelme became first secretary. At this point anarchist influence upon the Mexican working class reached a high point for the nineteenth century.

The remaining leaders of the almost moribund Círculo in Mexico City tried to discredit the Zacatecans with the rank-and-file workers by accusing them, with a degree of accuracy, of being partisan supporters of García de la Cadena for the presidency of the republic, but their charges fell upon deaf ears.[59] Most of the moderates supported García de la Cadena because of his sympathetic attitude toward the labor movement, but the militants of La Social and *El Hijo del Trabajo*, who now dominated the Congreso and the Sucursal in Mexico City, resisted them and issued a proclamation protesting the involvement of some members of the Zacatecas group in the political campaign. The writers for *El Hijo del Trabajo* attacked García de la Cadena for his political ambitions, in spite of his previous role as the savior of the Zacatecas Círculo when it had faced opposition from President Díaz.[60]

The ascension to power of Porfirio Díaz resulted in an alliance of such anti-Díaz labor groups as the anarchists, the former Lerdo supporters who would not accept the new president, and most of the moderates who initially rallied behind Díaz but soon became disenchanted and finally opposed him. These groups allied themselves in order to keep the labor movement free from the domination of the Díaz government. The Círculo of Zacatecas, and its Sucursal in Mexico City, served as an alternative to the Díaz-dominated Círculo in the capital. During the presidential campaign of 1880 the Círculo in Zacatecas declared its support for García de la Cadena. The anarchists anticipated this move and opposed it. The majority of delegates to the Congreso followed their lead, but at this time an increased sense of unity in the working-class organizations as a result of the effort to face up to the Díaz regime prevented the groups from breaking over the issue. The political advocacy was on the behalf of a democratic socialist opponent of a mutually hated government; and the candidate, García de la Cadena, was well liked by the working-class movement and even by the anarchists who, although they disapproved of anyone's candidacy, respected him because of his radical and pro-working-class political position which he restated during the campaign.[61]

The depth of the anarchists' disagreement with those who supported political involvement on the part of the Círculo of Zacatecas, the Congreso, or the Sucursal resulted in a mass meeting that took place on December 14, 1879, at Columbus Park in Mexico City. The Congreso called for the meeting in order to install its newly elected officers, of whom José María González (vice-president) and José Rico (first secretary) were members of La Social. Some five thousand persons gathered replete with numerous red-and-black flags, some of which bore the inscription "La Social, Liga Internacional del Jura." A large black banner bearing the inscription "La Social, Gran Liga Internacional" covered the front of the speaker's platform. The meeting quickly turned into a debate among the leading figures over the issue of whether or not genuine "socialists" could take part in the activities of an organization, such as the Congreso, if it became active in politics.

Francisco de Paula González, the new editor of *El Hijo del Trabajo*; Carmen Huerta; Alberto Santa Fe, an agrarian advocate; Fortino C. Dhiosdado, of La Social; and Mata Rivera delivered speeches sympathetic to the policies of La Social. The new president of the Congreso, Manuel Ray y Guzmán, then urged the members of La Social to continue to support the Congreso even if they could not accept the idea of political participation. The speakers finally agreed to allow the affiliated groups and their individual members to make their own decision, and they resolved "that the separation of La Social from the Congreso would be prejudicial to the cause of the Mexican proletariat." The Congreso did not endorse García de la Cadena.[62]

Because the delegates to the Congreso constituted a strong link with the Mexican working class, the anarchists considered them to be an important vehicle for the continued development of their cause. One measure of their progress in this regard was indicated by the group's support of the anarchist position of no political involvement. Political conditions made it imperative for them to be as closely involved as possible with the Congreso in case pro-Díaz elements tried to infiltrate and dominate the organization. But, more importantly, the La Social membership intended to develop the labor congress into a massive "umbrella-type" organization. They planned a group that would be similar in nature to the Confederación Nacional del Trabajo that emerged in twentieth-century Spain. La Social was to provide ideological and organizational impetus from within the Congreso.[63] During 1877 and 1878, La Social continued to organize, reaching the peak of its strength in 1879–1882. In 1878 the organization claimed to have sixty-two regional sections working in urban centers throughout the country.[64] The anarchists had become, by far, the strongest force in Mexican labor. During the early 1880's they continued to dominate the Congreso which, in 1881, after its reorganization and official entry into the European-based anarchist International Workingmen's Association, claimed one hundred affiliated societies and a total enrolled membership of 50,236.[65]

The membership of the Congreso supported the anarchists between 1879 and 1882 in part because of the chaos and despair brought about by the civil war of 1876 and because some of them believed that the oppressive and disappointing policies of the Díaz regime fulfilled the anarchists' dire prophecies regarding the ultimately evil nature of the national government. The anarchists also succeeded in spreading their ideology because of the chronically desperate socio-political conditions of the urban working class and because of a persistent and intensive proselytizing effort by grass-roots organizers. One of their chief weapons was the working-class press. Besides the continuous effort made in newspapers like *El Hijo del Trabajo*, *El Obrero Internacional*, and *El Socialista*, La Social published *La Internacional* during the last six months of 1878. Edited by Francisco Zalacosta, it carried anarchist-oriented articles written by La Social members Rhodakanaty, Félix Riquelme, José Rico, and Francisco Tijera. Each issue carried their twelve-point program, which called for, among other things, "a universal social republic, autonomous government by the municipality, feminine rights, workers' falanges, abolition of salaries [workers' control], and equality of property holdings."

Savoring their new-found strength, the anarchists openly talked of a violent "struggle against the enemies of humanity." Although artisans for the most part, anarchist leaders always tried to identify themselves with, and to act as "the official spokesmen" of, the lowest and most oppressed elements of the people.[66] They were consistent in their opposition to government and in their call for a reorganization of political and economic power through the development of a cooperativist social order.

5. Nineteenth-Century Anarchism and the Agrarian Movement

During the second half of the nineteenth century, when Mexico began a slow drawn-out process of industrialization and urbanization, the seemingly quiet countryside experienced agrarian unrest of proportions unprecedented since the independence revolution of 1810. Trapped between increasing population on diminished *ejidal* and *pueblo* landholdings and ever-growing estates and demands of large property owners, *campesinos* throughout Mexico sought relief by an extraordinary mixture of tactics ranging from legal petitions and agrarian plans to insurrection. The agrarian disturbances which occurred periodically throughout the nineteenth century resulted from a long process of historical development and served as a prelude to similar and more famous occurrences during the fateful epoch 1910–1917. Their causes, nature, and significance are essential for understanding an important aspect of Mexican history and the Mexican Revolution.[1]

Intense peasant uprisings comprised an important part of the Spanish colonial experience in Mexico. Throughout the colonial epoch the *campesinaje* demonstrated a willingness to revolt that alarmed the authorities and caused them to take considerable security measures, including the creation of various rural constabularies.[2] But the agrarian population never successfully asserted itself prior to 1810. Its manifestations of unrest were always isolated by geographical conditions and poor communications. The uprisings were all defeated, for the rural population suffered not only from inferior weaponry but also from internal divisions. The rural working class rarely if ever confronted the great landowners as a unity. *Municipio* leadership often cooperated with the Spanish imperial order and opposed rebellious elements from the lower social strata of the village. Sometimes racial differences between mestizo and indigenous elements rendered deep, even violent, divisions within the villages. Communities contended with each other over land, water rights, and political jurisdictions. Rivalry existed between villages and the sometimes more fortunate hacienda laborers, who in parts of the Valley of Mexico received higher incomes than the free village inhabitants in addition to relief from the head tax which was paid by their *hacendado patrones*.[3]

Despite the uprisings, social banditry and Catholic millenarianism constituted the most frequent forms of Mexican agrarianism. Like the preindustrial, preideological urban crowd, preideological agrarian protest challenged not the state but rather abuses in administration, land seizures, and deplorable conditions encountered in the locality. Out of this social protest, plus the presence of some radical priest missionaries, the first agrarian ideology, Catholic millenarianism, emerged among the *campesinaje*. Some peasants believed that everything would be changed and the long-sought ideal of social justice would spread over the land. The effect of millenarianism in the Mexican countryside has not yet been treated adequately, but testimony to its presence is found in the religiosity of the Zapatista army of the revolution and in the spontaneous land redistributions carried out behind the advancing peasant armies led by the revolutionary priests Miguel Hidalgo and José María Morelos. The argument for spontaneity in these actions is enhanced by the lesser commitment of those two leaders to agrarian reform than that demonstrated by their "followers," who seized haciendas, killed their owners, and occupied the terrain.

Vasco de Quiroga began the Mexican agrarian Catholic millenarian tradition by creating an Indian commune at Santa Fe in the 1530's. Norman Cohn has quoted and described its extreme and contemporary form in Europe:

> "As Mine and Thine do not exist at Labor, but all possession is communal, so all people must always hold everything in common, and nobody must possess anything of his own; whoever owns private property commits a mortal sin." Taxes, dues, rents were to be abolished and so was private property of all kinds. There was to be no human authority of any kind: "All shall live as brothers, none shall be subject to another. The Lord shall reign, and the Kingdom shall be handed over to the people of the earth." And since the Millennium was to be a classless society it was to be expected that the preparatory massacres would take the form of a class war against the "great."[4]

The degree of militancy among the agrarian Catholic millenarians during the Mexican colonial era is not yet fully known, but during the independence struggle *campesino* rank-and-file elements in the armies of Hidalgo and Morelos anticipated the priest-led communal revolt at Yautepec in 1832 and the Zapatistas when they invoked the Virgen de Guadalupe and openly demonstrated deep religiosity while carrying out land reform in areas under their control.

During the nineteenth century the development of export-oriented agriculture in the traditional countryside intensified the growth of haciendas and threatened the village landholdings, *municipio* political independence, and indigenous precapitalist cultural values. The growth of the hacienda did not mean greater wealth in the hinterlands; rather it meant an increased flow of productivity and wealth to the cities, where the *empresarios* of the new export-oriented country estates lived, traded, and speculated. The cultural impact of the new countryside capitalism devastated the precapitalist indigenous farmers' former

value system. The traditional *campesino* worked and lived off the produce of the land. Its productivity satisfied his needs until the intrusion
of the outside world created new desires and concerns. He lost confidence in his former way of life, he sought the advantages of modern
nineteenth-century technology, and yet he resisted his loss of personal
freedom and the polarization of landownership. The prepolitical poor
believe in the rights of the common man based upon natural justice,
law, and custom. They resist infringement by outsiders or the rich.
The more serious *campesino* uprisings in central Mexico (excluding
Sonora, Chihuahua, and Yucatán) occurred in 1832–1834, 1842–
1844, 1847–1849, 1855–1856, 1868–1869, 1878–1884, 1896, and
1906. The *campesinaje* resistance deepened as the century progressed.[5]

After the mid–nineteenth century, free-contract and open-market
sales replaced the long-standing protection of Church and indigenous
municipio landholdings. The volume of land transfers increased until
it peaked during the Porfiriato. These changes catastrophically altered
the peasants' way of life. At the same time the contemporary agrarian
ideology of anarchism and other radical forms of thought reached the
Mexican countryside. Predictably, areas that previously produced social banditry—Chalco–Río Frío, eastern Morelos, and northwestern
Puebla—now produced heavily ideological agrarian revolutionaries.

Eric J. Hobsbawn has outlined the anarchist agrarian village movement in Spain as comprised of three groups—the periodically active
mass of the village population, the local militants, and the outside agitators.[6] Among the Mexican peasants, as in Spain, the third group
made an important contribution to the other two because it brought
agrarian revolutionary ideologies into a countryside already in periodic
revolt.

The serious agrarian unrest of nineteenth-century Mexico indeed
dates back to the independence struggles led by Hidalgo and Morelos
and the massive Oaxaca, Guererro, and Michoacán uprising of 1842–
1844, but the first ideological, coordinated, and well led and organized
agrarian uprising did not take place until 1849, when one thousand
poorly armed *campesinos* raided haciendas and seized Río Verde, a
town near Querétaro. The notorious rapine and savagery of this episode set a pattern for the struggles that followed. Most significantly,
the leader of these *campesinos*, Eleuterio Quiroz, set a precedent and
established a formative agrarian ideology by demanding, in writing,
the redistribution to the *peones* of the more populous lands of the *hacendados*. The *campesinos*, however, sustained their campaign for
only a few months and they offered no ideological-historical critique
of society as a basis for justifying their grievances or making their demands for change.[7] Agrarian tumult intensified and swept most of
central Mexico in 1856 as a result of the Ley Lerdo. The struggle finally merged with the incipient Wars of the Reforma (1858–1860). In

the late 1860's, after the French intervention and the liberals' return to power, agrarian disorders sharply increased and took on an entirely new dimension as a result of the appearance of a revolutionary doctrine. The important turning point toward the modern agrarian movement of the 1910 revolutionary era occurred with the ideological contribution of the Chávez López uprising of 1868–1869.[8]

During the years that followed the demise of Chávez López, agrarian adherents began an active campaign on behalf of the *campesinos* through the medium of the Mexico City working-class press.[9] Radicals, many of them anarchists, continued to develop the agrarian ideology by speaking of cooperative agrarian colonies independent of governmental interference and reinforcing their members' sense of local patriotism. José María González stands out as the leading spokesman for what might be called Mexican anarchoagrarianism during the 1870's.

Despite his importance, González' background remains largely unknown. However, the record of his public activities and the numerous newspaper editorials and articles he wrote during the second half of the 1870's have left behind a historical-ideological legacy and a limited amount of biographical information. He emerges as one of the most provocative and controversial figures of his time. González' descriptions of the more important agrarian confrontations of the epoch are the best expressions of a system of agrarian ideas then gaining widespread acceptance.

González became prominent in the mid-1870's bitterly denouncing and blaming the government, with his essays in *El Hijo del Trabajo*, for the hardships of the *campesinos*, artisans, and urban workers. He cited the omnipresent poverty, the chronic economic instability, and the continual political chaos as evidence of a corrupt and worse than useless Mexican government. Through these denunciations and his proposals for the betterment of society and the uplifting of the lower classes, he expressed in clear terms his anarchist ideology:

> The Social Revolution.
> What is the Object of that revolution?
> To abolish the proletariat.
> Then, cannot the government pass laws to bring about this goal?
> The government is unable to do anything.
> Why?
> Because it is the first enslaver.[10]

Openly challenging the very principle of government itself, González, a tailor, is a constant reminder of the negative reaction by many artisans to the economic and social impact of the evolving factory system of commodity production.[11] On a few occasions he acknowledged those persons who played an important role in the development of his political consciousness. Santiago Villanueva, whom he encountered

during the early years of the Gran Círculo when González first became
involved in the urban labor movement, probably wielded the greatest
influence upon him. Later González remembered him as "my old
friend, an artisan, the founder of the Mexican fraternal societies."[12]
The founder and first editor of *El Hijo del Trabajo*, José Muñuzuri not
only exerted powerful influence upon González but also serves as an
example of the Spanish anarchist impact upon the Mexicans. González
began his journalistic career under the tutelage of the well-grounded
and erudite Muñuzuri.[13] The only other person who had an acknowledged role in the development of González' anarchist creed was an
anonymous figure known as Santibañez (a name assumed on occasion by Rhodakanaty), whom González credited with having contributed greatly to his understanding of Proudhon. It is illustrative of the
organizing techniques used by Mexico's nineteenth-century socialists
that they met as a study group in the Santibañez home where they
read and discussed *What Is Property?* and other works.[14]

González' frequent discussion of agrarian conditions and of his anarchist ideas in *El Hijo del Trabajo* always received featured status
and sometimes occupied the entire front page and more. An illustra-
tion of his creative thinking, González' variation of the cooperativist
theme represents a part of his contribution to nineteenth-century Mexican agrarianism. Like some agrarian advocates, he sought escape
from the social exigencies of a harsh industrial society, from an unprecedented rate of urbanization, and from what seemed to be an increasingly corrupt government into a utopian countryside modeled
upon the socialism of Proudhon and Bakunin. González, in his approach, integrated Mexico's traditional agrarian sense of identity with
the locality, or *patria chica*, and the artisan guilds' self-help heritage
with European anarchist ideological conceptions. González recommended that a mass movement away from the capitalist economy be
started by forming independent, self-sufficient equalitarian associations at the village level:

> They [the workers] will . . . purchase land and settle colonies,
> and a sense of patriotism will develop for the colony to which
> one is born. Then, when prosperity smiles on the colony, there
> will be schools for the instruction and education of both children
> and adults which will be attended perfectly and will produce a
> higher morality that will . . . eliminate the vices that affect other
> societies. In this way government will no longer be necessary,
> with its imperfect schools, its manner of calling to the fore the
> emotions and wars caused by hunger, which is the cause for the
> multitudes of criminals found in our jails.
> [A] cooperative company can be formed with ample capital by
> means of installment payment plans. With the money obtained

in this manner one can establish stores stocked with high-priority consumer goods.

Once the funds are sufficient . . . the worker can continue independently of the capitalist. . . . By the same means land is then purchased in order to form colonies. . . . [After success] we believe that the inferior status of the middle-class woman would disappear forever, that beggary would have no reason for being, that the abuses perpetrated by the government upon the working class would be ended, that the moral character of the workers would be revealed, and that all people would enjoy respect because they would be part of a real social entity.[15]

Describing goals based upon ideology proved to be easier, however, than successfully formulating a realistic plan to bring them about. González proposed a program in which groups of associates would amass sufficient capital in order to purchase land and equipment to begin the system of agrarian collectives. He concluded with a premature appeal for thousands of agrarians and workers to join the project, which he predicted would "amaze" people:

In order to prove that what we propose is not a mere utopian scheme, we are going to set up an example. One hundred associates are able to create a capital amount of ten thousand pesos in two years if each of them saves one hundred pesos. This can be undertaken by fixed monthly payments, i.e., each member would have to give approximately four pesos and sixteen centavos monthly. In the first month four hundred and sixteen pesos would be collected and the funds would be placed into a savings account immediately. Calculated at 3% interest, the savings would provide a gain of twelve pesos and forty-eight centavos, an increase that would continue to grow from month to month. These figures are very small, almost miserable, because we do not wish to deceive but to convince. If this was done with complete enthusiasm and on a greater scale, i.e., with such a number of participants that in the first collection one thousand pesos were gathered, then one would see with amazement the immensity of the project.

What! Are there not ten thousand intelligent workers in the capital that understand their interests and will unite in order to achieve that high ideal of their emancipation, of their betterment? We believe that there are! . . . and very quickly all of the workers' societies in the republic will follow their example. . . . A moment of calm reflection will be enough for the regeneration of the workers. To those men of heart, to those who love Mexico, to those who have children and want to see them happy, to those who suffer from consumption caused by the fatigue of working

hours that are too long, to those who eat bread soaked with the
sweat that drips from their brows, to them we put this question:
Will you passively submit to your unhappy present and not
think of the future? [16]

González, widely read, helped to popularize developing agrarian concepts. His idea of autonomous agrarian collectives with control over
cash resources, to be used for land development and the provision of
needed farming implements, took hold and reappeared in later agrarian demands. The effort to build a system of agrarian cooperatives
within the conceptual framework that he proposed continued into the
1890's.

Two prolonged agrarian struggles that resulted in the expulsion of
campesino families from disputed land almost obsessed the Mexico
City advocates of agrarian reform during the 1870's. Contrary to the
emerging agrarian ideology, the great estate owners, or *hacendados*,
involved in these cases expanded their territories at the expense of two
campesino pueblos. The agrarian essayists in the Mexico City working-
class press became nearly hysterical in their denunuciations, while
whipping up the emotions of their supporters and calling their rivals
thieves and robbers.[17] But they failed to stop the land seizures and,
during the struggles that ensued, the agrarians became desperate. The
public dissemination of their ideas and the push to peacefully develop
agrarian collectives seemed to get them nowhere. Some came to believe that they had not gone far enough, questioned the adequacy of
their program, and placed their faith in violence as the necessary remedy.

A major crisis developed when González charged that José Ives Limantour, the proprietor of Hacienda La Tenería in the state of México,
forcibly seized the farming lands of the *pueblo* San Simonito Tlaco-
mulco in 1869 without legal sanction. In 1876 the *campesinos*, hope-
ful that the new president, Díaz, would help them, petitioned him for
return of the land. But by 1877 Limantour, who had supported former
President Lerdo, had proven his ability to survive political upheaval
by leading a campaign to collect private loans to the Díaz regime in
order for it to pay the government's debt to the United States. Limantour gained the support of the Díaz regime in the settlement of the
dispute and kept the property—this time with the sanction of the
courts. González reacted by printing the pathetic petition sent to Díaz
by the *pueblo* and then summarized his feelings:

. . . [A]s one can see from this document, Sr. Limantour has
committed an unjustifiable abuse. It certainly was not necessary
for him to increase his holding with the lands of the San Simonito *pueblo*. . . .
Well, then, do we have to wait until the powerful might feel

remorse, in order that without violence, or when with a sense of justice, they might return that which does not belong to them? That is to wait in vain![18]

For nearly two years the agrarian advocates in Mexico City campaigned for the return of lands lost by a *campesino* community to Hacienda de las Bocas in San Luis Potosí. In fact, the series of incidents on Hacienda de las Bocas led to some of the most fierce agrarian attacks against the Díaz government. González led the critics, referring to the regime as a group of "oppressors and gangsters" who used the *rurales* to support the *hacendados*.[19] According to the working-class press accounts (the other newspapers ignored the land disputes), these land acquisitions assumed almost classical patterns. They claimed that in 1864 the *hacendados* obtained a series of court decisions based upon the Ley Lerdo that adjudicated the land to them. With the courts' decisions, or perhaps before the courts' decisions, they obtained the support of the local, state, and national authorities. The *hacendados* involved, the "wealthy and powerful" Farias family, caused the *campesinos*, who had originally occupied the land early in the previous century, to be legally declared squatters.[20] This new settlement, a common phenomenon as the rural population continued to increase during the century, had received recognition in 1792 as the *pueblo* of Ahualulco; and the town archives indicated construction of the village church in that year. During the court proceedings, none of the town's citizens could provide testimony regarding the legal rights under which the town had been established, and they possessed no documentary proof. Officials of the Maximilian government then expelled them from the property.[21]

Later, during the tripartite civil war between Díaz, Lerdo, and Iglesias, agrarians believed that Díaz had at least partially adopted their ideology because they thought he had promised land reform to the poverty-striken *peones* of the Mexican countryside. González, for example, referred to this commitment when he wrote: "[T]he plan of Tuxtepec promised us the independence of the municipality, but it was just a promise to lure us."[22] The former citizens of Ahualulco acted upon the assumption that the land would be returned to them, and they reoccupied it.[23] Unfortunately for them, by 1878 the Díaz government and the local and state authorities decided against them. The *campesinos* were once again forcibly removed, their buildings razed, and their belongings lost.[24]

La Internacional's correspondent read the contents of a telegraphic message sent from the *rural* official on the scene; the reporter then forwarded the report from the town of Moctezuma to his paper, and it appeared in the next day's edition: "Commandant F. Rodríguez: Yesterday the removal of *morenos* began from Rancho de San Vicente, upon the orders from the owners of Hacienda de las Bocas; today the expulsion of all the families was completed. Joaquín Flores."[25] The message caused a furor among Mexico City's agrarians. Outraged, *La Internacional*'s editors commented:

> Six hundred families have been thrown off this land in Rancho de San Vicente, upon the orders of the usurpers from Hacienda de las Bocas.
> This horrible act is nothing more than a repetition of what previously occurred in 1869 when this vile *hacendado* threw out others, including old men, women, and children. . . . The rich, with but few and honorable exceptions, lead lives filled with vice and crime . . . at the price of onerous sacrifices on the part of the workers. But when the workers realize this, they will then be able to emancipate themselves from the rule of private capital by joining associations and creating cooperative societies. . . .
> ¡Ay de los vampiros de Oro! ¡Pueblo, justicia para el Proletario![26]

The growing animosity of agrarians toward the Díaz regime reached the boiling point. By 1877 González and others called for a mass uprising, La Revolución Social, in their articles that treated the disputes between *campesinos* and *hacendados*.[27] But the most important result of the agrarian disputes during the 1870's was the emergence of a more sophisticated agrarian ideology.

By 1878, with years of debate and hundreds of revolutionary proposals behind them, the agrarians boasted a program that seemed elaborate in contrast to the ideological simplicity of Chávez López. Zalacosta, the editor of *La Internacional* and an agrarian who favored direct and violent action, endorsed and printed a plan allegedly proposed by La Social. The anarchist-Bakuninist organizing groups then claimed sixty-two branch sections scattered throughout Mexico.[28] La Social's agrarian program called for dissolution of the national government; autonomous municipalities; an agrarian law to provide for the measuring and demarcation of deamortized lands; liquidation of urban capital and interests in the countryside; gradual leveling and equalization of property ownership; ultimate abolition of the wage system and, meanwhile, procurement of higher agricultural wages by means of strikes; formation of territorial banks to secure the sale of agricultural products; and Falansterio Societario communal groups as the basic mode of organization for both urban and agricultural laborers.[29]

In the meantime, intense agrarian unrest built up in the central and northern areas of the country. Between 1878 and 1884 the most widespread *campesino* rebellions to that point in Mexican history broke out in the states of Michoacán, Guanajuato, Querétaro, San Luis Potosí, Durango, Sinaloa, Chihuahua, Coahuila, Hidalgo, México,

Puebla, and Morelos. The revolts resulted from widespread land seizures by speculators in conjunction with the development of national railroad lines and the government's wholesale application of Ley Lerdo land-claims procedures.[30]

The desperate plight of the villages and no expectation that his agrarian plan could be legally implemented caused Zalacosta and other *agrarista* radicals to form a Gran Comité Conmunero. Its task was to promote revolution in the countryside, and its delegates attended village congresses in the states of México, Guanajuato, and Hidalgo. Emissaries established communications with rebellious agrarians as far away as Michoacán and Chihuahua. Then, armed with the program of La Social–La Internacional and the manifesto of Chávez López, Zalacosta went to Chalco, where he managed to stir up a *campesino* rebellion in late 1878. During the next eighteen months he and a few hundred of his followers fought a running battle with the federal army and *rurales* through northeastern Morelos, eastern México, Querétaro, and Hidalgo. The rebels sacked numerous haciendas and redistributed their lands among the *campesinos*. Non-*campesino* towns were attacked and burned. Government forces finally apprehended Zalacosta near Querétaro, where he was detained and eventually executed.[31] The wave of unrest rose and fell until 1884, when the government once again gained military control of the situation.[32]

In the midst of the agrarian turmoil that gripped most of central Mexico, Colonel Alberto Santa Fe penned the most complex and sophisticated agrarian document yet seen. It marked the apex in the development of nineteenth-century agrarian revolutionary ideology. The proposal, known as the Ley del Pueblo, received wide publication in the working-class press.[33] Although one historian describes Santa Fe as "half Bakuninist–half Marxist," his Marxist experience was probably minimal.[34] Marx was hardly mentioned in the working-class press during the 1870's and the first translation of his work did not appear until *El Socialista* broke the silence in 1883.[35] Bakunin's philosophy, however, received frequent coverage in the pages of the Mexico City working-class press with which Santa Fe maintained a close relationship.[36] Porfirio Díaz called Santa Fe a "communist";[37] the reason for this reaction is not hard to find, since the preamble of the Ley del Pueblo stated that the *ley* was based upon the concept of human social and spiritual equality. Its program called for the distribution of parcels of land to the extent of 276 rods in length by 184 in width per minor son to each *campesino* family in Mexico as long as the family's total capital and property did not exceed three thousand pesos. The *municipios* would determine which lands would be seized from the haciendas. To obtain compensation, the *ley* required the *hacendado* to present a receipt for his lands to the nearest office of a

Banco Agrícola y Industrial, which in open and public hearings determined the property's value. The bank, which would be required to have at least one branch in every state of the Mexican union, would keep a record of how much territory the *pueblo* claimed in order to determine when, according to its population, sufficient acreage had been acquired. The *ayuntamiento municipal*, or village council, was charged with the responsibility of individual or communal plot distribution in accordance with local tradition. The recipient was required to repay the agreed-upon value of the land to the agricultural bank at a rate of 10 percent per year plus 6 percent interest on the unpaid principal for ten years. The land title could not be transferred to another individual until the terms of the agreement had been met. Further, the agricultural bank was charged with the responsibility of providing low-interest loans to the *campesinos* through the municipal councils for the purchase of agricultural equipment, seeds, and other necessary farming implements. Consistent with contemporary libertarian socialist ideology and cooperativism, the base of political power was to be the local *municipio*.[38]

Santa Fe's persistent advocacy of his *ley*, his association with the fugitive Zalacosta, and the use of his plan by the revolutionary General Miguel Negrete in the states of Puebla and Morelos led to his arrest in Puebla.[39] Further incentive to make the arrest stemmed from his open communications with agrarian revolutionaries in Guanajuato and Michoacán who had already faced the federal army in the field.[40] Accused of being a "communist," he was placed in the prison of Santiago Tlatelolco in Mexico City on June 8, 1879.[41] After his release he lived in the north of Mexico in "exile." Chastized, years later he won election to the Congress as a pro-Díaz deputy from Durango.[42] He proved to be a repentant sinner who never again muddied the water.

In 1879 the Ley del Pueblo inspired a serious rebellion led by General Miguel Negrete in Puebla, the Chalco area, Morelos, and Guerrero.[43] Negrete explained:

> I even opposed Juárez . . . because he failed to come to the aid of the people, then Lerdo, and now Díaz because of his betrayal of the people after raising their hopes, by surrounding himself with a gang of accomplices, not friends.
>
> I have fought whenever I saw public liberties in danger, and the workers of the city and countryside, as of now, are worse off than ever. . . . [T]he tyranny will end. . . . I hope to lead the last revolution, the one which will end these conditions.[44]

Between 1868 and 1890 Negrete was a potent force in the vast mountainous area extending across the states of Puebla, Morelos, and Guerrero.[45] He supported revolutionary sociopolitical programs and consistently sided with the urban labor and agrarian movements in their relations with the governments of Juárez, Lerdo, and Díaz.[46] He plotted the overthrow of Juárez in 1866 because he and his confederate, General García de la Cadena, both leading generals in the liberal resistance against the French, considered Juárez too conservative.[47] Negrete took this action despite his position as the chief field commander of the Juárez army;[48] the plot fell through because of the opposition voiced by Generals Francisco Naranjo and Juan N. Sáenz.[49] It is clear from the record that Negrete did not fit the pattern of an ordinary provincial *caudillo*. He alienated himself from the mainstream of post-Reforma liberalism, the compromisers and "practical men," with his consistent espousal of agrarian and urban labor reform.

In 1868 and 1869 Negrete provided logistical support for the Chávez López uprising in Chalco and conducted a campaign against government troops in the Puebla-Morelos area immediately to the south of Chalco.[50] He then supported the insurrectionists at Chalco who rallied to Zalacosta in 1879.[51] Consistent with his record, Negrete supported the Ley del Pueblo in 1879–1880. He barely managed to escape arrest in Puebla when federal troops surprised him and some of Santa Fe's supporters. The Mexico City newspaper *El Hijo del Trabajo* commented, "God save Don Miguel from the claw."[52] In 1880 Negrete helped to spread the anarchistlike ideology of the agrarian movement when he issued his own revolutionary agrarian program, which called for the emergence of the autonomous and sovereign *municipio libre* to distribute land and determine the outcome of the long-standing agrarian dispute.[53] He continued to hold out against Díaz until the early 1890's when advanced age forced him to abandon the struggle.[54]

In 1880 Rhodakanaty returned to Chalco with the intention of reopening his *escuela*, only to find the task rendered hopeless by the combined hostility of the government, the local *hacendados*, and Tiburcio Montiel, who founded a large *campesino* organization, the Liga Agraria de la República Mexicana.[55] The Liga, which held regular meetings and sponsored legal action against the territorial encroachments of *hacendados*, had members in the states of Hidalgo, México, Morelos, and Puebla.[56] Active in the agrarian movement since the early 1870's, Montiel assisted Zalacosta in the formation of the Gran Comité Conmunero in 1876.[57] In 1878 he wrote a particularly aggressive article in *El Socialista* which condemned agrarian injustice and cited specific attacks, land seizures, and even instances of cattle rustling commited by haciendas against *pueblos*. He concluded with the assertion that, if his resistance to *hacendados*' aggressions was "*communismo*," then so be it.[58] He obviously regarded Rhodakanaty as a rival when the latter returned to Chalco. Discouraged, Rhodakanaty returned to Mexico City; he finally gave up and returned to

Europe in 1886.[59] Unfortunately for Montiel, his dispute with Rhoda-kanaty attracted too much attention to him; the government identified him as a cohort of Santa Fe and Zalacosta and arrested him in August 1881. After a short-lived jail release, during which he joined Rhoda-kanaty and others as a temporary editor of *El Socialista*, the government again arrested Montiel and sent him into exile at La Paz, Baja California. In the meantime, the ever troublesome *campesinos* at Chalco, who supported him by resorting to the seizure of contested lands, were violently suppressed by the federal army.[60]

Agrarian clashes continued throughout Mexico from Yucatán to Sonora until 1910, although the historical record does not reveal any major attempts made by the *campesinos* or *pueblos* of Chalco or the nearby areas of Morelos and Puebla to redress their grievances outside legal channels. The last major agrarian uprising of the nineteenth century in central Mexico occurred at Papantla in Veracruz, where, despite overwhelming government strength, about one thousand *campesinos* demanding "return of their land" rebelled in 1896. Following defeat in an open battle with the federal army, the indigenous rebels resorted to a vicious guerrilla war that continued until 1906.[61] Resurgent agrarian unrest in other parts of Veracruz erupted in 1906 along with uprisings in northern Mexico under anarchist-oriented Flores Magonista–Partido Liberal Mexicano leadership. The Veracruz fighting continued on into the Mexican Revolution of 1910. The Díaz regime reigned supreme; yet, the agrarians, pushed by a relentless population growth and ever expanding hacienda system, had already developed that collection of ideas and attitudes known as agrarian ideology.[62] Don Porfirio and his *científicos*, with all the power they possessed, never succeeded in undoing the revolution that had occurred in the minds of the *campesino* population.

Despite claims that the Zapatista Plan de Ayala and Agrarian Law were "original," it is clear that the agrarian ideology developed in the nineteenth century, especially in Zapata's own area of operations, foreshadowed most of the concepts that appeared during the agrarian struggle of 1910.[63] The Zapatista program included features of the precursor's proposals, such as redistribution of land, conditions of compensation, *municipio* political autonomy, *municipio* authority over actual land seizures and the awarding of communal or individual plots according to local tradition, the formation of a regional agricultural bank, and the guaranteed provision of such basic farming implements as seed, plows, and oxen.[64] The Plan de Ayala, as a revolutionary document, was more elaborate than its nineteenth-century predecessors; but, after all, it was the end product of an agrarian movement with a long history. As Professor John Womack states: "The plan [de Ayala] was not an instant creation. As a statement of attitudes it had been evolving for at least fifty years, through the public lessons Juárez had given in the supreme importance of 'principles,' 'law,' and 'justice,' through the formation of national pride in the resistance against the French, through the exasperation with personal promises and political abuses during Don Porfirio's long reign, and lately through the abortion of hopes in the virtuous Madero."[65] There existed, however, other important elements in this evolutionary process. Leaders expressing varying degrees of libertarian socialist ideology, such as Chávez López, Rhodakanaty, Zalacosta, González, Santa Fe, Montiel, and Negrete, in their own indefatigable way, made significant contributions to agrarian ideology in their struggles during the darkest days of the nineteenth century. Their efforts were an important part in the development of Mexican agrarianism prior to the coming of the Mexican Revolution.

6. Decline and Perseverance

Despite what can only be described as considerable success during the 1870's, the Mexican anarchist movement suffered inherent weaknesses which rendered it exceedingly vulnerable to government attack during the next two decades. The anarchists demonstrated little preparedness for the sustained campaign conducted against them between 1880 and 1900. The government offensive was begun in 1880 by President Manuel González, who served in Díaz' stead until 1884 when the strongman took charge again.

A number of apparent weaknesses plagued the anarchists: despite the semisecret nature of La Social, the tactic of using the working-class press to publicize plans and actions made the revolutionary socialists openly visible and easy victims of official harassment. Their antipolitical doctrine disrupted the urban labor movement and left them open to counterattack from a government that offered the working class social and economic growth and stability for the first time in Mexican history, and even provided some financing for urban and rural cooperatives. They isolated themselves by claiming governmental incapability of initiating meaningful reform, something which some members of the regime actively sought to disprove.

Although operational anarchism theoretically does not require great numbers for its sustenance, organized masses are needed to protect anarchism from hostile government. The slow growth rate of the Mexican economy before 1880 and the restriction of industrial growth largely to the central area of the country affected too small a percentage of the population to provide adequate numbers or sufficient strength for a mass-based urban working-class movement capable of confronting a hostile government. The *campesinaje* thus constituted the only sector of the working-class population large enough to support such an encounter. When armed conflict between the regime and the working class did occur, it took place in the agrarian sector, but communitarian revolution in the countryside also occurred prematurely. After 1876 the Mexican government consolidated its strength behind the astute political maneuvers of President Porfirio Díaz, who, after a tenuous first four years, commanded the loyalty of most of the army and the regional strongmen. The Mexican peasantry, scattered and unmanageable, could not carry out a mass uprising. That kind of upsurge would have required many years of proselytization in the *municipios* and on the haciendas. For example, in Spain the organization of the peasantry, under much more favorable geographic and other circumstances, took place for two generations with only partial success before the unsuccessful revolution of 1936. Zapata, during the Mexican Revolution of 1910, despite widespread sympathy, found it impossible to attract mass support outside the four-state area of Morelos, Puebla, the southeastern portion of the state of México, and part of Guerrero. In fact, his area of operations covered little more than the territory over which Negrete had exercized hegemony and in part of which Chávez López had conducted his uprising.

A dispute within the urban labor movement over the question of involvement in national politics heralded the beginning of a troubled epoch. In January 1880 the representatives of the Zacatecas Gran Círculo steadfastly insisted upon their support for General García de la Cadena in his quest for the presidency of Mexico against the Díaz-sponsored candidate, General González. Meanwhile, anarchists continued to espouse the idea of noninvolvement in national politics. Despite the mass rallies at Columbus Park on September 16 and December 14, 1879, and the seeming agreements reached there, the labor congress eventually fell apart and had to be reorganized because of this issue. Between January and April, delegates representing more than fifty thousand working-class men and women in affiliated organizations attended its meetings. During these months the delegates consistently elected La Social representatives and their antipolitical supporters to the directorate of the Congreso. On February 1, 1880, the delegates elected Villareal as president, José María González as vice-president, Félix Riquelme as first secretary, and Juan Orellana as third secretary.[1]

By April 20 it became clear that La Social's dominance of the Congreso prevented its endorsement of García de la Cadena's presidential bid. Ramón Sandoval, one of the representatives from the Zacatecas Gran Círculo, announced to the assembled delegates on that date that, in view of the fact the Zacatecas group endorsed García de la Cadena and the Congreso denied him its support, the Zacatecas delegation had no choice but to withdraw. A number of sympathizers joined in the walkout and the disrupted congress adjourned. Then the editors of *El Socialista*, who originally endorsed García de la Cadena on January 8, 1880,[2] tried to rally his supporters with a proclamation on April 29 announcing their alliance with the Zacatecans in order to bring about his election.[3]

From the beginning of the campaign García de la Cadena demonstrated why he had such avid support with ringing denunciations of Díaz that included a program for social change virtually identical to that espoused by the Congreso. This platform included land reform controlled by the local *municipio* rather than at the national level, autonomy for local municipalities, encouragement for workers to organize cooperative and mutualist societies, and the right to strike.[4]

From a major presidential candidate such a program was unprecedented.

The urban labor opponents of political participation quickly reacted to the smaller faction that endorsed García de la Cadena. First, they reconvened the Congreso on May 8, 1880, and elected Carmen Huerta president and González first secretary. Then, in conjunction with the Gran Círculo of Mexico City, they published a joint proclamation in *El Hijo del Trabajo* which condemned *El Socialista*, the Zacatecas Círculo, and all working-class groups that supported García de la Cadena. The Congreso and the Mexico City Círculo represented the vast majority of organized Mexican workers. An indication of anarchist strength at this time can be seen by the fact that Huerta and José María González signed the proclamation for the Congreso; so did Juan Villareal as president, and Félix Riquelme as first secretary of the Mexico City Gran Círculo. All were members or sympathizers of the libertarian socialist faction.[5]

By the end of April the dispute between the supporters of García de la Cadena and those who supported the anarchists caused the complete rupture of the Congreso. The García de la Cadena supporters assumed the risk of the Congreso's destruction with their withdrawal because they felt the workers' only real hope of defeating Díaz lay in García de la Cadena's election.[6] At the same time the anarchists steadfastly refused to commit themselves to a candidate for national office. The presidency, they felt, would ultimately oppress the people regardless of the individual in power.[7]

What at first appeared to be only another episode in a seemingly endless series of disputes over participation in national elections ultimately proved to be a critical turning point for both the anarchists and the working-class movement. While the dispute itself was not fatal to either, the resultant organizational disunity and political factionalism served to isolate the anarchists from the moderates and drastically weakened them both. The task of the Díaz government when it moved against them and independent organized labor thus became much easier.

The Congreso did not die; on the contrary, it continued to gain strength for the next two years. By 1882 it regained its losses of 1880 and claimed 50,236 members in its affiliated organizations.[8] Several factors counted in this remarkable recovery: The greater unity of the remaining members permitted them to function more smoothly. They conducted an intensive campaign to establish new labor associations, especially cooperatives. Many García de la Cadena supporters later returned to the fold after his losing effort in the election.

But valuable time had been lost. Even though the Congreso appeared to be gaining strength, in reality the anarchists' and the entire independent working-class movement's downfall had been sown. The first setbacks occurred in 1878 when the Díaz regime, provoked by strikes, persistent political campaigns against his government, and agrarian insurrections, began to react. First, the Sociedad Artística Industrial, a group controlled by La Social, found that the building received as a gift from President Juárez had been given by Díaz to the then-moribund, pro-Díaz Mexico City Gran Círculo.[9]

Then, shortly before Díaz turned his office over to incoming President González, a series of political arrests took place. In June 1879 government troops apprehended Colonel Alberto Santa Fe in Puebla at the height of his campaign for agrarian reform. Shortly before his arrest, Santa Fe agitated against the government and persistently argued the validity of land claims by local *campesinos* against a hacienda owned by General Cuéllar in the valley of San Martín Texmelucan, mid-way between Mexico City and Puebla. Cuéllar had obtained the land during his stint as military commander of the area and Díaz supported his claim.[10] Santa Fe's Ley del Pueblo promised sweeping agrarian reform and gained him a considerable following in and around the state of Puebla. As a result, his followers constituted a genuine threat to the pro-Díaz *hacendados* of the area. Díaz moved against Santa Fe with confidence.

The president's optimism was well founded because, since coming to power in 1876, he had greatly increased the strength of the government. During the tripartite civil war of 1876 the *rurales*, or national rural police who supported a losing cause on behalf of President Lerdo, were decimated and scattered. In 1876 Díaz had been virtually without a law-enforcement agency. In order to consolidate his power he spent several years rebuilding both the *rurales* and the federal army. By 1879 he felt strong enough to suppress dissidents and also to step down for one presidential term as the constitution required and allow his supporter, General González, to serve until 1884.

The government's greater ability to maintain order in the countryside also resulted in the arrest of Francisco Zalacosta, editor of *La Internacional*, who had evaded the authorities for almost two years. The agrarian uprisings he stirred up were crushed by the federal army before his internment and execution in Querétaro in 1880. Federal forces also stifled two other agrarian revolts at the same time—one led by the radical General Negrete, who promulgated a plan patterned after the Ley del Pueblo; the other, by the supporters of Santa Fe after his arrest.

Tiburcio Montiel and his *campesino* followers in the Liga Agraria de la República Mexicana next felt the government's wrath. Montiel, active in the labor and agrarian movements since the early 1870's, founded the *liga* after serving as the lawyer for Zalacosta's Gran Comité Conmunero in 1876. Unfortunately for Montiel, his aggressive stand on behalf of the *campesinos* in the Chalco area implicated him in the agrarian uprising led by Zalacosta. Authorities arrested him in August 1881 after his aggressive essay "Comunismo" appeared in *El Socialista*. His complaints about agrarian conditions and specific charges of acts of violence, land seizures, and cattle rustling by large landholders against the villages of San Buenaventura and San Ignacio Nopala in the state of Hidalgo and Tepexpan and Yuxtepec in the state of México earned him the title of "Communist" and he went to jail for it.[11] Shortly thereafter he was sent into exile at La Paz, Baja California.

By 1882, with Zalacosta and Montiel eliminated and Rhodakanaty's *escuela* refused permission to reopen, the Mexico City leftists were isolated from Chalco and the Mexican countryside. Defeated in an abortive uprising after Montiel's arrest, the Chalco *campesinos* passed into a state of relative quiescence that endured until they rallied to the banner of Emiliano Zapata thirty years later.

The agrarian uprisings between 1878 and 1884 would perhaps have overwhelmed earlier liberal governments, but the federal forces moved with swift efficiency and defeated the revolts which spread to Querétaro, San Luis Potosí, Michoacán, and Chihuahua. Anarchist attempts to coordinate the uprisings failed with the elimination of Zalacosta's band.[12] The Díaz government depended on the *rurales* and the federal army for the extension of its control over the agrarian population. *Rural* patrols were set up to police the quelled *campesinos*.[13] The government completed its pattern of agrarian suppression with a campaign that nearly exterminated the troublesome Yaqui Indians in the northwest during the late 1880's and 1890's.[14]

The urban labor movement also felt the sting of the government's anger. In Veracruz on June 24, 1879, nine persons involved in a port strike under way in that city were shot and killed during a street demonstration. *El Hijo del Trabajo* loudly declared that the governor of the state, Luis Mier y Teran, had ordered the shooting. The newspaper concluded: "It is necessary for Mexico to rid itself of that kind of *bribón* [scoundrel] if it does not want them to continue killing and assassinating."[15] More important than the moral outrage felt by the *El Hijo del Trabajo* staff on behalf of the "Mártires de Veracruz" was the evidence that they were intimidated. A mourning frontispiece appeared on the front page of the paper for over a year and the names of the revolutionary essayists who used its pages were deleted from their articles and pseudonyms were attached.

The government's suppression of the labor movement, considering its belligerence and vulnerability, developed slowly. A high degree of tolerance toward organized labor seemed to exist during the period 1876–1879. *El Hijo del Trabajo*, as the voice of the Gran Círculo, first found the outer limits of government tolerance in 1876 when President Lerdo suspended publication from October 16 to December 14.

Following the Veracruz massacre *El Socialista* joined *El Hijo del Trabajo*, complaining of threats and adopting the use of pseudonyms,[16] but, after a brief period of editorial outrage, the papers fell silent.[17] Late in 1880, *El Socialista* endorsed Díaz for the governorship of Oaxaca.[18] In 1881, *El Hijo del Trabajo* endorsed General González as president of the Republic with this justification: "We were irreconcilable enemies of the past administration because its treatment of us was hard and unjust, but we will always be close friends of the present one, because we have always—to this time—been inspired by the ideas of conciliation, peace, and progress."[19] After this dramatic change in approach, *El Hijo del Trabajo* refrained from revolutionary themes and even ceased its coverage of labor news, a serious blow to the urban working-class movement.

The government waited until late in 1881 to finally close down the by then anarchist-dominated Mexico City Gran Círculo. President González temporarily lifted the suspension in March 1882, but the hard-put Círculo had to advertize to lease its meeting hall: " . . . the reasons for being suspended having ceased, the Círculo offers the use of its salon to those who might want to use it."[20] In 1883 the Gran Círculo de Obreros de México permanently closed and passed into history.[21]

The Congreso managed to avoid problems with the government for a considerable length of time. In typical fashion it issued an official statement that it intended "to be the expression of all the workers' societies in the country that send delegates. We support, in principle, the laws of the land. We hope for domestic tranquility and declare that insurrection will only be resorted to when it is intended that the rights of man be taken from him."[22] However, in 1881, the Congreso invited trouble with Díaz by affiliating with the anarchist international in Europe. Nathan Ganz, an American anarchist and publisher of the *Anarchist Socialist Revolutionary Review* of Boston, contributed some articles to *El Socialista* and served as the Mexican delegate to the London convention of the anarchist international in 1881.[23]

Near the end of 1882, shortly after reaching an all-time high in membership, the original Congreso passed into oblivion. No reports of its demise or of its activities after 1882 appeared, but several new organizations surfaced shortly thereafter and their involvements provide some insights. In late 1884 Pedro Ordóñez was praised as "a liberal, and president of the TRUE Círculo y Congreso de Obreros . . . and he is a property owner."[24] The TRUE Círculo y Congreso was created as a unified organization in 1884. It cooperated freely with the government in formulating a social reform program acceptable to both Díaz and moderates within the labor movement. The description praising the much toned down Ordóñez as "a property owner" was unprecedented in *El Socialista*. Urban workers, previously troublesome for the regime, now combined as government supporters under a leader who just a couple of years earlier had enjoyed great prestige among Mexican libertarian socialists and radical labor organizers.[25]

The government provided extensive financial aid to the TRUE Círculo y Congreso for the development of rural agrarian cooperatives. Some of these cooperatives soon featured surprisingly complex and integrated economies.[26] Although the TRUE Círculo y Congreso itself failed to become a viable and growing organization, the government-sponsored cooperatives survived until the mid-1890's. The government justified this blatant violation of laissez faire by arguing that the colonies ensured development, social tranquility, and immigration. Despite some successes, by 1897 the government abandoned the cooperatives in favor of the now-notorious development companies.[27]

Another, more militant, labor group also emerged in the wake of the Congreso's demise. The Junta Privada de las Sociedades Mutualistas de México, claiming the right to strike and seek "social justice," surfaced in the mid-1880's headed by Carmen Huerta, the former Congreso president and La Social member. Ordóñez also held membership. The Junta Privada, despite its more militant inclinations in contrast to the TRUE Círculo y Congreso, took pains to praise the government and the political system,[28] but it survived only a few years. The Díaz regime had gained nearly complete control over the labor movement.

The anarchists did not give up despite the setbacks. In July 1884 the Club Nacional de Obreros Libres announced its presence and invited working-class support. The leadership claimed the inviolate right to strike and urged workers to resort to this weapon if other means failed.[29] American anarchists from the Knights of Labor assisted the Club Nacional in its effort to organize among Mexico's textile workers during the middle and late 1880's.[30] The Club Nacional did not survive into the 1890's as an entity, but its adherents, reinforced by sporadic American support, continued their activities, especially in the north.

A small group of die-hard revolutionaries organized Los Grupos Revolucionarios de Emigrados Españoles en Varias Regiones in 1885. They issued a call "to all of the exploited in general, and to Spanish immigrants in particular . . . to rise up and throw off the yoke of the oppressor."[31] Government records list 9,500 Spaniards living in Mexico with immigrant status in 1887.[32] This organization provides another example of the influential role played by Spaniards, such as Muñuzuri and Villareal, in the nineteenth-century Mexican working-class movement. The anarchists, despite their defeats, had a residual strength that became the basis of their survival.

The government declaration rendering cooperatives illegal represents one of the hardest blows struck against the anarchist campaign for cooperativism in the nineteenth century.[33] When later legalized, the government ensured domination of the cooperatives with the proviso that all such enterprises were subject to government control and regulation. Government hegemony over all police and civil activities, including education, further limited their independence. No cooperatives of the type envisioned by José María González could exist under those stipulations.[34]

The consolidation of power by the Díaz regime affected the anarchists and the working-class movement in ways other than direct intervention. The most important episodes in this regard involved the regime's conflicts with Generals García de la Cadena and Negrete. Both men long supported revolutionary sociopolitical programs and frequently sided with the most militant elements of the urban labor and agrarian movements in their relations with the liberal governments of Juárez, Lerdo de Tejada, and Díaz.[35]

García de la Cadena, after years of opposition to Juárez and Lerdo from his Zacatecas stronghold, openly challenged Díaz for the first time in 1879 when the Zacatecas Gran Círculo received his support against the Díaz-dominated Gran Círculo in Mexico City.[36] García de la Cadena, an honorary guest at the inaugural meeting of the Zacatecas group, guaranteed the delegates that he would "protect them."[37] The Zacatecas Gran Círculo's quick success against its rival in Mexico City could only aggravate the injury felt by Díaz.

A short time later García de la Cadena published a letter in *El Socialista* which opposed Díaz over the issues involved in a proposed new tax on Mexican industry. The text provides insight into his political philosophy: ". . . it will mean hardships for the Mexican workers who will be laid off their jobs; . . . [the large estate owners] want this tax instead of one that would apply to them."[38]

Then, in 1880, García de la Cadena opposed González' candidacy for president with an appeal to organized labor. His rivalry with Díaz continued until 1886 when he supported an unsuccessful revolt led by Negrete. Federal troops invaded Zacatecas, captured García de la Cadena, and executed him. His fate had by then become a familiar story in Mexico. The government newspaper, *El Diario Oficial*, announced his death while "trying to escape"—the *ley de fuga*. An immediate public outcry led by several respectable newspapers in Mexico City followed the announcement. *El Siglo XIX* issued a typical commentary: "García de la Cadena has been killed by the *ley de fuga*; a good man has been murdered."[39]

After his abortive revolution of 1879–1881, Miguel Negrete enjoyed a reputation as a vehement opponent of Díaz and as an advocate of the agrarian cause. For the next five years Negrete chafed as he watched the dictatorship increase its hold over the country and the agrarian situation deteriorate. Finally, in 1886, he could tolerate no more and prepared for a final confrontation. He promulgated his reasons in a revolutionary plan that denounced the government's policies and called for the free autonomous village, the *municipio libre*, which he believed should be the fundamental political and economic unit of the nation. His proclamation called for a complete agrarian reform: land was first to be redistributed to the *municipios* and then the villages themselves would allocate it to individual farmers or retain it in common, whichever method was more consistent with local tradition. He proposed agrarian banks in order to provide necessary funds for irrigation, farming implements, and overall development. Negrete's new government offered the urban labor movement its support in order to establish a system of free cooperatives and mutualist societies. It also promised higher wages, the right to strike, and better working conditions.[40]

Porfirio Díaz, after the usual precautions of determining security in other areas, crushed the revolt. After a few nervous weeks Díaz managed to isolate other rebellious army units from Negrete. Then, in the summer of 1886, government armies invaded Puebla in a sustained and difficult campaign in which the federal troops experienced considerable privation.[41] Negrete finally retreated toward the south, but government troops intercepted and surrounded his forces and captured Negrete.[42] García de la Cadena, who had supported Negrete in 1864–1866 and 1868, violated Díaz' orders and fled the Federal District to Zacatecas in order to rally his troops. Pursued and captured by order of Minister of War Pedro Hinojosa, García de la Cadena died in the field at the hands of a firing squad.[43] Almost twenty-four years of armed resistance against the general politics and the labor and agrarian policies of Juárez, Lerdo, Díaz, and González had come to an end. With Negrete and García de la Cadena eliminated, the working-class movement lost its military allies and all immediate hopes for a revolutionary redress of workers' grievances.

7. The Resurgence

Introduction

During the late 1880's and 1890's, disorganization and demoralization plagued the anarchists. The continuance of difficult conditions for the working class, a few remaining adherents, student unrest, the flow of Spanish émigrés, a minor influence from anarchist members of the Knights of Labor in the 1890's, and a more significant influence from the Western Federation of Miners and the Industrial Workers of the World in the first decade of the twentieth century, however, helped to keep the cause alive. In the meantime, an aged Díaz regime encountered a deteriorating economy and mounting public resentment.

Despite a lack of leadership, Mexico's industrial workers showed militancy throughout the Porfiriato. In 1885 worker unrest resulted in serious textile strikes at El Valor in Tlaxcala, Cerritos in Orizaba, La Magdalena in Contreras, and San Antonio de Abad in Mexico City. The intervention of an older and more conservative Pedro Ordóñez, now a city *regidor*, highlighted the San Antonio de Abad strike. Instead of a five-peso strike fine being paid to the owners by the defeated workers, the money went to a workers' charity, La Casa Amiga de la Obrera. In 1888 a strike closed the La Victoria plant in Puebla for nearly three weeks. In 1889 walkouts closed the El Molino factory in Veracruz, San Fernando in Tlalpan, and Cerritos. The unrest during the period 1885–1890 usually resulted from salary reductions and involved workers fully aware of the almost routine hostility of the authorities and the omnipresent soldiery.[1]

In January 1890 the San Antonio de Abad workers went on strike again, once more protesting a cut in wages. The San Antonio de Abad situation was significant because the factory was the largest in the Federal District and its workers were beginning to build a record for radical working-class militancy that would continue through the revolution with their affiliation with the anarchosyndicalist-dominated Casa del Obrero Mundial and through the 1920's with the anarchosyndicalist General Confederation of Workers (Confederación General de Trabajadores, CGT). In 1892, in 1894, and twice in 1896 the San Antonio de Abad plant closed because of strikes. The issues ranged from salary reductions and increased working hours to management-employee relations.

Other plants with significant histories of worker militancy also experienced continuing unrest. La Colmena of Tlalnepantla, an older factory than San Antonio de Abad, whose workers Santiago Villanueva organized in 1868 and who affiliated with the workers' Círculos and Congresos of the 1870's and 1880's, was closed down by a strike in 1898. Seven hundred workers struck and won negotiated concessions, a rare victory. An even larger and more significant strike occurred in 1900 when El Mayorazgo in Puebla was struck and three thousand textile workers in the state of Puebla followed suit.[2] This walkout, Mexico's first "general strike," inaugurated the twentieth-century era of modern syndicalism. Mexican workers not only remembered their heritage and how to strike, despite the illegalities, but also, after twenty-four years of "Porfirian peace," utilized the most contemporary European syndicalist tactics. Nineteenth-century theory had become twentieth-century reality.

Americans from the Knights of Labor assisted in the campaign to organize the railroad workers of Nuevo Laredo in 1887, Monterrey and Puebla in 1898, and Aguascalientes and Mexico City in 1900.[3] During the first years of the twentieth century, members of the Western Federation of Miners began their radicalizing work at Cananea. Many of these men were part of a developing tendency within the United States labor movement which soon produced the theoretically anarchosyndicalist Industrial Workers of the World (IWW) in 1905. The IWW operated at Cananea in 1906. The Mexican Liberal party (Partido Liberal Mexicano), organized by Ricardo Flores Magón, a leader of the 1890's university student protests in Mexico City, included substantial anarchist elements and worked with the Americans. Beginning in 1904, the Magonistas, from their American sanctuary, began to send emissaries—revolutionary culture brokers—into the mining camps of the Mexican north and into agrarian villages as far south as Veracruz and Oaxaca.

The Díaz regime was concerned. The role of American anarchists in the organization of Mexican labor during the last decade of the nineteenth century, joined by the exile Magonistas during the early years of the twentieth century, was reflected in the Second Pan American Conference held in Mexico City 1901–1902. The Mexican government demanded uniform and severe extradition laws dealing specifically with anarchists and applicable to all of the American nations.[4] The conference delegates shared the belief that anarchists should be prosecuted, but the problem lay in finding an adequate definition of anarchism. The Mexican delegate, Alfredo Chavero, after several weeks' delay, admitted his inability to define it. Nevertheless, he submitted a list of twenty-two crimes which he insisted constituted anarchist acts. The cited offenses ran the gamut of criminal behavior, from murder and robbery to sabotage. The last crime listed was a catch all: "*los delitos de anarquismo*," still undefined. While delegates agreed with and adopted the first twenty-one offenses as anarchist crimes, they dropped the last category of "*anarquismo*" from the final declaration of the conference.[5] The other twenty-one charges were adopted and Chavero left only half-satisfied with the results.

The Resurgence: Social and Economic Factors

During the Porfiriato industrialization created a growing urban complex and an increasingly powerful urban working class. Increased economic activity stimulated the larger urban centers. Those totaling over 20,000 population grew at an annual rate of 2.5 percent between 1877 and 1910 while rural communities under 5,000 lagged behind at a 1.2 percent annual growth rate. Mexico City more than doubled in size during the Porfiriato from 230,000 to 471,000. Other industrial centers experienced even more spectacular growth; Monterrey increased by 461 percent and Veracruz by 490 percent. The growth of the cities was caused by increased trade, both foreign and domestic, and expanded factory production which provoked an influx of *campesinos* seeking urban opportunity. The rural-urban migration created an over-abundant labor supply, which, complemented by the general economic slump after 1906, drove industrial workers' real wages steadily downward from a high point reached in 1897.

In central Mexico an industrial worker whose daily income provided buying power of 1.92 pesos in 1897 found his daily real wages in 1907 reduced to 1.40 pesos, with no signs of recovery to console him.[6] Higher food prices undermined his economic position, although other crucial items, such as rents, fuel, and clothing, also increased in cost far more rapidly than the growth of industrial wage earnings. Until 1897 rising real income and active government mediation in labor-management disputes discouraged both revolutionary activism and the acceptance of revolutionary ideology. Then, after more than twenty years of steady industrial and agricultural production increases accompanied by stable prices for essential goods, the Mexican economy faltered. The following ten years were exceptionally difficult for the lower classes.

The relatively firm prices that prevailed before 1900 for consumer goods essential to the urban workers fell to inflation between 1900 and 1910. During the previous twenty-four years corn, bean, and wheat costs rose at an acceptable average of 4 percent per year. Cotton even decreased in price. In the next ten years cotton costs increased 98 percent, chiles 193 percent, and beans 64 percent. The final three years saw the problem reach a crisis stage. Between 1907 and 1910 corn prices went up 38 percent and wheat 20 percent. In addition to the steady decline in real wages, the urban workers also encountered a higher rate of unemployment during the last decade of the Porfiriato.[7] Increasingly difficult conditions alienated many workers and contributed to the urban labor unrest that surfaced in 1898, peaked in 1906–1907, and was reasserted after 1910.

In the agrarian sector, the unprecedented extent of village land seizures and the extreme development of latifundia during the Porfiriato created large numbers of landless rural workers, resulted in a search for crops which would maximize cash earnings, and left the Mexican domestic agricultural market vulnerable to fluctuations. That vulnerability was demonstrated between 1907 and 1910 when the reduced acreage still devoted to the production of essential domestic foodstuffs was afflicted by crop blight causing severe shortages. The number of haciendas increased between 1877 and 1910 from 5,869 to 8,431,[8] while the greater part of the 57,778,102 hectares of land given out by the liberal governments between 1853 and 1911 was distributed after 1877.[9] The more affluent recipients of those land grants, known as the "younger Creoles," pushed labor productivity to new heights in order to increase their returns. Sugar production, which took place in both the lowlands and the more densely populated highlands, increased from 629,757 tons in 1877 to 2,503,825 tons in 1907.[10] Spectacular increases were also recorded in other plantation products. Ward Barrett has demonstrated that the search for profits was a traditional aspect of the great estate in Mexico;[11] in the latter part of the nineteenth century that tradition was accentuated.

One insight regarding the overall impact of these trends upon the quality of rural village and urban worker life is seen in the increasing costs of corn, beans, and chile and, after 1907, in the sharp per capita decline in the production of these essentials. Meanwhile, throughout the Porfiriato, there were dramatic production increases of the intoxicants mescal and tequila, the consumption of which increased from 10,018 liters in 1877 to 26,068 in 1910, and pulque, which soared from 95,856 liters to 347,653.[12] Deteriorated economic conditions exacerbated pre-existing social tensions in the lower strata of the working classes and were an important factor in both the resurgence of Mexican anarchism in the early twentieth century and the coming of the Mexican Revolution.

Working-class revolutionary leadership in 1910 came from the artisans whose difficulties paralleled those of the less skilled workers. In addition to the higher costs of essentials, the rise of industrialism and industrial workers spelled the decline of competitive artisan crafts. *Sastres*, or tailors, composed one artisan group that especially suffered throughout the development of the textile industry. During the late Porfiriato the accelerated rate of change literally destroyed them. In 1895 there were 41,000 independent tailors and 19,000 textile factory workers. By 1900 the number of tailors decreased to 26,000 and the textile factory workers had reached an equal total. In 1910 only 8,000 tailors remained, and 32,000 factory workers labored in plants which became ever larger and more centralized.[13] The spectacular growth of the cement, brickyard, and typesetting industries spelled a similar fate for the typesetters, quarry workers, stonecutters, and stonemasons. The revolutionariness of the *tipógrafos, canteros,* and *sastres* during the early twentieth century did not occur by accident.

The artisan situation further deteriorated with the elimination of the *alcabala*, the principal legal bulwark supportive of the artisan's economic position at the local level, during the late Porfiriato. The *alcabala* was a state or local protective tariff on imported goods from which local governments obtained their necessary operating revenues. The rise of industry, however, carried with it concomitant political influence for the industrialists at the national level and an increasingly dominant free trade ideology. Once the national government could provide alternative sources of fiscal support for state and local administrators, the local political elites separated from their traditional pro-*alcabala* allies, the artisans. The Díaz regime accordingly abolished the *alcabala* in 1896.[14] Many local retailers and distributors welcomed the freer flow of trade. The artisans, isolated and outraged, organized in desperation.

Ricardo Flores Magón, the PLM, and the Prerevolutionary Strikes

In the early twentieth century, Mexican anarchism continued a pattern of development that roughly paralleled that of Europe. The developing factory system rendered the earlier organizational conceptions of mutualism and cooperativism obsolescent, and a larger urban labor force made the formation of an anarchosyndicalist union feasible. Mexican anarchism moved from the relatively escapist tendencies of the nineteenth-century cooperativists, who advocated withdrawal from the capitalist economy into independent societies and the joining together of capitalists and workers as brothers, to the anarchosyndicalists, who, alienated and belligerent, confronted capitalist society with such weapons as the general strike, sabotage, and workers' control of the factories.

The Díaz regime, because of its early successes, acted something like a filter against the full transmission of the Mexican anarchist tradition.[15] As a result, the twentieth-century Mexican anarchists turned, not to their nineteenth-century predecessors, but to Proudhon, Bakunin, and Kropotkin. The movement was once again stimulated by the presence of Spanish anarchists, and they played a comparable role to that of the previous century.[16]

The first powerful twentieth-century anarchist organization developed around the Liberal party led by the Flores Magón brothers. Ricardo Flores Magón first read Kropotkin at an early age and testified to the strong impression that he received. Between 1900 and 1910, Flores Magón and the Liberal party posed the only serious challenge to the Díaz regime and they became a symbol of resistance. The "Liberal party" actually operated as a revolutionary resistance against Díaz and not as a group devoted to political campaigns or activities normally attributed to political parties. Most PLM members and activists were not anarchists. Some were socialists, but a majority simply wanted democracy in Mexico. The majority abandoned the anarchist-dominated PLM Junta and supported Francisco I. Madero once the revolution against Díaz began.

Ricardo and Enrique Flores Magón were the sons of a *porfirian* army officer and landowner in the southern Mexico state of Oaxaca. Their parents, imbued with the political ideals of nineteenth-century Mexican liberalism, violently rejected the dictatorship of Porfirio Díaz as a violation of liberal principles. Both Ricardo and Enrique moved to Mexico City where they received training in the law. Ricardo first surfaced as an opponent of the Díaz regime in 1892 with his arrest for leading an antigovernment student demonstration. Only nineteen years of age, he served one month in prison. It is likely that he received his introduction to anarchism and became aware of the anarchist tradition within the Mexican working class during his next few years as a student, but his activities and political beliefs between 1892 and 1900 are unrecorded. By 1900 he already professed anarchist beliefs, but his communist-anarchism did not emerge publicly until many years later while he was living in exile in the United States.

In 1900, Ricardo, more radical than the youthful student leader of 1892, assisted in the publication of a new anti-Díaz newspaper, *Regeneración*. Later that year Ricardo and Enrique participated in the creation of the Students Liberal Committee (Comité Liberal de Estudiantes) in Mexico City. In February of 1901, Ricardo, acting as a delegate from the Comité, attended the nationwide "Liberal Congress" organized in San Luis Potosí by the antidictatorial social reformer Camilo Arriaga. During a speech to the congress, Ricardo repeatedly labeled Díaz and his aides "a pack of thieves" and he emerged from the congress as one of the new liberal movement's most prominent spokesmen. In April he took part in the formation of a new liberal club in Mexico City, La Asociación Liberal Reformista, which affiliated with the San Luis Potosí Liberal Congress.[17]

During the next three years he suffered repeated arrest and fines, and the government permanently closed *Regeneración*. Finally, in 1903, confronted by the choice of constant police surveillance and frequent arrests or the abandonment of their convictions. Flores Magón and his closest liberal associates chose to continue the struggle from across the border in the United States. In February 1904 the Flores Magón brothers, Juan and Manuel Sarabia, Santiago de la Hoz, Librado Rivera, Antonio I. Villareal, Rosalio Bustamante, and Santiago R. de la Vega met in Laredo, Texas, and formed the Club Liberal Ponciano Arriaga as an organization through which to carry on their campaign against Díaz. *Regeneración*, published in San Antonio and intended to stimulate Mexicans on both sides of the border against Díaz, reappeared in November 1904.[18]

Police and Furlong Detective Agency harassment caused the liberals to move from Texas to Saint Louis, Missouri, after one year in Laredo and San Antonio. On September 25, 1905, they formally announced the creation of the Mexican Liberal party in Saint Louis. The announcement included a call for the development of a network of underground revolutionary cells throughout Mexico in order to bring about the overthrow of the Díaz regime. The membership of the governing Junta of the new party consisted of Ricardo Flores Magón, president; Juan Sarabia, vice-president; Villareal, secretary; and Enrique Flores Magón, treasurer and included as *vocales*, full members of the directorate, Rivera, Manuel Sarabia, and Bustamante.[19] During September 1905 their newspaper, *Regeneración*, reached twenty thousand copies per edition.[20]

By this time President Díaz and United States Ambassador to Mexico David E. Thompson fully realized the presence of Ricardo Flores Magón, the PLM, and their intentions. The "Pinkertons" (Furlong) had already informed Díaz that Ricardo was "a dangerous anarchist." Their report continued: "The Flores Magóns, Sarabia, and Villareal have always appeared to me as men fanatical over one idea and for that reason they are dangerous, as are all persons that one encounters with that obsession . . . they are always talking of tyranny . . . of the rich classes, in particular of the *hacendados* and industrialists, who exploit the workers."[21] A few months later Ambassador Thompson informed the United States Department of State that the PLM "worried" President Díaz, "harmed United States business interests," and advocated "anarchism."[22]

In reality the Liberals had long been divided on the question of political perspective. Of the original Junta only Ricardo, Rivera, and Enrique developed an anarchist ideology. While in Laredo and San Antonio in 1904, some of them, a minority, sensing Ricardo's deepening radicalism, rejected it and supported the moderate social reforms advocated by the wealthy Arriaga. During the Liberals' year-long interlude in Saint Louis, Ricardo, Juan Sarabia, Rivera, and Villareal hosted frequent meetings with American anarchist Emma Goldman and with Spanish anarchist Florencio Bozora. These conversations deepened the anarchist convictions of Ricardo and Rivera, but Sarabia remained much more of a social reformer and Villareal tended toward an orthodox socialism which the Junta's anarchist majority temporarily tolerated.[23] Enrique's anarchist convictions were real although less profound than his brother's. In 1923, after Ricardo's death, Enrique returned to the forefront, urging anarchist ideology and tactics upon striking CGT textile workers in Orizaba. Although arrested, he remained outspoken on the subject thereafter.[24] During the intense campaign to develop a broad and multi-social-class base of support in Mexico against Díaz, the PLM leadership expediently decided not to expose its anarchist beliefs.[25] Despite continued Furlong interference, arrests, and frequent flights in order to maintain their freedom, the PLM Junta members continued to promote and organize considerable revolutionary momentum in Mexico. In 1906, in the midst of widespread labor strikes, *Regeneración*'s circulation increased to thirty thousand.[26]

By 1906 the PLM had forty-four clandestine guerrilla units and Liberal clubs operating within the five zones into which they had divided Mexico. The northern sector, zone three, aided by intense activity on the American side of the border, was the best organized and comprised the states of Sinaloa, Baja California, Sonora, Chihuahua, Coahuila, Nuevo León, and Tamaulipas. A *camarada de confianza* who carried the title of *delegado* commanded in each zone. A national commander-in-chief who reported to the Junta in the United States directed the five zone *delegados*. Beneath the zone *delegado* was the guerrilla unit commander (*jefe de guerrilla*) and his assistant, the *subjefe*, the only two members of the local units who knew the identity of the zone *delegado*. Urban and rural working-class volunteers primarily comprised the guerrilla units, which varied in size, some as large as two hundred to three hundred members, but averaged somewhat under fifty. The volunteers elected the *jefe* and *subjefe* from among their own numbers. In that manner the PLM built a popular mass following, gave the members a sense of full participation, and maintained organizational security at the lower levels.[27] The Junta and *Regeneración* were funded for the most part by small donations collected from all parts of Mexico. Despite full prisons, the Díaz regime failed to significantly compromise the security of the PLM clandestine infrastructure within Mexico. Rather, the PLM was spied upon at the top when agents of the Furlong Detective Agency, hired for the task by Díaz, infiltrated the exile Junta in the United States and almost completely compromised it.[28] Also, the American authorities consistently frustrated PLM plans.

The major occasion of worker unrest in which the PLM played at least a partial role involved the Cananea Copper Company strike of 1906 in the state of Sonora. Because of the contending forces involved, the Cananea strike achieved far greater significance than could normally have been expected. Sonora was the bailiwick of the infamous Governor Rafael Izabal, the protegé of Vice-President

Ramón Corral. After their seizure by the revolutionaries, Izabal's haciendas revealed torture chambers and forced labor conditions for Yaqui Indians. At the time of the strike the company was jointly owned by the Anaconda Copper Company and former proprietor William D. Greene, a financially beleaguered promoter who continued to manage the daily operations of the mine but who maintained direct telegraphic contact, regarding important decisions, with John D. Ryan of Duluth, Minnesota, one of John D. Rockefeller's most trusted and talented aides. Greene accepted a partnership with Anaconda in order to obtain the funds to remain operating. Anaconda, in turn, carried substantial influence with the territorial governor of Arizona, Joseph H. Kibbey, whose appointment the company had endorsed and who controlled the Arizona Rangers. Considerable PLM activity at Cananea preceded the strike. During the spring of 1906, Lazaro Gutiérrez de Lara of the PLM formed and served as president of the Club Liberal de Cananea. Strike leaders Esteban Baca Calderón, Francisco Ibarra, and Manuel Diéguez headed another Cananea liberal club, the Unión Liberal Humanidad, founded to support the PLM and to organize the workers.[29] Baca Calderón envisaged the development of the Mexican working class as a base of support for the PLM. Writing Villareal two months before the strike, Baca Calderón said:

> . . . the miners here should know . . . that the dictatorship is their worst enemy and they should feel the just desire to overthrow it. In this respect I have an idea: . . . to found a miners union, without a hostile stance or political manifesto, at least for now. Later we would invite all of the miners in the Republic to found their respective unions so that we might all then merge into the Liga Minera de los Estados Unidos Mexicanos. All of these unions will have the obligation to form a basis in order to help [workers] in similar conditions as indicated by the directing Junta [of the Liberal party] whenever necessary. These unions will then join the Liberal party providing it with mass resolute support.[30]

On June 1, 1906, the workers at Cananea suddenly went on strike, demanding an eight-hour work day and a higher minimum wage and protesting racial discrimination against Mexicans in housing, job promotions, and rates of pay. Two days of rioting ensued in which buildings were burned and the Mexicans continued to resist with firearms from inside the workers' living district. The PLM members, local union organizers, and the Cananea authorities were all taken off guard by the workers' action, but both sides responded quickly and the significance of remote Cananea deepened accordingly. The mine management and local officials immediately tried to break and then repress the strike. PLM and other labor "agitators," including nine Mexicans and seven Americans, were identified "visiting the mines scandalizing and procuring new disturbances."[31] The two days of gunfire, sabotage, and rebellion followed these actions.

Jesús González Monroy, a PLM member and striking miner at Cananea, explained the extreme actions then taken by the public authorities: "The rulers of Sonora correctly saw the Cananea strike as something more than a manifestation of protest against the company . . . it was necessary [in the authorities' view] to terminate it quickly and completely if they did not want to see the fire of popular discontent communicated to every part of the national territory."[32]

The strike reached the national consciousness more quickly than the editors of *Regeneración* could have hoped for when American vigilantes crossed the border from Arizona led by Captain Thomas Rynning and five other Arizona Rangers. A greatly exaggerated account of attacks upon Americans telegraphed across the frontier by Greene had provoked the American action. The Arizona territorial governor made a half-hearted public attempt to discourage the vigilantes when he declared that they acted on their own.[33] The routine United States Army cavalry pursuit of Apache Indians across the frontier, an activity carried on for years with the full knowledge and approval of the Díaz regime, established precedence for the border violation.[34] The Cananea management and Sonoran officials wanted American intervention because the nearest Mexican army and *rural* detachments were more than a full day of travel from the scene.

The strike and rebellion ended on June 6 when Governor Izabal, backed by two thousand Mexican troops, threatened the forced conscription of the striking workers into the army and to send them to southern Sonora to fight in the Yaqui Indian war going on there. Between thirty and one hundred Mexicans lost their lives in the five days of fighting. The results of the sensational events in Cananea were multiple. The government suffered a severe setback in national popularity, especially with the usually sedate Mexican middle class, because of the "foreign invasion" of national territory. Nationwide workers' unrest was further stimulated and the alarmed Mexican and United States governments began a concerted drive to break the PLM and its revolutionary "anarchism" before it was too late.[35]

The Liberal party platform, promulgated on July 1, 1906, attempted to claim a broad base of support from all social classes. Its working-class provisions included demands for a national minimum wage, a six-day work week with Sunday rest, cash wage payments rather than company script monies tenable only in company stores, the abolition of the company store (*tienda de raya*), the abolition of child labor, owner-management payments for industrial disability expenses, and the establishment of minimum standards for job safety and working conditions. For the rural workers the platform provided for redistribution of unproductive lands held by great estates and thus appealed to *campesinos* while minimizing the alarm it caused with the landed elite. Another important proviso, steeped in Mexican history, demanded the restoration of usurped *municipio* political authority (article 46).[36] The party platform heralded what the Magonistas hoped would be the revolution.

To bring about that revolution, the PLM, under the field leadership of Praxedis Guerrero, mobilized its forty-four clandestine guerrilla groups for a series of coordinated uprisings scheduled for the fall of 1906. The PLM hoped that these revolts would trigger a larger mass upheaval. Ricardo Flores Magón and the Junta secretly moved their headquarters to El Paso in September in order to be closer to the scene of action. However, the alarm caused by the Cananea strike in the highest levels of the Mexican government had its effect. American authorities cooperated with the Mexicans in a massive roundup of PLM members in Douglas, Arizona, and Rio Grande and El Paso, Texas. The Mexican government's arrest of hundreds of Liberals disrupted the planned revolution, but three PLM attacks did occur. In September at Acayucan, Veracruz, three hundred men led by Donato Padua attempted to seize the town. Repulsed, they retreated into the countryside to begin a guerrilla campaign that spread into the state of Tabasco and continued until the forces led by Santana Rodríguez (Santanón) joined them to take part in the revolution of 1910. In October 1910 they launched a series of attacks that antedated the Madero-led revolution a month later. The composition of the Padua PLM–Santanón forces was largely *campesino*. PLM-led Indian uprisings in 1906 also failed at Chinameca, Minatitlán, and Ixhuatlán in Veracruz. Some of the remnants joined forces with Padua. The third attack, against Jiménez, Coahuila, originated in Del Rio, Texas. It ended in failure. The composition of the Del Rio forces, like most PLM units in the north, consisted of a cross section of Mexico's lower and middle social strata. A PLM detachment was also defeated in October near Ciudad Camargo, Tamaulipas. A plan to seize Ciudad Juárez across the border from El Paso never materialized because of the devastating effects of coordinated police raids and arrests that took place in the two cities during mid-October. Ricardo barely escaped and fled to Los Angeles, where the Junta reorganized.[37] It took the PLM two years to recover from the setbacks of 1906.

The textile strike, lockout, and workers' rebellion of 1906–1907, known as Río Blanco because of events that took place at that factory in Orizaba, had a minimum of visible PLM involvement and no identifiable anarchist participation. Yet, like Cananea, Río Blanco is significant in the history of Mexican anarchism and the working class because events there revealed the growing working-class unrest that fueled the PLM, the coming of the revolution, and the resurgence of Mexican working-class anarchism.

The Orizaba area became a site of worker unrest as early as the 1870's. Later, the textile workers there were involved with the anarchosyndicalist labor federations, the Casa del Obrero Mundial, and the General Confederation of Workers. In 1906, Orizaba, an intensely industrialized area in comparison with most Mexican population centers, because of its relatively small population was one of the few areas in Mexico where the industrial proletariat constituted a sizable percentage of the populace. During the 1890's large new textile factories had been constructed at Río Blanco and Santa Rosa that counted 35,000 and 33,000 spindles and 900 and 1,400 looms, respectively.[38] Río Blanco was the largest textile employer in the nation with 2,350 industrial workers in 1900. Santa Rosa was also unusually large with 1,100 employees in 1898.[39]

The Orizaba-Puebla textile industrial area experienced increasing worker unrest beginning with the late 1890's when the state of Puebla suffered Mexico's first general strike. Most of the factory owners were French, something the workers did not forget. In 1901 the Río Blanco workers formed a "libertarian mutualist-cooperative society," and a secret "resistance group" to regain their "lost rights." Two years later, in 1903, the workers in the Río Blanco plant protested the abusive behavior of a supervisor, struck, and closed down the factory.[40] In 1904 the workers elected Manuel Avila their leader and created a "Gran Círculo."[41] In the winter of 1906 a protestant evangelist preacher, José Rumbia, opened a tabernacle near the Río Blanco factory and attracted a considerable number of workers to his congregation during the first few months. His sermons were a mix of fundamentalist Christianity and a radical-populist critique of the foreigners, "Roman Catholic church, and bourgeoisie."[42] Early in the spring a Magonista-PLM revolutionary culture broker (*luchador obrero*), José Neira, arrived in Río Blanco, obtained a job in the factory, and began attending the Protestant lectures. Soon the pastor had Neira leading political discussions after the sermons.

Together with Rumbia, Neira and a nucleus of twenty-seven workers met at the home of Andrés Monta on April 2, 1906, and launched the Gran Círculo de Obreros Libres (GCOL) in Río Blanco.[43] At their first meeting they voted to affiliate with the PLM Junta then in Saint Louis. Neira was elected president of the GCOL, which vowed to open branch Círculos at the nearby factories of Santa Rosa and Nogales. Neira and his followers enjoyed quick successes at both installations. The GCOL also began to publish a newspaper, *La Revolución Social*, which featured articles predicting the "holocaust" (*el holocausto*) and which branded both government and Church as criminal and corrupt.[44]

The GCOL and its newspaper stirred up worker unrest, and the nervous Díaz regime promptly reacted by declaring the GCOL subversive and ordering the arrest of its leaders. *Rurales* armed with rifles duly surrounded the GCOL meeting place in Río Blanco on *jueves de Corpus* in June or July 1906 only to find it empty. The leaders had fled, including Neira and Rumbia. The *rurales* captured only Pablo Gallardo, whose wife revealed his hiding place. The authorities subsequently sent Gallardo to Quintana Roo as a forced military conscript and dissolved the GCOL, but many workers had been affected by the experience.[45]

Several months later, José Morales, a foreman in the Río Blanco plant, founded a new GCOL and served as its self-appointed president. With the endorsement of President Díaz, the state governor of Veracruz, Orizaba political boss (*jefe político*) Carlos Herrera, and local judge Ramón Rocha, Morales vowed that he and the GCOL would "support the governor" and not involve the workers in politics.[46] He also expressed his affection for Díaz. Labor historian Luis Araiza has described the leader of the new GCOL as "more concerned with the interests of the industrialists than those of the workers." With little opposition, the Morales-led GCOL quickly organized branches throughout the textile regions of Orizaba, Puebla, and Tlaxcala. Radicals were denied entry to the GCOL Río Blanco meetings.[47]

In the meantime, the owners of ninety-three factories in the central region of Mexico, which included all the major textile mills, organized a textile industrialists' group known as the Centro Industrial Mexicano. Late in November the factory owners issued a new ruling applicable to the industrial workers in Orizaba, Puebla, and Tlaxcala which prohibited friends and relatives from bringing uncensored reading materials into the otherwise untainted company towns for the workers to read in their homes. In addition, all workers were required to carry black passbooks that would contain their identification and employment discipline entries. This ruling, working conditions, and hours were argued and negotiated in November and December by the GCOL leadership and the Centro Industrial Mexicano.[48] Morales and the other union leaders came under tremendous pressure from the rank-and-file at large meetings to reject the new ruling and to insist upon at least some concessions.

On December 7 the GCOL held a large strike meeting in Puebla. About three thousand workers gathered to draw up their grievances and to request President Díaz to arbitrate. The list of workers' demands included the release of workers at 5:30 P.M. on Saturdays instead of the usual 8:00 P.M., additional time for eating, a number of holidays, a pension plan, overtime pay, control of worker abuse by supervisors, the right to read newspapers, the entry of GCOL representatives into the factories as observers, and the prohibition of company stores and child labor (120 children were employed in Río Blanco alone).[49] A number of speakers addressed the weary crowd but an anonymous orator received tumultuous applause when he declared that thus far Mexico had experienced only two revolutions, those of independence and La Reforma, and that there was going to be a third one, "that of class war (*la lucha de clases*)."[50] The workers then developed a plan to strike against factories in selected regions. A strike by six thousand textile workers in Puebla ensued. A few days later, eight hundred more workers in Tlaxcala joined the effort. The textile industrialists, urged on by José Limantour, decided to shut down all the member plants of the Centro Industrial Mexicano, citing an accumulated warehouse supply inventory that required depletion as the reason for the closure. The plaintive GCOL leadership may have bargained in good faith but found itself caught between angry workers and intransigent factory owners.

The lockout began on December 22, 1906, and affected 22,000 workers in Puebla, 10,000 in Orizaba, and 25,000 more in and around Mexico City, Veracruz, Querétaro, and Guadalajara. The GCOL strike fund of 25,000 pesos lasted only four days. Some Puebla-Orizaba workers suffered extreme privation. About 2,050 of them migrated to other parts of the country seeking relief. The GCOL leadership had unsuccessfully petitioned the Díaz government to arbitrate the dispute on three separate occasions earlier in the month before the lockout began. Finally, when the government agreed to arbitrate, the industrialists predictably turned down its request. On December 31 the capitalists agreed to accept government arbitration.[51] By then the desperate GCOL leadership was ready to accept almost any settlement in order to reopen the factories.

On January 4 the stern terms of the accords became public. The only proviso that even hinted at compromise by the employers was the cynical abolition of child labor for those under seven years of age, but child workers were already normally older than that. The prohibitions on reading materials and the other rules, including the required passbooks, remained in effect. On January 6, Pascual Mendoza, the GCOL leader in Puebla, addressed the assembled workers there and, citing the endorsement of the archbishop, "God," "Church," and "Country," he gained majority approval for the new agreements. But in Orizaba a large and loud minority shouted down and denounced Morales after he gained a majority vote. In PML-like rhetoric the protesters shouted out, "Death to Porfirio Díaz!" and "Down with the dictatorship!" Leaders of the Santa Rosa GCOL, president Rafael Moreno and vice-president Manuel Juárez, led the opposition to the accords.[52]

On January 7, Mexico's textile factories reopened and events passed normally except in Orizaba. At 5:30 A.M. the first contingent of workers, arriving early at Río Blanco to get the plant ready for the first shift, confronted an angry crowd of dissidents; men, women, and children threw rocks at the buildings and shouted their protests. The sentiments expressed in the beginning are not known. Later that day the shouts clearly expressed rebellion against the government, as they had during the previous night. The arriving workers turned back and some of them joined the crowd.[53]

As the crowd grew in front of the factory, Jefe Político Herrera tried to disperse it, only to be shouted at and stoned. Some of the women felt a deep grievance against the management of the large monopolistic and virtual company store, the Centro Comercial, run by Frenchman Victor Garcín and Spaniard Manuel Díez. There are various explanations of the provocation which led the workers to attack it, including the killing of a female worker-shopper and several accounts of verbal insults offered by Garcín against the strikers. At 9:00 A.M. Margarita Martínez called upon the angry crowd gathered in front of the factory, "¡A la tienda! ¡A la tienda!" The crowd sacked and burned the Garcín-Díez-operated store. The smashed merchandise littered the ground around Orizaba for days afterward. At that point a unit of the 13th Infantry Battalion arrived on the scene reinforcing a small force of *rurales*, who, caught up in the feelings of the crowd, had refused to take action. The soldiers took the *rurales* into custody and opened fire on the workers, killing seventeen and wounding eighty.[54] Eleven of the *rurales*, including their commander, Lieutenant Gabriel Arroyo, later died before a firing squad, shot for their actions. With the store sacked and burned, some of the workers marched to the center of town, shouting "Death to Porfirio Díaz," seized the jail, and released all the prisoners. The strike-lockout had turned into a working-class rebellion.

Another large segment of the crowd, still led by Martínez, headed toward the Nogales and Santa Rosa factories, several miles away, shouting rebellious slogans: "Death to the dictator Porfirio Díaz!" "Long live liberty!" "Long live Mexico!" "Down with the oppressors and company stores!" About two miles outside Nogales they linked up with the workers from the Santa Rosa and Nogales factories who had heard of the events in Río Blanco and came out to meet them. The crowd, led by Santa Rosa GCOL leader Manuel Juárez, attacked the Nogales and Santa Rosa installations, burning down the company stores.[55] Returning on the road from Santa Rosa, they encountered Colonel José María Villareal and his units from the 13th Infantry Battalion. The troops opened fire on the workers, killing scores in the largest single massacre of nonindigenous people in the history of the regime.

By late afternoon the remnants of the Nogales and Santa Rosa protesters struggled back to Río Blanco. In the meantime, the workers there, many of them with guns, seized the nearby railroad station and engaged in one-sided battles with the army. With the bitter remnants from Nogales and Santa Rosa assisting, the crowd tore down and burned the cluster of houses in Río Blanco where Morales and others in the GCOL leadership resided. Morales, fully understanding the situation, fled early in the day to Atlixco in Puebla. The contagion was not easily controlled. The military rounded up eighty workers from the Cerritos plant after they sacked and burned a pawnshop in Orizaba. Other armed workers formed roving bands. The one-sided gun battles between workers and soldiers continued through the night.

By January 8 an armed peace settled over Orizaba. Hundreds of workers resided in jail and 800 infantrymen, 150 local police, and 60 *rurales* patrolled the streets, roads, and factories. On the ninth, a crowd of still-angry workers gathered in front of the Santa Rosa plant. The troops opened fire, killing five workers. Santa Rosa strike leaders Juárez and Moreno also died that morning. Some reports allege that they fell in action. Others claim they were executed in the ruins of the burned-out company store at Santa Rosa as an example to the others. On the ninth, 10 workers were summarily executed in the Río Blanco jail.[56]

The Río Blanco strike–workers' rebellion resulted in almost 200 workers killed and countless casualties. Four hundred became prisoners, among them a number of women, including Martínez. About 25 soldiers died and 30 to 40 suffered wounds. Employers terminated or suspended over 1,500 workers in the Santa Rosa, Río Blanco, El Yute, San Lorenzo, and Mirafuentes factories.[57] Newspaper reports of Río Blanco, however distorted and muted, resulted in a severe loss of prestige to the government. Despite the praise offered by the American consul from Veracruz to the military commanders on the scene, "for decisive action," the regime's popular acceptance suffered. In the relatively calm aftermath of 1907, the country watched and waited.

With order restored, Limantour fired the *jefe político* of Orizaba, Herrera, for his failure to act. The government viewed the entire affair as the work of outside agitators. Justo Sierra, a high-ranking intellectual member of the regime, felt that infiltrators had contaminated the workers with "collectivist" ideas. Francisco Bulnes, another of the *científico* braintrust, saw the movement as "communist."[58]

The Cananea and Río Blanco "strikes" cannot be understood in all their complexity by the mere description of objective events or of PLM activities. They revealed the compounding problems that drove Mexico toward the revolution of 1910: a growing national economic crisis, intensifying nationalist resentment against foreign businessmen, a restive working class, and the work of revolutionary precursors led by alienated segments of the urban middle class and provincial elites.

On January 9, 1907, *El Imparcial*, an important pro-Díaz newspaper, reported, in a lengthy article, on the "rebellion" in Río Blanco. It complained of "anarchist propaganda" circulated among the workers for months before the uprising occurred. *El Imparcial* attacked anarchist reasoning as invalid because it confused the economic order with the social order, two aspects of the human condition which the writers for *El Imparcial* felt were entirely separate. The propaganda, the newspaper claimed, "inculcated hate of the rich." It concluded by asserting the need to "limit" access by the workers to "socialist, communist, or anarchist ideas . . . It is necessary that everyone understand that the rights of free thought and expression are not unlimited." [59]

After the Río Blanco rebellion of 1907, working-class unrest continued to smoulder and erupt in the Orizaba, Puebla, and Mexico City areas until the outbreak of the revolution in 1910. Heavy troop concentrations became necessary in Orizaba and, occasionally, in Mexico City to keep the situation under control. In Puebla the government created a new workers' organization, the Gran Confederación de Obreros, out of the remains of the GCOL to help pacify the workers. The confederation's bylaws prohibited strikes, stressed cooperation with employers and government, and threatened expulsion for any worker who advocated strikes. Despite the new *charrismo*,[60] workers continued to demonstrate their dissatisfaction.

In January 1907, shortly after the termination of the Río Blanco rebellion, the workers at the La Magdalena textile factory in San Angel near Mexico City—a site of documented anarchist-led workers' militancy between 1876–1882 and 1911–1931 and continued strikes in the 1880's–1890's—struck and the installation closed down. The nearby La Hormiga plant workers briefly followed suit, but the strike failed with the arrest of five worker-leaders after the *rurales* occupied the factory. The owners of La Magdalena and La Hormiga blamed Río Blanco infiltrators for the trouble and strikes because hungry refugees from Río Blanco invaded San Angel during December 1906 and January 1907. In April of 1907 a strike once again closed the Nogales and Río Blanco factories, despite the formidable number of soldiers in the area. The workers still protested the hated passbooks, necessary for employment and designed to eliminate "troublemakers," and the prohibitions against workers' reading materials. The strike failed when the employers, backed by the army, threatened to bring in fifteen hundred strikebreakers from Oaxaca.[61]

Strikes in Mexico City, Puebla, and Orizaba continued through 1908 with the focus on another serious dispute in San Angel. The owners of La Hormiga tried to expel fifteen hundred workers from the company-owned housing area after the workers struck and refused to permit the expulsion of the fifteen selected strike leaders. The owners insisted that the fifteen were infiltrators, outside agitators, from Río Blanco. With the aid of troops and police, the management evicted all fifteen hundred of the workers from the housing area, at least temporarily.[62]

In 1909 workers struck and shut down perhaps the largest textile factory in Mexico, San Antonio de Abad of Mexico City, on two separate occasions. The first time, the dispute between workers and management stemmed from the summary dismissal of an employee. The reasons for the controversial firing are not known. Later in the year a reduction in salaries resulted in another strike. Both efforts by the workers failed. The Puebla area experienced recurrent strikes and worker unrest despite the presence of the Gran Confederación de Obreros and its *charro* leadership. The Río Blanco workers tried once again to redress their grievances in 1909. They justified their strike by claiming abuses at the hands of their French employers, but the Río Blanco workers found the authorities impatient. Strikebreakers were quickly brought in from neighboring states and the plant reopened with new personnel.[63]

During the period 1907–1910, strikes frequently occurred in the textile mills, Mexico's most developed industry. Sometimes mass arrests of strikers took place, but usually a show of armed force by the government sufficed. The last and most serious strike of the prerevolutionary 1907–1910 period took place at the Santa Rosa factory in Orizaba. In July 1910, with PLM guerrilla activity under the direction of Padua and Santanón being conducted in the adjacent rural areas, six hundred Santa Rosa workers went on strike. Troops arrived on the scene, and the owners used selective firing and the threat of more strikebreakers to coerce the workers back to their posts. The revolution would have to come from elsewhere.

In 1907, the PLM, despite the setbacks of 1906, intensified its efforts. Under the direction of anarchist Praxedis Guerrero, the PLM collected arms and prepared clandestine groups to once again launch the revolution. However, in August a raid by the Los Angeles police and Furlong Detective Agency representatives resulted in the arrest of virtually the entire PLM Junta. Police took Ricardo Flores Magón, Librado Rivera, Antonio Villareal, and Modesto Díaz into custody. While American radicals rallied to assist in their legal defense, the most opportune moment for the PLM revolution, the fall of 1907, passed. Despite the difficulties, Praxedis Guerrero and Enrique Flores Magón continued the mobilization of secret armed groups in Mexico well into 1908.[64]

By June 1908 at least thirty armed groups planned to launch coordinated attacks later that month. But, once again, American and Mexican police intelligence compromised the PLM plan. On June 18, authorities rounded up a group of twenty PLM revolutionaries in Casas Grandes, Chihuahua, and on the twenty-third a successful police raid at the El Paso home of key PLM military leader Prisciliano Silva shattered the PLM's chances. In addition to confiscating Winchester rifles, 150 homemade bombs, and more than 3,000 rounds of ammunition, the police arrested PLM members. Simultaneously, United States cavalry troops deployed along the border opposite Las Vacas, Coahuila, one of the PLM's planned targets for attack. On the twenty-sixth the Las Vacas PLM unit contested for control of the town with the local army garrison. At the same time a PLM group of about fifty men in Casas Grandes launched a futile attack against Palomas near the American frontier. The expected aid from PLM groups crossing the border from the United States did not materialize. A series of small PLM uprisings failed at Los Hornos, Matamoros, and La Sierra de Jimilco, Coahuila. The PLM leadership carried out a prodigious task of military preparations, but their lack of security at the very top compromised the Junta and disrupted the entire organization.[65]

The arrested Junta members, after spending months in a Los Angeles jail, saw the charges against them finally dropped, but instead of gaining their freedom they were transported to Tombstone, Arizona, where a corrupt trial process featuring racial bias and perjury resulted in their conviction. Ricardo received a sentence of eighteen months' internment at the territorial prison at Yuma, Arizona.[66] Field commander Praxedis Guerrero then carried on the enormous task of planning and preparing the next insurrection. He began by organizing Mexican workers living in Arizona, New Mexico, and Texas and gathering funds at public meetings. In the meantime, PLM guerilla units operated in Veracruz and Coahuila.[67]

But 1910 was the year of Francisco Madero's spectacular candidacy for the presidency of Mexico. Landowner, businessman, and financier, Madero had the resources to conduct a strong campaign. His reformist and idealistic approach attracted a strong following among the bourgeoisie and Mexico's already disaffected populace. His defeat, protest, and revolutionary pronouncements drew away many former PLM adherents. The Mexican Revolution finally came in 1910, but the PLM was at a disadvantage. The Junta was in jail and, after initial military victories at Casas Grandes, Chihuahua, and other sites, the dynamic and strongest remaining PLM leader, Praxedis Guerrero, was killed at Janos, Chihuahua, on December 30.[68]

Other PLM military commanders, some important and highly successful, such as Luis A. García with his three hundred men and José de la Luz Blanco, carried on a highly successful guerrilla campaign in cooperation with Madero's chieftains. However, they were eventually overshadowed and outmaneuvered by Madero who, unlike Ricardo, was able to visit Ciudad Juárez immediately after its fall. Many PLM moderates and orthodox socialists, tired of the anarchist Junta, accepted Madero's entreaties and joined his forces, thus eroding PLM strength. Then Madero arrested the most powerful and successful PLM military leader, Prisciliano Silva, in a purge of potentially dangerous left-wing elements within the revolutionary movement. In the following months, successful PLM units in the center and south of Mexico declared their support for the seemingly broad-based and open revolution under Madero. The only sector where the PLM established independent military control was in isolated Baja California during the winter and spring of 1911. Following Madero's victory in central Mexico, the federal army easily retook Baja. Ironically, in mid-1911, after years of struggle, as a result of the Baja California episode where American radicals took part, many Mexicans regarded the PLM as a group of filibusters and as traitors to the revolution. The bulk of Mexico's population credited Francisco Madero with the winning of the revolution. The upper-class Madero, his upper- and middle-class supporters, and his basically peasant army not only defeated the army of Porfirio Díaz but also survived the internecine struggle against the lower-middle- and working-class revolutionaries of the almost leaderless PLM.[69]

The PLM represented more than a mere precursor of the Mexican Revolution, however. A leading element in the early stages of the revolution, it continued to be important until after Madero's victory in 1911. The significant difference between the PLM, the Madero-led revolutionaries, and the Constitutionalist movement of Venustiano Carranza that succeeded Madero was that the PLM represented a workers-peasant revolution. Between 1905 and 1910 the PLM helped to recruit working-class participation in the revolution. After 1911 its significance diminished as workers, in the liberalized climate that followed the collapse of the dictatorship, began to organize on their own without the assistance of the exile-based PLM. The only direct PLM influence on the emergent workers' organization, the Casa del Obrero, in 1912 stemmed from the presence of former PLM members Antonio Díaz Soto y Gama, Lazaro Gutiérrez de Lara, Manuel Sarabia, and Santiago de la Vega.

In 1910 the Mexican Revolution unleashed social forces far more complex than Madero or the PLM could hope to understand or control. The PLM and Madero were made possible by social contradictions that would require many more years of struggle for resolution. The forces that brought about the revolution can be briefly noted:

1.   Militant and revolutionary elements within the urban working class: An enduring hostility, its roots can be traced to the Mexico City *tumultos* of the colonial period, artisan discontent, and the extreme hardship for lower-class workers that left them alienated and without hope.

2.   Intensified agrarian revolt provoked by the Díaz regime's sponsorship of an increased rate of village land seizure that saw a concomitant rise in the resistance offered by the rural working class: This resistance to the polarization of landownership was long standing and can be traced back to agrarian and Indian revolts in the colonial period, the intense social banditry, and the

first agrarian insurrections of the nineteenth century. Control of the countryside had long consumed much of the government's energies.

3. An alienated elite in the provinces caused by frustration with the Díaz regime's unresponsive attitude toward its felt and expressed needs: Indeed, to some sectors of the provincial elites the government seemed to pursue policies inimical to its interests. After consolidating his rule in the nineteenth century by defeating opposition *caudillos* in the provinces, Díaz found rising opposition from a new generation at the end of the century. Their exclusion from the decision-making process and the regime's open collaboration with foreigners moved many of them to oppose Díaz.

4. An alienated intellectual class in the capital city and provinces: The young intellectuals, disappointed in the regime's failure to meet their expectations for political democracy and social justice, both rejected and ridiculed the regime when it failed to meet their standards.

5. Lowered real wages for both urban and rural workers which steadily diminished between 1897 and 1910: Mexico's dependent and neocolonial status drained the country of raw materials, distorted development and wealth distribution, caused a long-range food-price crisis, and made short-run food shortages triggered by crop blight possible between 1907 and 1910 through the excessive growth of export-oriented agriculture. These conditions were exacerbated by economic setbacks caused by a world-wide silver crisis in 1902, a world-wide economic recession in 1907, and localized crop failures.[70]

6. The intrusion of European revolutionary ideologies which provided the alienated and increasingly desperate opposition sectors of society with answers for their dilemma.

7. The stagnation of the regime itself: Díaz was increasingly feeble, his political and economic advisors were discredited, and his military staff was aged in the extreme. His administration failed to deal with the dissent in the efficient manner demonstrated throughout the nineteenth century.

Given the developing contradictions of Porfirian society, one sees the anarchist PLM's contribution of a revolutionary organization and ideology as crucial to the coming of the Mexican Revolution.

During the course of the revolution the interactions of the forces noted above released the latent power of the Mexican urban working class. For the first time, Mexico's proletariat acted in a definitive manner on the stage of history, and the urban workers were mobilized for the most part by the anarchists.

8. Anarchism, the Working Class, and the Opening Phases of the Revolution

The Organization of Labor

In the great central area of Mexico, anarchism revived and grew within the crucible of growing Porfirian weakness in 1909. An enfeebled government allowed underground workers' groups to operate that only a few years earlier had experienced ruthless suppression. Shortly before the revolution, a Catalan political exile, Amadeo Ferrés, initiated clandestine meetings of artisans and other urban workers. A devout libertarian socialist, Ferrés resolutely carried the doctrine of anarchosyndicalism to the Mexican working class. In undertaking such an ambitious project, Ferrés joined many other Spanish anarchists who set out to proselytize Spanish America in the early twentieth century, with the declared goal to eventually convert the workers of the world to anarchist ideology. Anarchosyndicalism was to be their mode of organization. Ferrés reflected these aspirations in his Mexican activities. Shortly after the formation of the anarchosyndicalist Casa del Obrero, he wrote, "Workers, laborers, proletariat of the world, we are transforming conditioned and unresponsive beings into thinking and autonomous individuals."[1] Because of his leading role in the teaching of libertarian dictums, his admiring contemporaries sometimes referred to him as the "apostle."

Ferrés possessed sterling qualifications for his monumental task. Well educated and persuasive, he had an intimate knowledge of Spanish anarchist concepts of organization and tactics beginning to produce impressive successes in his homeland. During the last months of the Díaz regime, he began the seemingly hopeless task of organizing an independent anarchosyndicalist Mexican labor movement, free of government influences, by arranging small secret meetings of workers from the typographic industry in Mexico City.[2]

Beyond the degenerating social, economic, and political situation and the general labor unrest, Ferrés succeeded in his efforts with the *tipógrafos* because of a dynamic personality and oratorical and essayist skills which fascinated his followers. His ideology echoed the anarchist concept of the "free man," "natural law," and the work ethic. In order to avoid personal corruption, man "should always be thrifty" and "work for his own sustenance." Ferrés' version of natural man explicitly declared that man should work as a part of nature, respecting and attempting to preserve his natural environment. Ferrés predicted that when man reached the highest levels of perfection human society would function as though the world comprised a "single building." Ferrés regarded the nation-state as an agent for the "defense of privileges enjoyed by a leisure class," and a gross, corrupt violation of his objective. He urged his followers to join him in order to achieve "regeneration, emancipation, redemption, and manumission and to escape degeneration."

In the essentials Ferrés reflected a classical anarchism: philosophic, nonviolent, and visionary. His plan for the betterment of the Mexican working class, based upon the ideas of a rich assortment of European anarchist intellectuals, began with an assessment of the nation's ills:

> The Mexican government and all governments now in existence fail to provide just and equal administration of the law to the working class because the governments are dominated by holders of great wealth to whom government administrators grant special privileges.

> The laws, which are imposed upon the masses by these governments dominated by the privileged few and which are for the benefit of the elite, violate the "natural laws" that ultimately govern man and nature. Unable to associate freely as in nature, natural man is left in chains.

> Government tyranny is caused by capitalist oppression and the insatiable greed of the bourgeoisie, which, in search of profits, has left the working classes of both city and countryside in wretched condition.

> Religion reinforces this order by rationalizing the status of the workers and assuring them of relief in another world. It is a mythology intended to coax the worker into giving up earthly desires in hope of a better condition after death. The evil cooperation of Church and state in the oppression of the worker is a logical combination, but the dogma of religion itself is unacceptable.

> Politicians are grasping, egotistical, materialistic, and corrupt. They really seek power and wealth, however idealistic their pronouncements may be. Many of them are ready to take advantage of the productive class in order to enlist it in their personal advancement. They will promise virtually anything in order to gain that support, but they will always side with the bourgeoisie in a real crisis.[3]

Despite the bleak picture that Ferrés described, he recognized the Madero-led revolution as an opportunity for greater freedom to organize: ". . . the wind of freedom is blowing." He argued that the scientific revolution provided an example of new human knowledge that touched all aspects of life and that the full cultural, economic, and political impact of this greater enlightenment would spell the end of a privileged class. Convinced of the inevitability of sweeping changes,

Ferrés cited public support for the democratic Madero in his struggle against Porfirio Díaz as a product of this new knowledge.

Ferrés claimed that the Mexican worker became more sophisticated as the means of production changed and that the transformation of the economy toward the factory system placed ultimate power within the grasp of the working class. In order to correct all the abuses and resultant ills of society caused by the corruption of government, capital, and clergy, the workers—the only producers—must assert their power. Workers transformed all material things intended for human use, and, Ferrés concluded, the production of material objects was the principal factor in human progress in both the technological and spiritual realms.[4]

He postulated the necessity "to awaken the workers, to uplift them." With "rational education" the worker becomes enlightened; he becomes a "responsible being." With each elevation of the worker's consciousness, the projects for which he will permit his labor to be used become increasingly beneficial to mankind. The worker, with his upgraded morality, would then "make history rather than be a victim of it." The producer's high standards and morality would be the impulse for a new and better civilization.

The workers would be "titans of good will." They would produce those things necessary for the good of humanity and not mere frills, while lacking essentials. Thus, the bourgeois and his government represented the corrupt enemy because they produced for their own advantage, sought profits which they hoarded, failed to respect nature, and limited production of necessities while the mass of humanity sank into depravity. The worker had to "struggle for the revindication of his class" (*lucha reinvindicadora*), not for revenge against the bourgeoisie, but for survival; "without the principle of mutual aid we are condemned to oblivion."[5]

Only when the worker understood the meaning of "union and fraternity" would he comprehend his importance and that of his work. Ferrés claimed that unity through the workers' syndicate provided the individual worker with the strength to resist "the greed, viciousness, prejudice, and venal influences of the bourgeoisie and its despots." The "rationally educated" worker, as a "titan of good will," would be willing to sacrifice himself for the organization and advancement of his brothers. Ferrés reckoned that the working class "*sabio*" must abandon all personal ambition, all egotism, and dedicate himself to the organization of the working class. That would liberate all mankind.

Ferrés repeatedly warned his adherents of the absolute need to separate working-class organizations from politics. They must always guard, he insisted, against politicians "claiming to be noble and devout adherents to the principles of workers' rights but only hoping to enlist working-class support in pursuit of their private political ambitions."[6]

In 1911, after Francisco Madero's insurgent forces captured Ciudad Juárez and just one week before President Díaz resigned, the typographic workers of Mexico City, led by a nucleus of anarchists, organized the Confederación Tipográfico de México. A short time later the indifference of the interim regime of Francisco León de la Barra permitted the *tipógrafos* to hold a general meeting of their Confederación in order to begin an organizing campaign on behalf of the Mexican labor movement. Addressed first by Ferrés and then by firebrand anarchist Antonio Díaz Soto y Gama, the *tipógrafos* voted to create a *sociedad de resistencia* out of the confederation in order to take the lead in the organization of the Mexican working class.[7] Once again, as occurred during the nineteenth century before the Díaz dictatorship imposed severe discipline and sophisticated labor management policies, working-class radicalism made headway against a backdrop of national political confusion and social and economic instability.

Two of the *tipógrafos* in attendance, José López Dónez and Rafael Quintero, later emerged as important leaders of the labor movement during the revolution. Trained by Ferrés, both became outspoken adherents of his doctrine.[8] They and their fellow printers developed a heavy sense of mission with a self-image as apostles leading the less-enlightened workers to salvation.[9] Ferrés stressed the importance of the *tipógrafos* as a catalyst for the organization of the entire Mexican working class. López Dónez echoed that belief and the conviction that "the *tipógrafos* are the apostles, those called upon to instruct the others."[10] Quintero, later a principal leader of the Casa del Obrero Mundial, revealed the same line of thought when he described the *tipógrafos' sociedad de resistencia*: ". . . the brotherhood to which we belong is destined to be the most important one for the [future of the] civilized world." The assumption of intellectual superiority and the sense of mission among the highly literate *tipógrafos* is understandable when viewed within the context of the 84 percent rate of public illiteracy reported by the Mexican census of 1910. Despite their vision of self-importance, López Dónez and Quintero rejected the role of "leaders," as did Ferrés. They claimed only the duty of asserting themselves in order to bring about a "free and just society" with "neither god nor master."[11]

The best educated men among the *tipógrafos* found Ferrés' teachings especially attractive. These men, called the *obreros intelectuales*, included, besides López Dónez and Quintero, several others who later assumed important roles in the Casa del Obrero: Federico de la Colina, Enrique H. Arce, Fernando Rodarte, Lorenzo Macías, Pedro Ortega, and Alfredo Pérez. The *obreros intelectuales* dominated the confederation of typographers. Ferrés called them the "tireless ones."[12]

Ferrés, like Rhodakanaty before him, favored much more conservative tactics than some of his more zealous followers. He employed the strategy of forming a small group of adherents who in turn were to organize and educate other industrial and agrarian workers until the masses composed a completely unified and mobilized body. During the early years, Ferrés wanted their activities to focus on working-class education and on the formation of legal, industry-wide syndicates involving massive numbers of workers. He anticipated that the syndicates would have tremendous power and the eventual ability to seize control of the means of production, but initially they would devote their efforts to uplifting the workers, providing mutual aid benefits, and defending urban labor against blatant injustices committed by employers. The libertarian anarchosyndicalist society was to be the product of careful preparation and a social evolution involving several decades.

Within a very short time, however, some of Ferrés' adherents began to exhibit much less patience and exerted mounting pressure in favor of strikes, labor agitation, threats of a general strike, and an active search for ways to "combat capitalism" and its "accompanying social institutions" through the formation of "resistance societies." Some even talked of sabotage. However, during the crucial first four formative years the *tipógrafos* operated within the law and avoided conflicts with government. Ferrés did not oppose such revolutionary tactics as the general strike, but he favored a long period of careful preparation. Ferrés successfully restrained the *tipógrafos* from premature revolutionary actions until after 1914. In that year, with his support, they joined the Casa del Obrero Mundial. In 1916 his long campaign to restrain aggressive working-class leaders from calling a premature general strike until the mobilization of sufficient numbers of workers failed. But he did succeed in teaching the men who led the labor movement during the revolution how to organize and administer large workers' syndicates as was done in Spain. That knowledge served them well in the early development of Mexico's first large modern industrial unions.

After its formation, the Confederación de Tipógrafos grew rapidly. In two months it had a total of almost five hundred members, with an average weekly increment of between fifteen and twenty new members. Within a short time most of the publishing houses of Mexico City were organized, and affiliates of the Confederación had been formed in the farthest reaches of the nation, including Monterrey, Tepic, Guadalajara, and Oaxaca.[13] Throughout the revolutionary period, 1910–1917, the provincial branches remained much less radical than the larger central group in Mexico City.

Four months after its inauguration, the confederation, led by the *obreros intelectuales* and Ferrés, began publication of its newspaper,

El Tipógrafo Mexicano, as an educational device for the organization of the working class. From the very first issue, October 8, 1911, Ferrés and the *tipógrafos* revealed a communications approach identical to that used by the radical leaders of the 1870's who published such newspapers as *El Socialista*, *El Hijo del Trabajo*, and *El Obrero Internacional*. They had the same objective in mind: the mobilization of the urban working class. The paper reflected Ferrés' moderate tactical approach and filled its pages with essays by a wide spectrum of European intellectuals, including Victor Hugo and Leo Tolstoy. The *obreros intelectuales* also authored articles urging syndicalism, "rational education," and "the uplifting of the working class." Too philosophical and written in a manner far above the comprehension of the average, barely literate worker, *El Tipógrafo Mexicano* never realized its potential with the rank-and-file. Two thousand copies were published every half month, with a total cash expenditure per edition of thirty pesos.[14] The established press of Mexico City, in the spirit of liberality that swept the country at the time, generally welcomed the sober new publication. In addition, representatives of the *tipógrafos* served as guest speakers and distributed copies of *El Tipógrafo Mexicano* at workers' organizing meetings.[15]

The editors of *El Tipógrafo* soon became well-known and highly respected spokesmen for the organizing workers of Mexico City. Beginning in 1911, letters poured in from neighboring and far away provincial cities calling upon them to assist in the formation of workers' societies.[16] López Dónez, whose devotion to anarchism survived long after the fall of the Casa del Obrero Mundial, enjoyed a reputation as a popular writer and made a great number of personal appearances. These activities included serving as the featured speaker at the inaugural meetings of Mexico City unions and attendance at organizing rallies throughout the country.[17] The *obreros intelectuales* of the *tipógrafos* assisted in the formation of a number of unions in 1911 and 1912, the most important being the radical stoneworkers' union (Unión de Canteros Mexicanos). The *canteros* organized around the demand for "better pay and the means to regenerate the workers." Radicals from the *canteros*, shortly after their organization, took a leading part in further working-class organizing through the secret anarchist group Luz, which founded the Casa del Obrero. For a short time the *tipógrafos* assisted the enthusiastic *canteros* in the publication of their radical newspaper, *La Voz del Oprimidio*.[18]

The Confederación de Tipógrafos grew and formed affiliates in other cities. As a result, the organization changed its name in July 1912 to the Confederación Nacional de Artes Gráficas in order to reflect its new national status. The secretary of the *canteros*, Severino Rodríguez Villafuerte, addressed the *tipógrafos* at the first meeting of the new Artes Gráficas and declared, in recognition of the crucial role they played in the organization of the Mexican labor force, that the *tipógrafos* and the *canteros* "were throwing off the heavy farce, the block of granite, that had been placed on the back of the productive class by the bourgeois octopus."[19]

The Confederación Nacional de Artes Gráficas was organized according to Ferrés' design. An elected board of directors, dominated by the *obreros intelectuales* and headed by a general secretary (*secretario de interior*), directed its activities. The general secretary supervised organizing efforts, called and chaired meetings, delivered special addresses to the delegates assembled from all over the nation, was responsible for minutes of the meetings and for treasury and public relations, and administered the election of delegates from the affiliated shops. Amadeo Ferrés served as the first *secretario de interior* of the Artes Gráficas.[20]

Under Ferrés' administration, the Artes Gráficas enjoyed considerable success, aside from the impressive growth in numbers. During 1912, general sessions of the Artes Gráficas met in the Rinconada de la Soledad in downtown Mexico City one evening each week, with a separate special-issues conclave held each Friday evening from seven until nine. The meetings, open to the general public, generally attracted a considerable crowd. Ferrés usually presided, and he and the *obreros intelectuales* used the opportunity to express their views on popular issues. The *tipógrafos*' treasury fared very well during the first few years. In August 1911 it totaled 249 pesos. By October it grew to 340 pesos and in November swelled to 497 pesos. It continued to grow and in March 1913 rose to 966 pesos. Dues payments remained very low, and in 1914, after considerable inflation and generalized unemployment, journeymen printers paid only 50 centavos per month and apprentices 25 centavos.[21]

In many ways the Artes Gráficas functioned as a syndicate. National in scope, organized industry-wide, and well disciplined, it was viewed by its members as an instrument of struggle on behalf of the working class. Through its emissaries and *El Tipógrafo Mexicano*, it did "ideological combat with capitalism." The self-proclaimed image of struggle with capitalism forced the Artes Gráficas to confront the question of violent tactics and strikes.

While the Artes Gráficas discouraged strikes and other precipitant actions which invited government repression, the *tipógrafos* immersed themselves in the turbulent milieu of the Mexican Revolution. Restless workers demanded immediate solutions. As a result, first the Confederación de Tipógrafos and then the Artes Gráficas supported a number of strikes when the tactical situation seemed to merit them. The management of La Prensa capitulated in 1911 during a dispute involving overtime pay when the linotypist members of the Artes Gráficas joined the other employees in a threatened walkout. The El

Modelo printing house also gave in during 1911 in the face of an imminent strike over the same issue.[22] The prestamped mailing envelope factory El Libro Mercantil was struck and closed down for three weeks in 1912 over the same and additional issues. The Artes Gráficas membership manned picket lines and distributed 617 pesos in strike-relief funds during the shutdown. A special nationwide fund collected for the El Libro strikers eased their plight. It garnered a total of 266 pesos in about two weeks with the Artes Gráficas branch in Sonora contributing 20 pesos to the effort. Finally, a linotypist strike in Torreón closed down the printing industry in that city late in 1912 and, despite the fact the fact that the Torreón workers were not affiliated with the Artes Gráficas, an assembly of three hundred members endorsed their efforts and approved the directors' decision to send 100 pesos in strike-relief funds because the Torreón strikers were "*compañeros*." During the opening years of the emergence of the Casa del Obrero these activities made the Artes Gráficas the principal bulwark of urban working-class militancy.[23]

Membership in the Artes Gráficas included conservatives who opposed strikes and related activities and radicals who wanted immediate action. López Dónez, ever true to the long-range planning and teachings of his mentor, Ferrés, opposed "prejudicial tactics" which "hurt the workers more than the capitalists" and "provoked violations of honor and unfaithfulness."[24] The more radical elements in the Artes Gráficas argued that "strikes, without doubt, are effective and are absolutely necessary as practical experience for the inevitable, definitive, and not too distant social revolution."[25] Quintero and other disciples of Ferrés among the *obreros intelectuales* became increasingly impatient. But the radicals were in the minority until the late summer of 1914 when the Artes Gráficas, led by Quintero and the *obreros intelectuales*, joined the militant and revolutionary Casa del Obrero Mundial. The Casa, an anarchosyndicalist working-class organization, many times endorsed in its proclamations the dictum, "all means necessary for the victory of the revolutionary working class."

The Casa del Obrero and the Madero Regime

The individuals who created the Casa del Obrero Mundial represented a far greater threat to the liberals who surrounded President Madero than the relatively respectable artisans who comprised the Confederación Nacional de Artes Gráficas. In early June 1912, Juan Francisco Moncaleano, a Colombian anarchist and political fugitive sought by the Colombian military, arrived in Mexico after a brief stay in Havana. A university professor in Colombia, he aroused the authorities by his organizing activities and his advocacy of violent revolution and an anarchistic society. During his approximately two years in Havana, Moncaleano wrote a series of articles about the martyred Catalan anarchist Francisco Ferrer Guardia, the man he admired more than any other figure in history. Moncaleano firmly believed in Ferrer Guardia's elaborate conception of a system of workers' schools sponsored by workers' syndicates known as the Escuela Racionalista. The Escuela Racionalista, a product of contemporary Spanish anarchist thought and advocated by the Spanish anarchist exiles who scattered over Spanish America in the early twentieth century, was seen as the principal mechanism for working-class and long-range organizing. To its advocates, it represented working-class control of ideas, values, education, and cultural development. Moncaleano and Amadeo Ferrés both operated on the assumption that the Escuela Racionalista was essential for the uplifting of the masses.[26]

Moncaleano came to Mexico from Cuba inspired by news of the Madero-led revolution, the work of the Confederación de Tipógrafos, and the agrarian uprising in defense of village integrity led by Emiliano Zapata. He went directly to Mexico City accompanied by three Cuban *compañeros* and his dynamic wife, Bianca de Moncaleano. After establishing some contacts, he attended meetings of the Artes Gráficas for several weeks and then solicited support from that group in order to establish a combination workers' central and Escuela Racionalista. Ferrés and the majority of the *obreros intelectuales*, despite their sympathy, decided against the venture because it involved an open and premature ideological conflict with both Church and state. The *tipógrafos* preferred not to antagonize the authorities. In addition, they already had more requests for aid from Mexican labor groups than they could handle. The *tipógrafos* praised Moncaleano for his efforts but turned him down as an unknown outsider. He eventually attracted a number of *obreros intelectuales*, including the important Casa del Obrero Mundial figures Anastasio S. Marín, Lorenzo Macías, Enrique H. Arce, and Ferrés, to his cause.

Undaunted by his initial failure, Moncaleano attended meetings of the small orthodox Marxist Partido Obrero Socialista, which only numbered about twenty regular members. He first questioned and then attacked the party's hope of success via the electoral route and managed to recruit its more radical members into the small group he formed. Moncaleano then visited the Unión de Canteros, where he gained four new supporters. These recruits to anarchy included some of the most prominent future leaders of the Casa del Obrero Mundial: Luis Méndez, Eloy Armenta, Pioquinto Roldán, and Jacinto Huitrón.[27]

Moncaleano's group numbered only eight members—Rodolfo García Ramírez, Eloy Armenta, Jacinto Huitrón, Pioquinto Roldán, Luis Méndez, Ciro Z. Esquivel, and J. Trinidad Juárez—when they began holding secret sessions in his home and in the homes of the other members.[28] After his well-known meeting with the Artes Gráficas membership, Moncaleano resorted to secrecy because Madero government authorities warned him to cease all political activities or face expulsion as a troublesome foreigner. Dedicated to the Escuela Racionalista as the means by which to uplift the masses, Moncaleano and his supporters decided at one of their first meetings, June 29, 1912, to create such a learning center. Symbolically, they named their group Luz (light—meaning hope and enlightenment).[29]

They tried to publish a newspaper, *Luz, Peródico Obrero Libertario,* but it proved too expensive and time consuming and failed after three issues.[30] Without Artes Gráficas' financial backing, such efforts could not hope to succeed. *Luz,* however, was a remarkable newspaper. Moncaleano used it to publicize the hopeless cause of Flores Magón and the Partido Liberal Mexicano, the anarchist program of which he enthusiastically endorsed and whose leader he deeply admired. More importantly for the soon to be born Casa del Obrero, Moncaleano's group published through *Luz* their Manifiesto Anarquista del Grupo Luz. It carried ten points that can be summarized:

1. To enlighten an enslaved and ignorant people.
2. To overthrow the tormentors of mankind: clergy, government, and capital.
3. To not serve the ambitions of any political charlatan, because no man has the right to govern another.
4. To make known that all men are equal because they are all ruled by the same natural laws and not by arbitrary ones.
5. To demand explanations from the opulent rich regarding their wealth, from the government regarding its lying authority, and from the representatives of the bandit god of the bible for his celestial powers.
6. To devastate the social institutions generated by torturers and loafers.
7. To gain freedom for the enslaved worker.
8. To use truth as the ultimate weapon against inequity.
9. To struggle against fear, the terrible tyrant of the people.
10. To march forward toward redemption, toward the universal nation where all can live with mutual respect, in absolute freedom, without national political father figures, without gods in the sky or the insolent rich.[31]

Finally, the Unión de Canteros decided to support Moncaleano's efforts. With a donation that left the *canteros'* treasury empty, he published a series of Ferrer Guardia essays in pamphlet form. Distributed to union and artisan groups, the tracts outlined the Escuela Racionalista—a preschool program for younger children, a workers' library, and the development of a complete educational system operated in co-operation with the workers' syndicates. Ferrer Guardia described the Escuela Racionalista as free of government influence and "devoid of dark theology and politics, both of which impede real learning."

Moncaleano's activities immediately aroused the ire of the Madero regime. Luz's planned opening of the first rationalist school and workers' central on September 8, 1912, failed to materialize because of a police raid that resulted in the mass arrest of the membership and in Moncaleano's immediate expulsion from the country. His principal assistants in the workers' central–school project—Pioquinto Roldán, Jacinto Huitrón, and Alfonso Ortega—along with five other Luz members, were incarcerated in Belén prison. The anarchists won release two weeks later after leading a tumultuous protest demonstration which broke out behind prison walls on September 15 and continued for several days.[32]

On September 22 a meeting of Luz members, the released prisoners, and their supporters commemorated the opening of the first center of the Casa del Obrero and Escuela Racionalista. In this modified program the Casa served as a workers' central council to be used for organizing, cultural, and propaganda activities. The Casa leadership, comprised of Luz members, planned, coordinated, and carried out these efforts. The crowd of supporters in attendance at the Casa inaugural consisted largely of stoneworkers, typesetters, other members of organized labor, and some middle-class intellectuals. The speakers all paid tribute to Moncaleano as the Casa's founding martyr. From its inception, the Casa held open public meetings on Sundays, conducted classes with open enrollments weekday nights, and even opened a small library of predominantly anarchist literature, the Biblioteca de la Casa del Obrero.[33]

The free classes offered by Luz members attracted so many workers that Luz prepared an enlarged program. The Casa became a studies center that featured courses in modeling, personal hygiene, architecture, chemistry, arithmetic, physics, English, Spanish, music, literary composition, public speaking, and history. In addition, Luz members taught ideology in classes called "*conferencias obreras para obreros,*" "*unión instructiva para la mujer obrera,*" "*ciencia, luz, y verdad,*" and "*equalidad, libertad, y amor.*" All classes met weeknights from six to nine, with enrollments left open for the duration.

On Thursdays and Sundays during late 1912 and 1913, special daytime sessions discussed syndicalism, philosophy, and economics. On Sunday nights a festive game of casino provided a welcome diversion. A private group of citizens called the Independent Civic Confederation (Confederación Cívica Independiente) offered some of the classes, and the others were given by Luz members, including Pioquinto Roldán, Antonio Díaz Soto y Gama, Rafael Pérez Taylor, and Jacinto Huitrón.[34] The sizable attendance and the cooperation of nonaffiliated civic groups and intellectuals with the Casa educational program manifested the Mexican government's miserable failure to provide public services in the field of education.

The Luz membership functioned within the Casa as a Bakuninist-type control group. By January 1913 its successes compared favorably to those experienced by its nineteenth-century precursor, La Social, which worked within the Sociedad Artística Industrial, the Gran Círculo de Obreros, and the Congreso Nacional de Obreros. At first, the Luz radicals focused their energies on the Casa educational program. They avoided criticism of a nervous Madero regime that had already expelled Moncaleano and summarily arrested his supporters.

The Casa became a national sensation and its initial successes in the capital city provoked enthusiasm in the outlying cities. In March a group in Monterrey formed calling itself Luz and began to publish a newspaper of the same name on April 1, 1913. Each edition involved five hundred copies with a total publishing cost of 6.50 pesos. Individual copies sold for 2 centavos. The Monterrey membership consisted principally of radical workers from the Carpenters Union (Unión de Carpinteros) and the stoneworkers.[35] They claimed loyalty "to the teachings of Ferrer Guardia," the martyred Catalan.[36] The Monterrey group demonstrated a confusion of ideas and ideologies, but they were the first reflection of the growing influence of the Casa in the Mexican hinterlands.

For several months, Luz succeeded significantly in its task of building an educational and recruiting program for the Casa. As time passed, an increasing number of workers affiliated and many became highly politicized, active participants in the Casa program. As a result, in January 1913 the Luz control group enlarged its membership in order to incorporate the new adherents. Luz also changed its name to Lucha (struggle) and began an active program to organize anarcho-syndicalist unions on a national scale. These syndicates would have national representation in the Mexico City–based Casa and would be composed of self-governing autonomous locals at the factory or provincial level. The organization of local syndicates into regional *casas* or their maintenance as separated solitary unions depended upon the strength of anarchosyndicalism in the given geographic region. The change of name from Luz to Lucha and the ambitious new program indicated the growing militancy and confidence of the Casa's directors.

From the Casa's inception, it met with government competition and opposition. High-ranking Madero regime officials had little but scorn for the working-class anarchosyndicalists and never bothered to find out the substance of their ideas. To the contrary, they regarded the Casa leadership as little more than a gang of ruffians and troublemakers. Nonetheless, they saw the Casa's radical influence on urban labor as a problem meriting police scrutiny and government participation in the labor movement.

Initially, Madero, shocked to see large numbers of workers drifting toward an ideology that rejected any legitimate role for the government or government-sponsored activities, created a Department of Labor (Departamento de Trabajo), which in turn supported the development of a labor union central that would cooperate with and support the regime, the Great League of Mexican Workers (Gran Liga Obrera de la República Mexicana). Some of the liberals around Madero advanced the Gran Liga as the best means to undermine urban working-class radicalism, but it never succeeded in gaining more than a token number of members.

Anarchists disrupted its initial meetings by taking the floor to denounce the directors for their politics and brand the Gran Liga as a mere front for the government. Unfortunately for the Gran Liga, Madero had already lost most of his popularity among the Mexico City workers by late 1912 and, thus, a majority supported a Lucha-led anarchist takeover during the election of officers in January 1913. The newly elected Lucha directors then expelled the deposed former officials of the Gran Liga from the meeting hall. The meeting and its aftermath descended into a tangle of charges and countercharges, the liberals claiming that the whole affair resulted from a late meeting during which most of the voting members had gone home. Lucha had no interest in perpetuating its role in the Gran Liga and later withdrew. The liberals claimed that "agitators" disrupted and discredited their organization among the workers. The anarchosyndicalists from Lucha felt they had simply exposed the Gran Liga as a fraud. The majority of the workers either believed Lucha or, at the least, lost interest in the Gran Liga. They affiliated with the Casa.[37] The Gran Liga's surviving conservative elements had no appreciable effect on the labor movement, despite building donations and continued funding from the government.

Lucha's position stressed the uselessness and immorality of seeking government arbitration or assistance in disputes with employers. Claiming the greater effectiveness of "direct action" (*acción directa*) via strikes, boycotts, sit-ins, and demonstrations, Lucha anxiously awaited an opportunity to test its strategy. In the winter of 1913 the Mutualist-Cooperative Union of Restaurant Employees of the Federal District (Unión Mutua-Cooperativa de Dependientes de Restaurantes del D.F.) and the radical Free and Cosmopolitan Workers (Empleados Libres y Cosmopólitas) invited the Casa to help in a strike against the Café Inglés of Mexico City. Lucha decided that this highly publicized encounter provided the test the Casa needed in order to prove its tactics and gain new support. The combination strike–sit-in filled the restaurant to capacity and disrupted service. The management quickly yielded to the workers' wage and hour demands.[38] The events at the Café Inglés gained the Casa its desired public success.

Other occasions for "direct action" soon followed. The most publicized incident took place at La Ciudad de Hamburgo, a clothing store owned by the foreign concern Struck and Company. The Casa accused store manager Gustavo Struck of working his employees twelve hours per day and paying "miserable wages":

> Don Gustavo was cruel and despotic. He worked his employees more than 12 hours [daily] and paid them miserable wages. It was necessary for them to be on their feet all of the time, especially those who waited on customers. He maintained a vigilant and harsh watch over the help. When approached with a question or asked for help, he either turned his back or ordered the employee back to his position with an irritated expression and harsh tone. His immediate assistants, also foreigners, were as illdisposed as he.[39]

When Struck dismissed an employee because of the latter's union activity, he provoked the Lucha membership and they called for a protest demonstration by the Casa del Obrero. On February 2, 1913, a crowd of two thousand, called out by the Casa and its local affiliate, the Sociedad Mutualista de Obreros Libres, the labor group responsible for the organization of Mexico City's store clerks, gathered in the street in front of the Ciudad de Hamburgo. The situation became tense because Casa crowd tactics quite frequently led to the stoning of store windows and violent encounters with the police. A further complication was the delicate location of the Ciudad de Hamburgo on the Calle de Plateros near the Zócalo and the National Palace. Nervous army troops guarded the nearby government offices.

The Madero government acted quickly and, with expressions of "concern for justice," appointed a special commission to investigate the dispute. The commission strongly rebuked the company and ordered the management to pay the striking clerks' union 1,000 pesos' compensation and accede to its demands.[40] These and other successes of *acción directa* helped Lucha recruit a number of new unions and several thousand additional workers into the Casa during January and February 1913. The newcomers included the workers' groups involved in the Café Inglés and Ciudad de Hamburgo disputes—La Unión Mutua-Cooperativa de Dependientes de Restaurantes del D.F., for restaurant employees, and La Sociedad Mutualista de Empleados Libres and the Sociedad Cosmopólita de Dependientes, representing retail store employees in Mexico City. The demonstrations continued, and a short time later the weavers and clothmakers of Mexico City were successfully organized into the Federación Obrera de Tejedores and affiliated with the Casa.

Acción directa succeeded in making the Casa the omnipotent labor organization in Mexico by early 1913. Lucha proudly announced each success in its "official" Casa periodical named, appropriately enough, *Lucha*. Casa growth allowed expansion of its school library, which now contained the "best works" of Mikhail Bakunin, Pierre J. Proudhon, Peter Kropotkin, Max Stirner, Luis Fabri, José Prat, Anselmo Lorenzo, and Enrique Malatesta.[41]

The pro-Madero newspaper *Nuevo Era* criticized anarchist themes published in *Lucha* in January 1913, but after expressing initial liberal hostility, it ignored the Casa press. By February, government officials and the liberal press demonstrated more concern with the imminent collapse of the Madero regime than with what they perceived as the growing threat of organized labor.

The Casa del Obrero and the Huerta Regime

With the fall of Madero's government and the assassination of both the president and his vice-president, José María Pino Suárez, the directors of the Casa del Obrero refrained from public comment with the justification of *"no participación política."* Lucha members had been circumspect, after their early difficulties, in avoiding a confrontation with the Madero regime. They refrained from political criticism and stressed their "educational program." This policy of restraint continued during the first days of Victoriano Huerta's new military dictatorship. Fearing repression, Lucha protested that the Casa was an educational institution, albeit one that preached against the three "octopi" of clergy, government, and capital.

Slowly, however, the Lucha control group revealed more radical tactics and moved toward open opposition to Huerta. Directing its attention to the working class, Lucha indirectly attacked the Huerta regime, without naming it, by the declaration that "the working class is to blame for the deplorable state of affairs that allows a corrupt religion, state, and capitalism to govern them." Capitalism, Lucha declared, would not fall easily even after full mobilization of the workers, for "it still has the government, clergy, the police, and the soldiers. Together these forces have converted free mankind into a slave of bastard ambitions."[42] Rafael Pérez Taylor, usually an orthodox socialist but one of the Escuela Racionalista's most steadfast adherents, in an obvious allusion to Huerta and his army followers, offered a solution: ". . . all one has to do is enlighten the soldier in order for him to cease being one."[43] Considering the Casa's vulnerability, these attacks constituted a tactical belligerency that invited repression.

Lucha's emerging ideology was clear. Speaking for the Casa, Pérez Taylor explained the majority view of the clergy: "We want to abolish the clergy because it consumes much and produces nothing, spending its life corrupting consciences and sowing discord." Timoteo García summed it up: ". . . the bourgeoisie has converted a beautiful world into a vale of tears." [44] In Lucha's stronger attacks on the Mexican establishment, it identified the culprits as the Church, state, capitalism, large landowners, village strongmen (*caciques*), overseers (*mayordomos*), businessmen, tyrants, despots, oppressors, assassins, and enslavers—all of whom, Lucha claimed, supported and received support from the state.

Lucha offered the same solution earlier advocated by Ferrer Guardia, Ferrés, and Moncaleano: "The triumph of those opposed to all authority [*ácratas*] will represent for humanity the triumph of love and peace built on the ruins of hate, war, misery, and hunger." The victory would be won, not through violence, but by the enlightenment of their "ignorant" working-class brothers. Once that higher consciousness had been achieved, Lucha predicted that massive and powerful syndicates would develop, a process deemed already underway. Lucha warned that the Casa would not accept help from government or from politicians, that no nonworker could join the Casa, and that no one in their group would ever serve as a "leader," because it was immoral. Lucha reserved special scorn for the small Marxist-oriented Partido Obrero Socialista.[45] Unaffiliated groups, such as the Confederación de Artes Gráficas, began to view the impressive successes of Moncaleano's successors in the control group Lucha and its growing umbrella organization, the Casa del Obrero, with increasing admiration.

In the next two months the Casa organized new syndicates among the restaurant workers, retail clerks, and weavers. Its growing strength caused the Casa to look confidently forward to Mexico's first large May Day march since the nineteenth century. Elements of the small orthodox Marxist socialist Partido Socialista and other labor groups, including the *tipógrafos*, not affiliated with the Casa joined in a march of thousands across downtown Mexico City. Lucha seized the initiative in organizing the affair, and Eloy Armenta and Rafael Pérez Taylor joined the prominent Madero government representatives and Casa sympathizers, Isidro Fabela and Heriberto Jara, in addressing the crowd. The principal speakers and the bulk of the signs carried by the marchers emphasized the "bread-and-butter issues" of the eight-hour day and six-day work week.[46] Size estimates of the May Day celebration varied, with the largest figure set at thirty thousand. A sober estimate based on concurring eyewitness testimony provides a more likely figure of twenty thousand.[47]

Despite the radicalism of Jara and Fabela, their participation caused a division in the ranks of both Lucha and the *tipógrafos*. Some Lucha members joined Ferrés, leader of the *tipógrafos*, in a boycott. Loyal to his Spanish anarchist heritage, Ferrés refused to take part because of the presence of politicians like Jara and Fabela, regardless of how radical they might be. The reasoning was clear: the danger of Casa "political involvement." The intensely ideological Spaniards in the Casa usually expressed their refusal to participate in political activity more strongly than did the Mexicans. Madero's early expulsion of Moncaleano and Huerta's later removal of many Spanish leaders of Lucha would be fatal for the anarchosyndicalist principle of "no political participation" for the urban working class. In May 1913 working-class resentment toward Huerta rose to such an intensity that the Lucha majority considered the action worthwhile. Despite Lucha's fears, Huerta, perhaps because of his tenuous political situation, proved exceedingly tolerant.

Simultaneous May Day demonstrations occurred in Río Blanco, Mérida, and Monterrey. Violence marred the episode at Río Blanco when the district military commander, General Velázquez, directed his troops to fire after the crowd ignored his order to disperse. The Mérida and Monterrey observances were relatively small and took place without incident. The Casa leadership group rejoiced at their support in Río Blanco and protested the repressive actions of the local military commander.[48] Following the May Day demonstration, Lucha amplified the name of its labor organization to include *Mundial* in recognition of a world-wide proletarian movement and affinity with the libertarian socialist International Association of Workers (Asociación Internacional de Trabajadores, AIT) headquartered in Amsterdam.

Several new syndicates joined the Casa during the euphoria of success that prevailed in Mexico City in the days immediately after May Day. On May 5 the tailors (*sastres*) of Mexico City formed a syndicate affiliated with the Casa.[49] The adoption of the classification of syndicate meant that they intended to deny the legitimacy of state rule, that they rejected political activity, and that they thought the government could eventually be overthrown by *acción directa*. Casa doctrine once again openly advocated the tactics of strikes, sabotage, sit-ins, street demonstrations, and boycotts. The *sastres'* enthusiasm placed them into immediate conflict with one of Mexico City's largest department stores, El Palacio de Hierro. They charged the paymaster (*contador*), José Burko, with dishonesty and insulting behavior and demanded his dismissal. When the management refused their demands, the *sastres* expressed their disgust with "bourgeois insolence" and went on strike. They picketed the store, organized a boycott, and crowded inside during business hours.[50] The final outcome of this dispute has not been preserved for posterity, but, more importantly, a significant artisan group was committed to the Casa.

On May 3 the weavers and textile workers (*tejedores*), a union that already belonged to the Casa, publicly adopted syndicalism. At the same time they struck and closed down the San Antonio de Abad, Miraflores, La Colmena, and Barron textile factories. An insight into the thinking of the strikers was revealed by a strike declaration which, in reference to one of the factory owners, stated the hope "to tumble that insolent Frenchman out of the clouds." A few days later, on May 8, the quarry workers and stonecutters (*canteros*) of the Mexico City area joined forces as a Casa syndicate. On May 24 the carpenters, cabinet-makers, and wood engravers followed suit. Despite the presence of government undercover agents and at least one police raid of the Casa meeting hall, the strikes and meetings, during which increasingly outspoken criticisms of the Huerta regime were heard, continued until nearly the end of the month.[51]

During May, Lucha members began a series of clandestine meetings with nonlabor opponents of the Huerta regime in order to prepare antigovernment demonstrations in the capital. Among the planners for the demonstrations, scheduled for May 25, were Jesús Urueta and outspoken deputy Serapio Rendón. They met with some of the principal leaders of Mexican anarchosyndicalism and the braintrust of Lucha—Díaz Soto y Gama, Pérez Taylor, Pioquinto Roldán, Jacinto Huitrón, Eloy Armenta, José Colado, José Santos Chocano, and Miguel and Celestino Sorrondequi. The crowd in attendance, although smaller than that of May Day, totaled several thousand. Eight Lucha members addressed the assembly and condemned "military dictatorship and usurpation" without mentioning Huerta directly. They appealed for a "return of democracy."

Despite Lucha's caution in avoiding an overt call for the removal of Huerta, its activities exhausted the dictator's patience. He could not allow unrest in Mexico City while fighting revolutionaries in the north and south. Huerta's officers arrested about one dozen Casa leaders. Using article 33 of the Constitution as his legal basis, Huerta then deported several of the speakers at the May 25 rally as undesirable aliens, including Spanish-born Lucha members Eloy Armenta, José Colado, and the Sorrondequi brothers. José Santos Chocano, a Peruvian writer for *Lucha*, joined the Spaniards in flight. The deportations seriously weakened Lucha and the future development of the Mexican anarchosyndicalist working-class movement. Mexicans arrested included Anastasio S. Marín and two of the most militant workers, Luis Méndez and Jacinto Huitrón, whom the authorities held in Belén prison for over a month.[52]

The intimidated remnants of Lucha petitioned Congress in the name of the Casa for the release of the imprisoned leaders and called for repeal of article 33. Pro-Huerta critics of the Casa rejected its appeal and described it as a "center of conspiracy" (*foco de conspiración*). Huitrón, Méndez, Pérez Taylor, Díaz Soto y Gama, and others denied involvement of the Casa in any political conspiracy. They claimed that "syndicalist by-laws" prohibited such activities. Serapio

Rendon and Belisario Domínguez spoke on behalf of the arrested Casa leaders before Congress and condemned the Huerta regime's methods, only to be kidnapped, executed, and buried in a soon-discovered grave. Prior to the discovery of the bodies, an adamant Congress demanded a full explanation and refused to adjourn. Huerta reacted by dissolving both houses.[53]

With Lucha disrupted and demoralized, Casa urban labor organizing activities subsided until August of 1913 when the leadership of the *tipógrafos'* Confederation of Graphic Arts, the *obreros intelectuales*, decided to bring their group into the Casa. Among the leaders who decided to bring the Artes Gráficas into the Casa were Amadeo Ferrés' original disciples, Rafael Quintero, Federico de la Colina, Anastasio S. Marín, Pedro Ortega, and José Barragán Hernández. Some of the *tipógrafos'* leaders already held individual membership in Lucha, but the entry of their syndicate into the Casa brought new, more prosperous, and somewhat more sophisticated members into the rank-and-file membership as well as into the Lucha leadership group. Lucha, the Casa, and *tipógrafos* now came under the dynamic leadership of Rafael Quintero. The merger was a major advance in the struggle for a strong anarchosyndicalist labor movement.

The entry of the Artes Gráficas into the Casa caused a breakup of the *tipógrafos'* membership. The *tipógrafos'* organization had been rife with disputes since the radical innovations of Amadeo Ferrés began in 1909. The divisiveness and the task of winning over the majority of the membership had exhausted Ferrés and, compounded by his illness, precipitated his resignation as their leader. In late 1913 the majority of *tipógrafos* voted to declare their organization a syndicate with all the revolutionary connotations of that label and to enter the Casa del Obrero Mundial. At that point the more conservative members objected to the commitment of their mutual aid funds to strikes and "resistance" activities which they considered "ill conceived." A general meeting of the *tipógrafos* assembled, and when the majority voted to syndicalize and join the Casa, the minority formed a new, more conservative union called the Unión Cooperativa Linotipográfica. They rejected all appeals for unity and never did join the Casa or accept its revolutionary-anarchist precepts.[54] Some *tipógrafos* who did join the Casa had difficulty accepting the most revolutionary anarchosyndicalist dictums. One of these men, Rosendo Salazar, advocated Proudhonian cooperativism; he also supported the move to anarchosyndicalism and elicited the condemnation of the conservatives in the Artes Gráficas. However, his less than wholehearted acceptance of the antipolitical ideology of the anarchosyndicalists earned him their distrust.

The *tipógrafos* gave the Casa new life. Using their professional skills they published a newspaper, *El Sindicalista*. The newspaper's name imitated the identical rubric of a contemporary anarchist periodical published in Spain. The principal administrators of the new "official" periodical of the Casa and Mexican anarchism included Quintero, Salazar, and Epigmenio H. Ocampo. Lucha members Santiago R. de la Vega and Díaz Soto y Gama and the sympathetic Pérez Taylor contributed regularly to its issues. Considering the difficult economic situation and the unstable political conditions which might have been conducive to far more radical appeals, *El Sindicalista* pursued neither extreme nor provocative policies. The periodical devoted most of its pages to anarchist philosophy, the defense of syndicalism through the defense of antipolitics, the workings of cooperatives within the Confederation of Graphic Arts, and the right of the workers to organize "in their own defense." Many of the essays in *El Sindicalista* were reprints of articles that had appeared earlier in *El Tipógrafo Mexicano.*[55]

An indigenous Mexican anarchism came of age in the pages of *El Sindicalista.* Edited by Rosendo Salazar and José López Dónez, *El Sindicalista* used the positivism of Agustín Aragón to prove the inevitability of libertarian socialism.[56] Aragón and the Lucha leadership believed that a new order of freedom and equality was coming in Mexico because of "the Natural Law of progress" and because man had now achieved the final stage of positivist human social development. One of the leading exponents of the cause then offered a definition: "Anarchism is an absolute absence of government, [a society with] neither God nor master [*ni Dios, ni amo*]. . . . in order for a sizable collectivity to achieve that condition, the highest degree of culture is essential; [a society] perfectly conscious of its actions fulfills the function of God, government, laws, and everything else within its naturally harmonious order. When it reaches that highest level of development it will be anarchistic [*anárquico*]."[57]

Casa anarchosyndicalism took on clearer shape near the end of 1913 and the pages of *El Sindicalista* explained the process to the workers. Anarchists urged workers to join syndicates in order to escape their "exploited condition" because "unity will provide the strength to attack the problem with practicality."[58] Trade guilds were organizing into syndicates and, consistent with artisan tradition, maintaining their independence from other trades. When workers of a given profession suffered unacceptable conditions, they could strike with the expectation that their fellow tradesmen in other syndicates nationwide would support them by means of Casa-directed tactics. The short-run objectives of the limited strikes emphasized improved working conditions and higher salaries. Anarchists perceived the general strike, involving all syndicates at once in order to disrupt the national economy, as working-class war on the state and capitalism.

Once the syndicates sufficiently developed they would be in a position, through the mechanism of the general strike, to paralyze and

take over entire national industries and trades in order to operate a
new "Industrial Republic," without capitalists. Anarchists rejected the
state, parliamentary legislation, and political activity because politicians, they believed, had vested interests in the already exising
socioeconomic order which rested upon the exploitation of the working class: ". . . the politicians will never save the working class in
spite of all their promises. Democratic politics is a painful lie [*burda
mentira*]."[59] They also rejected the socialist state as being oppressive:
"If authoritarian socialism has taken it upon itself to fan the historic
process of class struggle by seizing political power for the proletariat,
. . . libertarian socialism, before and after this process, will continue
struggling so that the principle of authority will not impose on the individual conscience a new mode of slavery."[60]

The strike constituted the only real weapon held by the workers.
Díaz Soto y Gama explained its utility: ". . . it is impossible for bourgeois society to survive without the labor of its slaves or the consumption [needs] of the exploited."[61] Partial or piecemeal strikes prepared
the way for the great general strike which would end capitalism and
its political system. One writer declared that in 1913 Mexican anarchosyndicalism had "barely begun to show its red petals."

In October 1913 a divergent version of Mexican working-class anarchism emerged, Christian Communism, principally enunciated by
Díaz Soto y Gama. In his view, Jesus Christ, "the vagabond carpenter
from Galilee," favored "equality" and opposed "slavery." By positing
the principles of "harmony, fraternity, and justice among the free and
equal," Christ was "the first libertarian socialist."[62] Díaz Soto y Gama,
despite his religious zeal, expressed overt hostility to the established
Roman Catholic church in Mexico. One of his partisans declared that
"the true Christian must look . . . to the Bible and never to the falsi-
fiers that have imbued prejudice into the thinking of the workers."[63]
Many anarchists joined Díaz Soto y Gama in his attacks on the
Church; a few joined him in defense of religious faith. He and Pérez
Taylor presented a series of Casa-sponsored classes and issued public
denunciations of "the false ministers of God, those who have profaned
the maxims of Christ." To the Casa anarchosyndicalists, Christ was a
very human proletarian revolutionary.[64]

By the end of 1913 the pitiful economic condition of the Casa's
working-class membership forced a change in organizing and propaganda tactics. Without funds, *El Sindicalista*, the Casa newspaper,
ceased publication and the harried anarchists instituted mass meetings as a means of recruitment. A popular group of orators known as
the *tribuna roja* held sway. Leaders in the *tribuna roja* included Quintero, Díaz Soto y Gama, and nonanarchists Pérez Taylor and Aragón.
They addressed massive crowds that overflowed into the street in
front of Casa headquarters.

Surprisingly, general economic misery and Casa financial bankruptcy had a beneficial effect on the Casa's recruiting efforts. The
mass meetings succeeded in gaining new members to an unexpected
degree and apparently reached the mass of average illiterate workers
much more effectively than *El Sindicalista* and its literary predecessors. The *tribuna roja* era, beginning in late 1913 and ending in late
May 1914, represented the most successful period of membership recruitment yet enjoyed by the Casa. The crowds, often excited and un-
ruly, vigorously applauded attacks against the Church, capitalism,
and the state.[65]

Despite these successes, the Lucha leadership group felt a printed
publication was essential in order to give the Casa's message wider
range. By May 1914 the Casa recovered sufficiently to attempt new
programs. On May 1 and 15 a newspaper, *Emancipación Obrera*, began publication in an attempt to reach the greater Mexican working
class. The editorial board, including Quintero, Marín, and Salazar,
emphasized worker recruitment and education and blamed workers'
ignorance and lack of ideology as the major obstacles to organizing.
The newspaper dedicated itself to the solution of the dilemma. As a
part of this effort, the Casa reopened its school, the Rationalist Cultural Center (Centro de Cultura Racionalista). Pérez Taylor explained
that "anarchist doctrines are so elevated that a maximum degree of
culture is necessary in order to give them understanding." The economically disadvantageous and politically conservative position of re-
ligiously oriented working-class women resulted in a rationalist course
on "the equality of the sexes" taught by Paula Osorio.[66]

The successful tactic of mass meetings, however, continued. A large
May Day rally and several other meetings ensued during the month
which protested the government raids of May 1913. The attacks on
Huerta suddenly became bitter and provocative. The crowds grew
larger and more threatening. The government responded decisively.

On May 27, Commander Ignacio Machorro, in a repetition of the
action taken almost at the same time a year earlier, led a multitude of
police on a raid of Casa headquarters. The police arrested between
fifteen and twenty persons and destroyed the Casa offices, records,
library, classrooms, and other facilities. Detained Lucha members included Barragán Hernández and Marín. Quintero, Méndez, Salazar,
and Huitrón escaped arrest through the efforts of Federico de la
Colina, who sequestered them in a house located in the *barrio* of
Tepito. Normal Casa activities, including the publication of *Emancipación Obrera*, ceased as a result of suppression by the Huerta government until the arrival of the revolutionary Constitutionalist army
two months later.[67]

9. The Casa del Obrero Mundial and the Constitutionalists

After the defeat of Huerta, the Constitutionalist forces loyal to Venustiano Carranza and Alvaro Obregón moved quickly to recruit urban labor support against their provincial rivals led by Francisco Villa and Emiliano Zapata. The active diplomacy of Obregón became the most effective link between the Constitutionalists and the organized working class.

The Treaty of Teoloyucan, signed on August 15, 1914, formally transferred political authority to the Constitutionalists and permitted the peaceful entry of Obregón's troops into Mexico City. Because of Huerta's closure of *Emancipación Obrera* and Casa headquarters, the Lucha leadership group regarded the arrival of the Constitutionalists as the "liberation" of Mexico City and hailed the Constitutionalists, some of them quite radical, as the "liberators." On August 20, the date of Carranza's triumphal entry, Lucha leaders held a "liberation celebration" at Casa headquarters. The new government sent a sizable contingent of representatives noted for their prolabor sympathies to the ceremony, including ex-Magonista Antonio I. Villareal. The assembled Casa members and their guests then heard a series of discourses on "proletarian revolution" and anarchosyndicalism delivered by Roldán, Huitrón, de la Vega, de la Colina, and others. The government delegates did not appear intimidated by the radical rhetoric of the Casa leadership and assured the assembled workers of the social nature of the Constitutionalist revolution and that the desperately poor living conditions and food shortages experienced by the urban workers were the primary concerns of the new government. They called for working-class support for the "Revolutionary Government" which they claimed acted on organized labor's behalf.[1]

On September 26, Obregón followed up these initial contacts with the Casa by donating to it the building of the former Jesuit convent of Santa Brígida as a meeting place. The Casa accepted the gift, and in less than five weeks the urban labor leaders seriously compromised their ideological pledges of nonpolitical involvement. The close working relationship established by Obregón with the Casa, the unusual political conditions that prevailed, and an openly sympathetic government overruled allegiance to an unmodified anarchosyndicalism. Cooperation with Obregón, under what they believed to be their own terms and exercized in their own interests, seemed advantageous to both rank-and-file members and a majority of the Casa leadership.

In the fervor of "liberation," anarchosyndicalist leaders who later disavowed the Regional Confederation of Mexican Workers (CROM), because of "government domination," accepted Obregón's gift, apparently without dissent. Because of difficult conditions, anarchists considered the acceptance of such donations from a supportive government to be wise and not necessarily compromising.[2] From the Constitutionalist government's point of view, urban labor constituted a sizable and potentially powerful force. The donations cost the government little and they helped create good will among urban workers.

The reopening of the Casa in late August 1914 precipitated an intense organizing campaign in which Lucha representatives visited factories and artisan shops in Mexico City, Guadalajara, Monterrey, and the other principal centers of industry nationwide. The basis for the reconstruction of the Casa was prepared during its months of banishment under Huerta by means of an underground system of committees and emissaries sent out from Mexico City to cities all over the central Mexican plateau, including the states of Puebla, Michoacán, Hidalgo, Guanajuato, Querétaro, and San Luis Potosí.

During the last months of 1914, anarchists formed regional *casas del obrero* in Guadalajara and Monterrey and these branches sent emissaries to the central Casa in Mexico City. The Monterrey Casa included the local syndicates of painters, carpenters, stonecutters, confectionery workers, drivers and conductors (*motoristas y conductores*), bakers, smelter workers, tailors, matchmakers, textile workers, and electrical railway workers. The Monterrey Casa organizers included Vicente Aldana, Carlos García, José Spagnoli, F. Rivera, and G. Cervantes Lozano. They began publication of their own newspaper, *Ideas*, in November, stating ". . . our ultimate desire is the happiness of all, without gods, capital, or tyrants." Anarchosyndicalism, they believed, would achieve "victory" in the Mexican Revolution and, among other things, bring about the emancipation of women and the defeat of "fanaticism." The syndicates in secondary population and industrial centers, such as San Luis Potosí and Aguascalientes, were less powerful and ambitious. Originally stimulated by the visits of Casa proselytizers, including Celestino Gasca and Rosendo Salazar, they joined the Mexico City Casa.[3]

The Casa moved toward a more refined and elaborate national structure composed of affiliated syndicates. The syndicates operated as autonomous nationwide groups affiliated with the Mexico City Casa at the national level and a local Casa del Obrero in those towns where the syndicate locals organized. At both the national and the local level the syndicate remained "self governing." Any action taken in concert with the national Casa occurred at the syndicates' and regional *casas'* discretion. They affiliated with the national Casa for armed defense through local workers' militias and armories. However, this design existed largely in theory because of minimal coordination of the self-defense committees and the isolation of many syndicates. Thus, Casa

social services—such as general nutritional aid and hygenic education, organizing assistance and ideological direction, and cooperation
and coordination of syndicates during strikes—only partially developed and functioned most effectively in the larger cities.

The leadership of the national syndicates integrated with the national directorate of the Casa in Mexico City and increased the total
number of Casa directors to more than seventy-five. As the directorate
of the national Casa grew, the former Lucha leadership group increased in number until it became so large that Lucha disappeared
as a separate entity. In the late months of 1914 the rubric "Lucha"
fell into disuse. Casa growth required an increasingly complicated
organizational structure. Eventually, Casa activities were conducted
by twenty-three committees run by unpaid secretaries who held membership in the national directorate.

The more important national urban working-class and artisan
groups which joined the Mexico City Casa as syndicates included the
tailors (*sastres*), restaurant workers (Sindicato de Dependientes de
Restaurantes), weavers, stonecutters, textile factory workers, carriage
drivers, mill workers, chauffeurs, shoe factory workers, mechanics,
blacksmiths, school teachers, plumbers, tinsmiths, beltmakers, buttonmakers, retail clerks, bakers, models, draftsmen, seamstresses, and
bookbinders. The Casa was a mixture of the middle and lower economic strata of the employed work force. The *Tipógrafos* remained
the single most influential syndicate in the Casa, and they increased
their strength through the assimilation of the linotypists' union. The
new syndicate styled itself the Sindicato de Tipógrafos y Gremios
Anexos. Jacinto Huitrón, a linotypist, served as the Casa delegate to
the Anarchist International Conference in 1914.

Beginning in late 1914, rapid unionization, the continuing turmoil
and instability of the revolution, extreme inflation, and high urban
unemployment rates contributed to labor unrest and led to strikes in
the major cities. Serious strikes closed down the Mexico City rail
transit system, the electrical company, and the telephone and tele-
graph company. The syndicates involved, all affiliates of the Casa, had
developed a strong sense of workers' unity and, because of the crucial
public service nature of their industries, they possessed unusual
strength. The Carranza government found a solution for the power
company strikes by giving the union a partial management role in
order to restore service. One new leader, Luis N. Morones of the electrical workers' syndicate, suddenly emerged with enormous influence. The Casa leadership applauded these developments because to
them they represented workers' control of industry. But Morones did
not embrace anarchosyndicalism and began to discreetly develop a
close working relationship with the government. He established friend-
ships with many high-ranking government officials and, without

alienating Lucha veterans, subtly prepared the way for his future rise to power.[4]

The leaders of the new syndicates also included some Casa veterans, such as Celestino Gasca and Spanish anarchist Juan Tudó. The newcomers cooperated with and supported the Lucha old guard and the principal of no political compromise in the Casa directorate. However, despite their declarations of anarchist ideology, in late 1914 and early 1915 the new leaders reinforced the resolve of Quintero, Salazar, Gasca, and the rest of the leadership as they led the Casa into closer "revolutionary unity" with the Carranza-led Constitutionalists against Francisco Villa and Emiliano Zapata. In addition, less militant new leaders, such as Leobardo Castro and Samuel Yudico, moderated and openly supported Morones after 1916 as he led organized labor into a position subordinate to the Carranza, Obregón, and Calles governments.[5]

Due to the complexity of events in Mexico, interpretations of their significance varied widely and led to disputes between the participants in Mexico City and the anarchist Flores Magonistas residing in Los Angeles, California. The latter attached greater immediate significance to the fall of the Huerta government and the growth of the Casa than did the Mexican urban working-class leaders themselves. Casa writers sometimes violently rejected the tactically more radical Magonistas and their revolutionary claims. In one case, a writer described them as "renegades thousands of miles away who are exaggerating events in Mexico" and asked, "How can it be expected that Mexican workers could be carrying out the social revolution [as the Magonistas claimed], if they were not yet even organized or politicized? How could Mexican workers be expected to achieve this if it had not yet been possible in Europe where the workers were much more advanced?"[6] The Casa leadership's evident hostility toward the PLM intelligentsia in exile prevented official contact between them.

Despite their scorn for the revolutionary predictions of the far-removed Magonistas, a growing sense of urgency drove the Casa directorate on in its rush to organize and ideologically indoctrinate a maximum number of workers as quickly as possible. In order to facilitate this effort, the Casa published another newspaper, *Tinta Roja*, as a replacement for the Huerta-suppressed *Emancipación Obrera*. Salazar, Arce, and de la Colina edited *Tinta Roja*. The exclamation "there is no time to lose"[7] explained the situation. A dual program of teaching anarchosyndicalist ideology to the workers while seeking cooperation with the lenient Constitutionalist government emerged. The Casa therefore temporarily discouraged strikes, despite difficult economic conditions and employer refusals to raise wages, because of its desire to avoid alienating the tolerant Constitutionalists. Strikes called in search of short-run benefits were condemned as long-run errors. The

Casa moved quickly to organize as many workers as possible while impressing the government with the need for urban working-class support in the face of Villa's superior military strength. Many of the Casa directorate realized that the bulk of the organizing had to be achieved while the Carranza regime still regarded the urban workers as useful allies.

Most of the Casa leadership still distrusted government in general and Carranza in particular but displayed an increasing willingness to cooperate. The eventual alliance between the Casa and the Constitutionalists stemmed from the government's aggressive courtship of the urban workers, the desire of the Casa directorate to organize the workers quickly while the Constitutionalists still needed them, the important losses due to exile and repression which the old Lucha leadership had suffered at the hands of the Madero and Huerta governments, and the departure of the minority *agrarista* Lucha leaders from Mexico City in the early months of the struggle against Huerta to take up arms for Zapata in Morelos or the Constitutionalists in the north.

The Casa was already deeply indebted to the Carranza movement before the advance of Villa's forces in late 1914 forced the Constitutionalists to withdraw from Mexico City. The relationship began when Carranza's Constitutionalists occupied Mexico City and the Casa reopened, admitting many new members grateful to and sympathetic with the Constitutionalist cause. These men viewed the Carranza-led movement as friendly to labor and believed less tenaciously in the anarchist antigovernment ideas of no political participation than did the old membership. The radical Casa leadership hoped to mold the workers into a formidable anarchosyndicalist force prior to an inevitable conflict with Carranza. Meanwhile, Obregón carried out an aggressive courtship of organized labor among both non-Casa-affiliated workers and the Casa itself. The government took a giant step toward gaining greater short-run rapport with the Casa through its decision to issue paper notes in place of five-, ten-, and twenty-centavo coins then in short supply.[8] The measure provided considerable relief to the most desperately poor of Mexico City's working class.

In one major labor contract agreed upon in late 1914, the government served as arbitrator between Puebla textile workers and management. The workers received the eight-hour day as a result. Similar gains occurred in the Federal District and impressed even members of the Lucha old guard. Against the aura of Constitutionalist radicalism, the immediate sense of good will with the Casa created by the Carrancistas, and the conciliatory diplomacy of Obregón, the Villa northerners and Zapata-led agrarians seemed very remote to most Casa members.[9]

The absence of many Lucha *agraristas* also contributed to the Casa's ultimate decision to join the Constitutionalists. The agrarian-oriented leadership of the Casa for the most part had left Mexico City prior to the time the Constitutionalist recruiting effort headed by Obregón got under way. Severiano Serna and Joaquín Hernández traveled to Puebla and attempted to foster "resistance societies" against Huerta there, only to be apprehended and executed. During Huerta's reign, Anastasio Marín, the Flores brothers, Enzaldo Díaz, Eleuterio Palos, Elías Tinajero, and Díaz Soto y Gama joined Zapata in the south and what they regarded as an indigenous liberation movement in support of the *municipio libre*. In late 1914, Luis Méndez joined Zapata. Jacinto Huitrón also became an avid agrarian and worked in a Zapatista electrical plant. Some radical Lucha members—Eloy Armenta, Colado, and Roldán—joined the Constitutionalist movement much earlier. They enrolled in and helped to organize a miners' militia in Coahuila in 1913.

Between November 2 and 24, as the forces of Villa and Zapata advanced on Mexico City, the Constitutionalists withdrew toward Córdoba and invited the Casa to declare its support. At first the leadership of the Casa, surveying the situation, declined to transmit this request to the general membership or to the affiliated regional syndicates. But on the twenty-fourth the Zapatistas entered the city and the Casa directors witnessed what they considered a pitiful spectacle as the Zapatista troops humbly begged tortillas on the doorsteps of "bourgeois homes." The Casa leaders also objected to the ceremonial meeting of Zapata and Villa at the National Palace. They complained that the leader of the northerners acted suspiciously like a "personalist."[10]

Cultural and economic factors also played an important part in the ultimate decision by the Casa to reject Zapata and Villa in favor of the Constitutionalists. Urban workers, like their colonial-period and nineteenth-century ancestors, considered themselves citizens of Mexico City and much more sophisticated and modern than the *campesinaje*. As constituents of Mexico City, they enjoyed the way of life and the general wealth of the metropolis even if an unbalanced distribution of income gave them only peripheral advantages, such as public transportation and parks, sewage disposal, and other public services. The Casa found the religious devotion of the Zapatista revolutionaries and their acceptance of the clergy particularly aggravating. Religious arm patches and banners, such as the Zapatista Virgin of Guadalupe, especially galled the Casa "rationalists."[11] Villa's personal habits soon earned him the label of "villain," and rumored church support of his cause lent to the rubric "the reaction." These impressions were gross simplifications and unfair caricatures, but in the minds of the Casa leadership the agrarians and the Villistas seemed to represent "*la reacción*," the cultural values of a bygone age.

By January 1915 the sentiment that Villa and Zapata were enemies had taken hold of most of the anarchosyndicalists' thinking. Near the end of the month, when the Zapatistas temporarily evacuated Mexico City and units loyal to Alvaro Obregón appeared, the Casa committed itself to the "Constitutionalist cause" and the armed struggle.

The Casa's final commitment of the urban working-class movement to the Mexican Revolution came about because of a convergence of interests on the part of the Casa, which wanted to advance working-class organizing, and Obregón, who needed troops. He sent friendly emissaries, such as Gerardo Murillo (Dr. Atl), Adolfo de la Huerta, and Antonio I. Villareal, to the union's headquarters for consultations. Obregón offered the Casa the old Jesuit monastery of San Juan de Letrán, the Colegio Josefina, and the publishing facilities of the daily newspaper *La Tribuna* in order to better carry on its organizing activities and to demonstrate his support of the syndicalists.[12] The Casa accepted the donations. Jacinto Huitrón, an avid agrarianist Zapata supporter and one of the most dedicated of the Mexican anarchists, accepted the keys to the Colegio Josefina from Obregón at a public ceremony. Huitrón agreed to allow the clerics and their students one additional day to evacuate the building. The following day Huitrón and some Casa members distributed the *colegio*'s food stores to a hungry crowd that had gathered outside. Conservatives criticized him for "provoking disorder." Inside, the Casa occupiers stripped the walls of religious images, tore apart confessionals, and otherwise eliminated all vestiges of religiosity. Obregón's support of the Casa during this episode, despite some public resentment regarding the occupation of the religious buildings, made a strongly favorable impression upon the Casa leadership. Even the usually implacable Huitrón openly sympathized with the general.[13] Obregón's efforts were well timed. The Casa anarchists had begun to have serious doubts about the seemingly radical Dr. Atl, who served in the delicate role of emissary between the Constitutionalists and the Casa. They noted that he always apologized for Carranza and denigrated the Constitutionalist movement's "bourgeois" leadership. Hence, a deep suspicion developed regarding the direction of all three main factions—Zapatista, Villista, and Constitutionalist—in the Mexican Revolution.

On February 8, 1915, the Casa directors met in their Santa Brígida headquarters and cautiously decided to reject affiliation with the Constitutionalist movement because of its "bourgeois" nature and their general distrust of government. Speakers criticized both Atl and Carranza during the meeting. They also dismissed support of the Villa or Zapata movements as impossible in view of their religiosity and primarily "agrarian" orientation. The Casa was caught in the middle. At the end of the meeting, however, the urgency of the situation and Obregón's "support of syndicalism" persuaded the directors to allow Dr. Atl to make a special appeal on the following day.[14]

Twenty-three syndicate secretaries and forty-four other members of the directorate attended the session. Dr. Atl rose to the occasion. In an impassioned and radical appeal for the "proletariat of Mexico" to come to the aid of "The Revolution" in the face of the serious "reactionary" challenge of the Villista and Zapatista movements, he conceded the right of the Casa to organize the workers nationwide. The directors discussed, debated, and finally overwhelmingly approved a declaration of armed support for the Constitutionalists. All the anarchosyndicalists present, including Quintero, Salazar, Barragán Hernández, and the *agrarista* Huitrón, voted in favor of the resolution.[15]

On February 11 the directorate convened a general assembly of the Casa membership at the Teatro Ideal in Mexico City. A series of speakers endorsed the resolution of February 9; the only protest came from Aurelio Manrique, a member of the ultra radical Unión de Estudiantes, a Casa affiliate. He reminded the assembly of its principle of nonpolitical involvement, but ideology was more forcefully used to justify working-class participation in the revolution. The Casa saw its chance to become a major force in the revolution and feared for its existence if the armies of Zapata and Villa won the upcoming struggle. Enrique Arce and a half-dozen others opposed the decision of the majority and, in anticipation of the eventual outcome, they boycotted the Teatro Ideal meeting. *Agraristas* such as Díaz Soto y Gama continued to support Zapata, but the mutual affection between them and the Casa transcended the conflicts of 1915, and after Villa's defeat they were welcome to return.

On February 18 a Casa delegation consisting of Quintero, Salazar, Gasca, Rodolfo Aguirre, and Roberto Valdés traveled to Veracruz and negotiated with Carranza representatives for several days. The discussions resulted in the famous Veracruz pact of February 20, 1915, formally committing the Casa to the Constitutionalist military effort. The delegation's explanation for this commitment went far beyond the mere condemnation of the forces of Villa and Zapata as "the reaction" because of their alleged "Church and banker" support. They reasoned that the agreement ushered in a new era of anarchosyndicalist working-class organizing and working-class consciousness. They interpreted the pact as an agreement giving the Casa full authority to organize workers' councils throughout the country. The Casa intended to immediately establish anarchosyndicalism as the organizational basis of the Mexican working class. The Casa delegates expected a later showdown with Carranza and his "bourgeois" supporters, but they already represented fifty thousand workers nationwide and felt that they controlled the situation.[16]

The return of the delegation to Mexico City signalled an intensive recruiting effort that resulted in the departure in early March of seven thousand Mexico City workers for the Constitutionalist military induction training center in Orizaba. They were organized into six "Red

1. *Red Battalion artillery unit stationed on the road from Cuernavaca to Juitepec to guard against Zapatistas. (Photo gift of Ernesto Sán-chez Paulín)*

Battalions." The nationwide total of urban workers who took part in the revolution is uncertain, but the most reasonable estimate is twelve thousand, which included workers' militias from the inception of the Constitutionalist revolution in the north and contingents from Monterrey and Guadalajara. They constituted a massive augmentation of commanding general Obregón's Constitutionalist army. The workers acquitted themselves well at the major battles of Celaya, León, and El Ebano.[17] Commentators have disagreed with regard to the militias' fighting capacity. But neither side in this dispute has produced any evidence to support assertions that must be regarded with caution by analysts. One should note the logistical shortages on all sides and the limited training available to all units, as well as seek a realistic perspective.

Taking advantage of the organizing concessions granted by its pact with the Constitutionalists, the Casa leadership formed a Propaganda Committee (Comité de Propaganda) comprised of Mexico City and provincial syndicate heads. The committee, which numbered about eighty members, was divided into fourteen commissions of six members each. Each commission included a few members noted for their speaking and organizing abilities. Their task was threefold: first, to open preliminary talks with unorganized workers and to explain the national political situation and the Casa's support of the Constitutionalists; second, to form local affiliates of the Casa and to neutralize the potential hostility of the local elites and press by not revealing revolutionary ideology or long-range plans to them; and, third, to obtain from the Constitutionalists "help and guarantees for the new adherents."[18]

Despite the fact that the organizers carried credentials issued by the Constitutionalist government, or perhaps because of it, about ten died while carrying out their task. Rosendo Salazar and Celestino Gasca labored in Guanajuato while others carried on intensive organizing in Oaxaca and Orizaba.[19] In Morelia a delegation managed, after fifteen days of effort, to establish a Casa del Obrero Mundial with an affiliated union membership of thirty-five hundred. A general strike immediately ensued, and the Constitutionalist government adroitly responded by creating artisan workshops for carpenters, saddlemakers, cobblers, bakers, and tailors.[20] The painters received a commission to paint all of the city's public buildings. Public anticlerical demonstrations were held and heralded the Constitutionalist cause as the "social revolution." The successful Morelia organizing delegation then moved on to organize *casas del obrero mundial* in Uruapan, Zamora, and Tlalpujahua. In Mérida, Yucatán, the local unions merged into a Casa "which pursues the same ends as that in Mexico City."[21]

In spite of the overt cooperation that existed, even dependence on the Constitutionalist army, the most devout Casa anarchosyndicalists thought they could control the situation and not fall victims of government domination. Jacinto Huitrón could still declare that "the struggle between capital and labor is fatal and will continue to exist as long as money remains the regulator of society."[22] The most vehement anarchosyndicalists joined in calling the Constitutionalist movement "the social revolution."[23] They perceived the Constitutionalists in the radical perspectives offered them by Obregón and Dr. Atl, the able propagandist assigned by Carranza to the task of maintaining urban working-class support for the government and keeping the Casa in line. Atl, an effective speaker and the early mentor of some of Mexico's greatest mural painters, including Diego Rivera, delivered "Jacobin-like" speeches at many Casa gatherings. A completely sincere revolutionist, he claimed that his newspaper, *La Vanguardia*, represented the Constitutionalists, the workers, and the revolution. The result was a feeling among the anarchosyndicalists that the Constitutionalist movement was "radical," "Jacobin," and, despite Carranza, anxious for "La Revolución Social." Atl called upon the workers to take "Direct Action," and he impressed upon them the need for immediate results. He convinced many that the Constitutionalists and the Casa represented the working-class revolution that was shaping the future of Mexico.

The Constitutionalist-Casa military alliance paid quick dividends. With two Red Battalions in the campaign, Obregón's forces won a series of strategic victories over their principal antagonist, Villa, and drove him northward into Chihuahua. By late 1915, Villa, isolated and in disarray, posed only a regional problem. The Constitutionalist forces controlled all the larger cities in Mexico, and the Casa established branches in Córdoba, Jalapa, San Andrés Tuxtla, Tlacotalpan, Tabasco, Tlaxcala, Puerto México, Oaxaca, Tapachula, Tehuantepec, Mérida, Puebla, Tezuitlán, Banderillas (Puebla), Pachuca, Querétaro, Guanajuato, Celaya, Orizaba, Aguascalientes, San Luis Potosí, Zacatecas, Guadalajara, Irapuato, León, Morelia, Monterrey, Linares (Nuevo León), Colima, Tampico, Arbol Grande, Villa Cecilia, Ciudad Victoria, Nuevo Laredo, Saltillo, Torreón, Hermosillo, and Chihuahua.[24]

By late 1915, with their opponents defeated, the Constitutionalist amalgam of revolutionary elite and urban workers began to unravel. Open Casa support for the "International Working Class Movement," and the existence of workers' militias, provoked the concern of industrialists and conservative public officials. Unquestionably, a volatile situation existed with urban food shortages, runaway inflation, unemployment, public demonstrations, wildcat strikes, and battalion-sized units of armed workers in the field.

Carranza and the Ministry of Government (Gobernación) led by

General Abraham González and Rafael Zubarán Capmany pragmatically attempted to deal with the growing crisis. In March 1915, the textile industry received government contracts theoretically designed to put thirty-five thousand workers back on the job. The Constitutionalists also passed liberalized labor laws which raised some workers' wages and protected them from sudden layoffs without notice. These measures not only failed to deal with the critical problems of food shortages and inflation but also had no noticeable impact on the specifics they attempted to treat.

The economic and social crisis continued to deepen, especially in Mexico City. Hundreds of small businesses in the Federal District closed their doors and many larger concerns reduced both their production and workforces. Thousands of formerly employed workers in the environs of the capital city found themselves reduced to poverty and charity. Beggars were omnipresent.[25] Counterfeiting and a loosely managed flood of paper currency contributed to an inflation which further exacerbated the situation. Middlemen merchandisers came under fire from the Casa for profits which reached 15 percent on beef, already in short supply. After the Casa accused "Spaniards" of monopoly business practices and hoarding,[26] acts of violence against Spanish businessmen occurred. The Constitutionalist government resorted to fines to bring the violators in line with new governmental profit guidelines. In the outlying states some governors resorted to price controls and to government distribution of basic foodstuffs and clothing. Fortunately for the Constitutionalists, the public seemed to believe that the economic problems stemmed from the continuing war with Villa and Zapata. The Mexico City press confidently asserted that with peace the economy would be stabilized.[27]

While the economic crisis haunted the government, the Casa recruitment program benefited. During the first six months of 1915, in the wake of worker hardships and Constitutionalist military victories, dozens of new syndicates emerged throughout the nation and thousands of new members swelled the Casa's ranks.[28] The newcomers had little ideological instruction. The propaganda committees had not yet taught them the concepts of anarchosyndicalism, antigovernmentalism, and the "class struggle." Significantly, in addition to the anarchosyndicalist ideologues, the newer members also heard appeals from less radical nonanarchist syndicate leaders, including Luis Morones.

During the second half of 1915, the heavy recruitment of new members into the Casa continued. Almost two dozen syndicates joined in November and December alone. The new syndicates continued to be organized in accordance with traditional artisan trade specializations which antedated the nineteenth century. Unlike the situation in northern industrialized western Europe, this tradition remained strong among the artisans, anarchists, and anarchosyndicalists of Latin Eu-

rope and the Spanish-speaking world. The new unions included the
dyers, the biscuit bakers, the bed manufacturers, and the tobacco factory workers. Organizing success made the Casa leadership even more
vocal and extreme in its propaganda. *Ariete*, the Casa's "official newspaper," welcomed the new syndicates to "anarchy and freedom." [29]

A wave of confidence swept the Casa directorate and the old-guard
former Lucha members. They exalted the new syndicates as adherents
of a "libertarian way of life" that would transform Mexico. The workers, "as are all those who are oppressed, all of those who feel as we do,
. . . are marching dizzily [*vertiginosamente*] toward true freedom. The
Casa del Obrero Mundial has opened the breach. That is where we are
going." [30] The serious deterioration of the economy, the newly found
sense of freedom on the part of urban labor, and the support of Obregón, Atl, and several other Constitutionalist officials all contributed
to a sense of optimism among Casa organizers and accelerated the
Casa's rate of growth.

On October 13, 1915, the Casa enthusiastically inaugurated the
Ferrés-Moncaleano goal of a full-fledged Escuela Racionalista at the
Casa headquarters at Motolinia #9 in downtown Mexico City. The un-
veiling of a bust of the school's theoretical creator, the Spanish martyr
Francisco Ferrer Guardia, highlighted the occasion. Dr. Atl, Agustín
Aragón, and Díaz Soto y Gama, among other speakers, addressed the
hundreds of spectators. The school employed seven full-time instruc-
tors, required no enrollment fee or course prerequisites, and emphasized "free learning" as the primary necessity "for the disappearance
of slavery." Although an inadequate attempt in the struggle to redeem
the Mexican working class, the school had considerable success. For
the first time since the defeat of Huerta a year earlier, the anarchosyndicalists implemented a part of their program which—as conceived
by Ferrer Guardia and developed by Ferrés, Moncaleano, Luz, and
Lucha in Mexico—the Casa national directorate considered to be crucial to the success of their effort to develop a class-conscious and fully
mobilized Mexican working class. To the anarchosyndicalists, the
Escuela Racionalista represented working-class control of the educational learning process. It meant the inculcation of the working class
with "libertarian socialist" ideals.[31]

The armed conflict phase of the revolution concluded in most of
central Mexico by late 1915. Most of the old-guard Lucha members
survived the tumult and once again united in the leadership group at
Casa headquarters. Quintero, Arce, López Dónez, and Tudó joined together as editors of *Ariete*. The paper's importance transcended the
brevity of its tenure. *Ariete* featured hard-line anarchosyndicalist ideology, including articles written by long-time Lucha members calling
for the restructuring of the society and the economy around the newly
formed Casa syndicates. Reproductions of revolutionary essays written

by famous European anarchists—including Proudhon, Bakunin, Kropotkin, and a plethora of Spaniards—supplanted the Mexican tracts.

Ariete's writers, editorializing for the Casa, anticipated that anarchosyndicalism would "break down the petty and selfish prejudices of trade unionism" and provide the Mexican working class with an expanded social awareness, an "advanced class consciousness," and "modern ideas." Mexican workers would then appreciate "national and international proletarian class unity" against the "capitalist exploiter."[32] According to *Ariete*, the syndicates were to serve as the new basis of politics and economic production in "Revolutionary Mexico." The Casa leadership defined the Mexican Revolution in extremely radical terms and espoused doctrines completely unacceptable to the more conservative elements within the Carranza government. Because of these ideological differences, the hostility between government and anarchosyndicalist-organized labor deepened.

Runaway inflation and food shortages remained the extreme symptoms of a troubled Mexican economy and fueled working-class discontent through 1915 and 1916. Grocery store closings and bare shelves, *Ariete* charged, were caused by corrupt "monopolists" (*acaparadores*) who were "starving the people in a relentless quest for gold." Inflationary prices further increased the tension. Organized labor reacted by demanding price controls, stricter regulation of currency, and higher wages. The government, convinced that it had already done enough, failed to respond. Consequently, a growing sense of workers' unrest resulted in a series of sudden strikes.

The first wave of strikes provoked by this crisis occurred in the early summer of 1915 when schoolteachers and carriage drivers affiliated with the Casa walked off their jobs. Then, on July 30 the Bread Bakers Syndicate forced the bakery store operators to increase bakers' wages, guarantee the ingredients in and the quality of their product, and lower prices, which the strikers claimed, had risen 900 percent in a few months.[33] The next flare-up took place in October when workers shut down the British-owned Mexican Eagle Petroleum Company (Compañía Mexicana de Petroleo "El Aguila," S.A.), turned to the Casa for support, and then joined it.[34] In October and November the Textile Workers Syndicate struck and received a 100 percent increase in wages, the eight-hour day, and the six-day work week.[35] The Mexican labor movement had never before acted with such audacity or experienced so much success.

In December 1915 the strikes became even more serious. The Casa carpenter's syndicate struck, paralyzed construction, and gained a 150 percent wage increase.[36] The buttonmakers and barbers followed suit and achieved immediate gains.[37] Striking Casa-affiliated miners, led by Elías Matta Reyes, a Lebanese immigrant, closed down the El Oro mining area on the border between the states of México and Michoacán.

When the predominantly German and French owners used strike-breakers and violence in an attempt to reopen the mines, the miners resorted to sabotage of the mining facilities. Both sides committed physical assaults. In 1915 the Casa activists among the miners numbered 150 and they wielded tremendous influence.[38] The anarchosyndicalist leaders of the Casa openly challenged both capitalism and government and yet expressed confidence in their course of action. No era in the history of Mexican labor had witnessed the militancy and belligerence that the Casa demonstrated in the last six months of 1915 and first eight months of 1916. The pressure and turbulence were building up toward the general strikes of 1916.

On January 13, 1916, during a period of increasing syndicate unrest and in the wake of Constitutionalist military victories, an alarmed President Carranza dissolved and disarmed the Red Battalions. When the discharged worker-soldiers returned to their homes, they found employment difficult to obtain and the Casa headquartered in the newly received, formerly prestigious House of Tiles in Mexico City. Jesús Acuña, minister of government and a member of the progressive Obregón-led faction of the Constitutionalists, had given it to the Casa as a token of his political good will. The returned veterans flocked to the House of Tiles for a seemingly endless agenda of organizational protest meetings and revolutionary lectures.[39]

The plight of the veterans of the Red Battalions, many of whom were unemployed and penniless, caused another abrasive dispute between the Casa and the government. The union leaders claimed that the men had been forgotten and cast aside. In January and February of 1916, the Casa petitioned for and demanded compensation not only for the impoverished veterans of the *batallones rojos* but also for striking workers whom it was claimed had been displaced by strikebreakers.

During the winter of 1916 Casa-sponsored street demonstrations, involving the veterans and other Casa members, criticized the government and demanded price controls, higher wages, and employment security. The demonstrations and protest marches usually began in front of the casa headquarters at the House of Tiles and often terminated at government or other office buildings. The veterans demanded government remedial action as compensation for their service to the revolution. On February 1, in reaction to the unrest, General González ordered his troops to close the House of Tiles meeting place and to arrest all those found on the premises. Simultaneous orders to close down regional *casas* went to the governors of some states. A number of Casa national directors were jailed at the military headquarters in Mexico City (Jefatura de las Armas). Jacinto Huitrón, among others, was held in detention for nearly four months. In the meantime, the Casa leadership planned a protest general strike for the Mexico City area to be carried out by the Federation of Federal District Syndicates (Federación de Sindicatos del Distrito Federal), an amalgam of Casa syndicates located in the Federal District of Mexico, which included the capital city. In Veracruz and Tampico angry members of regional *casas* staged street demonstrations, and the respective state governors declared a "state of siege" in order to regain control of the situation.[40]

During March 1916 the Casa continued its confrontation with the government by going through with plans begun in January for a "Preliminary" National Labor Congress to meet in the city of Veracruz. The congress was officially called by the Federation of Federal District Syndicates, which called upon the syndicates of the entire country to send delegates to help resolve the crisis which faced the Mexican urban working-class movement. Delegates attended from Guadalajara, the Federal District, and a number of cities in the states of Veracruz, Colima, Sinaloa, Sonora, Michoacán, Puebla, and Oaxaca. The raid upon the House of Tiles and the arrests of Casa leaders gave the congress, attended by representatives of more than seventy-three syndicate locals, an air of urgency when it convened on March 5.[41]

The governor of Veracruz, Heriberto Jara, a known radical in the Constitutionalist ranks, declined an invitation to address the congress, stating that the radical nature of the delegates' ideas "could in no way serve the interests of the people." Indeed, their radicalism far surpassed Jara's. In their final declaration, the delegates proclaimed "class struggle" as a fundamental principle, defined syndicates as "resistance societies," advocated "socialization of the means of production," and excluded "any kind of political activity from the syndicalist movement." The congress created the Mexican Region Confederation of Labor (La Confederación del Trabajo de la Región Mexicana), with headquarters to be established in the organized-labor stronghold of Orizaba, Veracruz. It was meant to be the Mexican regional organ in the long-held Spanish anarchist vision of an anarchosyndicalist world. The confederation, however, never really functioned. The congress, dominated by anarchosyndicalism, ended on March 17. It had not resolved the impending crisis in Mexico City.[42]

The Federation of Federal District Syndicates called the first general strike of 1916 to press home the long-sought Casa economic reforms and to protest the seizure of the Casa headquarters in Mexico City and the arrests of its leadership. It began during the early morning of May 22. All public utilities and public services ceased operations in the capital and most stores remained closed throughout the day. Thousands of workers marched toward Alameda Park in the heart of downtown Mexico City to hold a rally. General Benjamín Hill, commander of the plaza and charged with the security of the Federal District, met with a Casa delegation headed by Barragán Hernández, who

2. Meeting of returned and protesting veterans of the Red Battalions at Casa headquarters in the famous House of Tiles. (Photo gift of Ernesto Sánchez Paulín)

3. A group of workers outside the meeting rooms of the Casa in the House of Tiles. (Photo gift of Ernesto Sánchez Paulín)

4. *Part of the crowd which gathered in the Alameda Park on May 22, 1916, during the general strike. (Photo gift of Ernesto Sánchez Paulín)*

5. Negotiating meeting between General Benjamín Hill and the Casa
during the general strike of May 1916. (Photo gift of Ernesto Sánchez
Paulín)

gave him a list of demands addressed to the businessmen and industrialists of Mexico City. He listened as Barragán Hernández explained the workers' plight.

Hill agreed to act as an intermediary between the Casa and the employers and also between the government and the union. He then issued a threatening ultimatum to all employers concerned to attend the public negotiations with the Casa or face arrest by his troops. Late in the day the electrical power and other vital transportation services resumed operating by mutual accord. The parties agreed to continue negotiations the next day when Casa leaders could meet with the full contingent of businessmen and industrialists in an open conference.

On May 23 the rival groups, including the government, came together in the Arbeu Theater (Teatro Arbeu) and resolved the crisis. Concessions obtained by the Casa included the mandatory replacement of company scrip money with valid government currency (*gobierno provisional*) for the payment of workers' wages. The employers also agreed not to reduce the work force for at least three months in order to protect the strikers from retaliatory dismissals. The workers were to be paid for time lost during the brief strike. Finally, any company decision to close down factory operations required prior clearance with the local military commander. In the Mexico City area that individual was General Hill. The government agreed to give the Casa another meeting place in lieu of the House of Tiles and to examine the Casa's complaints regarding the arrests of some of its leadership but acknowledged no wrong doing and promised no further action. The Casa grudgingly accepted the building proffered by the government but never put it to regular use, because of its limited size and the belief that gifts from the increasingly hostile Constitutionalists should no longer be accepted.[43]

In the wake of the strike, progovernment liberals quickly attempted to bridge the widening gap between themselves and the Casa. Dr. Atl reflected liberal sentiments when he declared, "The strike . . . is not a reflection of discontent toward the government growing out of the Revolution, but a consequence of the [government's] proclaimed principles of that Revolution."[44] Successful government intervention during the first general strike of 1916 and the interpretation of revolutionary fulfillment given that intervention by the liberals were important steps in the development of the "official ideology" of the Mexican Revolution and eventual governmental control of the independent labor movement.

The general strike of May 1916 gained notable concessions for the Casa syndicate members; yet, rather than the strike heralding the final demise of the government and capitalism as the anarchists had predicted during the previous fifty years, the Constitutionalist regime demonstrated considerable flexibility in quickly settling the affair. At the time, the anarchosyndicalist leadership of the Casa sensed power and expressed confidence about the outcome. They did not see the inherent weaknesses in their organization, the lack of unity, and the virtually nonexistent discipline of the rank-and-file. Other labor leaders who signed the Casa-government agreement to end the strike, such as Luis Morones, the future leader of the Confederación Regional Obrera Mexicana (CROM), saw in the outcome the advantages of working with the Constitutionalists and enjoying their protection. The government thus built a bridge of confidence between itself and a new rising generation of pragmatic, less radical labor leaders.

Not all government officials were as sympathetic in their dealings with the Casa as Atl and Obregón. President Carranza and General González headed a conservative faction of the Constitutionalist regime in Mexico City that became increasingly hostile to organized labor. Significantly, government leaders saw the threat to their authority posed by revolutionary anarchosyndicalism. They also realized that the basis of the Casa's strength—capacity to organize and communicate with the regional *casas*—relied upon the leadership, the urban meeting halls, and the armories. The government responded to the threat decisively and crushed the anarchosyndicalists during the second general strike of 1916. The most powerful, however lukewarm, supporter of the Casa, Obregón, although in Mexico City at the time, made no move to intervene when the president, provoked by the general strike of July 31–August 2, moved against organized labor.

During the summer of 1916 an agreement among bankers, industrialists, and commercial houses, and consented to by the government, to set the value of the Provisional Government (*gobierno provisional*) peso at two centavos or one-fiftieth the value of the older gold-based currency, provoked urban labor unrest in Mexico City.[45] This action was probably taken to combat inflation, but it placed the major burden of that effort on the urban working class and wiped out the guaranteed wage gains made as a result of the May general strike.

Employers paid the majority of their workers in Constitutionalist currency; urban labor thus received a severe setback in real wages and a lowered standard of living. Strikes and angry, protesting street crowds became frequent.[46] The government rebuffed Casa appeals that it intercede on the workers' behalf with new monetary regulations.[47] The survival of the average factory worker and the underemployed now depended upon the traditional lower-class means of marginal subsistence on the fringes of the money economy. Families went without new clothing and were reduced to the most basic foodstuffs while their children begged and scavenged for wood to use as fuel. If a once-proud worker could no longer pay the rent on the one-room family apartment, the omnipresent squatter-shanty towns and *vecin-*

dades that enveloped the city were ready to receive him. Men who took pride in their skills saw their positions deteriorating to the lowest socioeconomic extremity.

Given the desperate condition of the urban working class, the Casa decision to challenge both the revolutionary government and the financially dominant elements of Mexico City with the general strike of July 31–August 2 was an understandable although premature action. The anarchosyndicalists, with their organization only beginning to establish firm direction for its many new members, were in no position to challenge the government and its army.

The directorate (Consejo Federal) of the Federal District Federation of Workers Syndicates (Federación de Sindicatos Obreros), noting the government and capitalist refusals to reconsider the two-centavos valuation of the Constitutionalist peso, voted unanimously to call a general strike.[48] The goal of the strike was to force the government and the employers of the greater Mexico City area to agree to the payment of workers' salaries in gold or its currency equivalent.

Syndicate leaders and organizers held secret meetings for several weeks in order to plan the strike and to avoid the perennial police observers at urban labor meetings. The general secretary of the federation, Barragán Hernández, a former Lucha member and one of the most forceful anarchosyndicalists of the revolutionary era, surreptitiously visited the various Casa syndicates in the Federal District and explained the strategy and the plans for the strike. Barragán Hernández also created three strike committees (Comités de Huelga). The second and third committees were to serve only if the first was put out of operation. The first committee included none of the principal syndicate leaders but did consist of ten militant Casa members: Esther Torres, Angela Inclán, Timoteo García, Alfredo Pérez Medina, Federico Rocha, Cervantes Torres, Casimiro del Valle, Ausencio Venegas, Cesar Pandelo, and Leonardo Hernández.[49]

Early in the morning of July 31, 1916, the lights, the telephones, the public transportation, the drinking water, and all other public services in the greater Mexico City area ceased to function. Factories shut down and the retail stores failed to open. The approximately ninety-thousand striking members of the Casa closed down all normal activities in the Federal District.

Later the same morning, striking workers began to assemble for a mass meeting at the Star Salon, a frequently used working-class gathering place in downtown Mexico City. The strikers, fearing police intercession, arrived in small groups. Chaired by Luis Araiza and characterized by forceful and determined speeches, it was an excited meeting. In the midst of the session Dr. Atl arrived, bringing with him an invitation from President Carranza for the Strike Committee to meet with him at the National Palace.

6. Strike meeting at the Star Salon shortly before the mounted police, acting on President Carranza's orders, attacked the crowd both inside and outside the meeting place, July 31, 1916. (Photo gift of Ernesto Sánchez Paulín)

After a brief consultation, the nine-member Strike Committee agreed to meet with Carranza, announced their decision to the assembly, and departed with Atl. A few moments later the mounted riot police (*gendarmería montada*), fully armed and still astride their horses, entered the theater attacking, beating, and dissolving the leaderless crowd. After some arrests, authorities closed the Star Salon and the rarely used "headquarters" given the Casa some two months earlier as a result of the May general strike and placed both under guard. In the meantime the Comité de Huelga, unaware of events at the Star Salon, met with the president. He denounced them as "traitors to the nation" (*traidores a la patria*) and ordered their immediate arrest. President Carranza declared martial law at 5:00 P.M. the next day.[50]

August 1, 1916, passed in ominous silence. All public activities in Mexico City remained at a standstill while the military patrolled the streets. Sentries guarded all Casa installations, the Star Salon, and the various working-class neighborhoods where disorders occurred. August 2 began with a massive military parade and show of strength through the downtown section of the city. At the conclusion of the march, the soldiers gathered in front of the National Palace to hear the formal reading of the proclamation of martial law by Lieutenant Colonel Miguel Peralta. The proclamation charged the syndicates with an attack upon "public order," "antipatriotism," and "criminal conduct." Citing the famous public order statute of January 25, 1862, article one threatened those who violated "public order" with the death penalty. A violation of "public order" was defined as participation in any form of strike activity at factories or other institutions determined by the authorities to be in the "public service." The penalties were to be dealt out in the summary manner prescribed by President Huerta's emergency decree number fourteen of December 12, 1913, which Huerta had issued in an attempt to deal with the revolutionaries trying to topple his regime. Authorities arrested a number of Casa leaders, but no executions followed; the prisoners were held in the national penitentiary.

Restoration of electrical service to the city following capture of Ernesto Velasco, an electricians' syndicate leader, proved to be a major turning point in the defeat of the strike. Under the threat of the most extreme punitive action, Velasco—whom police found in hiding, arrested, and roughed up—provided the military with the necessary technical information needed to restore electrical power. The restoraion of electrical power on the morning of August 2 demoralized the workers, and the poor status of Casa communications led many strikers to believe the strike was over.

On August 2, Barragán Hernández met with Obregón to ask for his assistance in guaranteeing the safety of the arrested members of the First Strike Committee and in opening negotiations with the government. Obregón, in what Rosendo Salazar regards as a fatal betrayal of the Casa, informed him that he underestimated the seriousness of the situation and warned that in order to avoid extreme punishments and further arrests the Federation of Federal District Syndicates and the Casa should "temporarily disband." Barragán Hernández reported Obregón's conclusions to the Second Strike Committee that evening. After a prolonged discussion, the committee voted to "recess" the Casa and the federation. The Casa was totally defeated.[51]

The strike failed because of a combination of factors: the use of strikebreakers from outside Mexico City in the operation of the restored electrical power plants, the devastating psychological impact upon the workers caused by the return of electricity, the arrest of the First Strike Committee, the closure of all Casa meeting places, the prevention of all street gatherings, the resultant lack of communications, and the intimidation caused by the extreme nature of the declaration of martial law accompanied by an overwhelming show of military and police force. A strategic factor in the failure of the general strike was its limitation to the Mexico City area. The Casa directorate did not dare to call upon the nation's workers because of a realistic recognition of urban labor's weakness in the states. The syndicates in other parts of the country simply did not enjoy sufficient strength to make a nationwide general strike work. Thus, the government, by concentrating its strength in the relatively industrialized Mexico City area, defeated the Casa.[52]

The trials of the twelve Casa prisoners before the military tribunal resulted in acquittal and release for all except Velasco, who received a death sentence. General Hill arrested the freed prisoners upon their release; a retrial also ended in acquittal. Public outcry and opposition to the extreme nature of Velasco's sentence from within the ranks of the Constitutionalists persuaded authorities to reduce his sentence on April 11, 1917, to twenty years in prison. Finally, through the intervention of Obregón, Velasco was released on February 18, 1918.[53]

Meanwhile, on October 10, 1917, the anarchosyndicalists received yet another crushing blow with the murder of Barragán Hernández. Attacked and wounded by a gun-wielding assailant in the street, he ran inside a nearby military station for refuge. His pursuer, José González Cantú, member of a prominent Mexico City family and a recently graduated class leader in a local military academy, followed him there and shot him to death. The onlooking soldiers did not stop or give chase to the murderer. The urban working class had lost one of its strongest leaders.[54]

10. The Aftermath of August 1916: Continued Activity

After the general strike of July–August 1916, the closure of the Casa, and the prosecution of many of its most active members, syndicalist organizing was stymied in the Mexico City area. Workers' meetings were not tolerated. On one occasion Jacinto Huitrón was arrested for holding a memorial gathering on the anniversary of Ferrer Guardia's execution. The syndicates fragmented. Nine months passed before new anarchist groups felt confident enough to surface in the capital.[1]

In June 1917 a new Grupo Luz was formed headed by Huitrón. Only a handful of the old leaders were willing to participate openly in Luz. Among them were José López Dónez, Luis Méndez, and Enrique Arce. Despite the lack of overt support, its newspaper, *Luz*, was popular and distributed four to five thousand copies per edition for a price of five centavos each. Among the writers who contributed articles —besides López Dónez, Méndez, and Arce—was Amadeo Ferrés, who sent an article from Tarragona, Spain.[2] By 1918 Luz was holding public meetings, cultural events, and fiestas. Sometimes the crowds numbered several hundred.[3] Luz and its newspaper helped sustain anarchosyndicalist morale in central Mexico from 1917 through 1920.

Other relatively less important and almost anonymous anarchist groups that formed in Mexico City during 1917–1918 were the Jovenes Socialistas Rojos, Los Autónomos, and Solidaridad. The latter was composed almost entirely of former members of the Federation of Federal District Syndicates. Luz and the other groups, in their totality, represented residual anarchist strength that would lead to the formation of the anarchosyndicalist General Confederation of Workers (Confederación General de Trabajadores, CGT) in 1921. The CGT, predictably, found the greater part of its hard-core forty-thousand membership strength during most of the 1920's and its peak enrollment of eighty thousand in 1928–1929 in the long-organized and traditionally militant Mexico City area.

While the capital was in flux, no less than twenty anarchosyndicalist groups continued to function or were formed in other parts of the country. They were the *casas del obrero mundial* of Guadalajara, Tampico, and Saltillo; Cultura Racional (1918) and Rebeldía (1918) of Aguascalientes; Germinal (1917), Vida Libre (1918), and Fuerza y Cerebro (1917–1918) of Tampico; Hermanos Rojos of Villa Cecilia near Tampico (1918); Alba Roja of Ciudad Victoria (1918); Francisco Ferrer Guardia of Nuevo Laredo (1918); Acción Consciente of Monterrey (1918); Acracia and Ni Dios Ni Amo of Ciudad Juárez

(1918); Acción Cultural Sindicalista of Zacatecas (1917); Ciencia y Libertad and Luz y Fuerza of Toluca (1917); Emancipación of Saltillo (1917); Hermandad Acrata of Orizaba (1918); and Grupo Cultural Libertario of Léon (1919).[4]

The most successful anarchosyndicalist organizing efforts outside Mexico City were in the Tampico area where sixteen syndicates were affiliated with the local Casa. Among the Tampico workers that organized were the day laborers, harbor boat crews, barbers, electrical workers, metal workers, carpenters, tailors, and *tipógrafos*. They formed a Federation of Syndicates (Federación de Sindicatos). The Tampico Casa and federation leadership formed its own control unit, the Grupo Casa del Obrero Mundial. In an editorial the leadership announced through its newspaper, *Tribuna Roja*, the desire to "break the hold of the bourgeois vermin [*bicho*]" and to attain "class equality."[5]

Germinal, one of the anarchist organizing groups in Tampico, was largely composed of the Tampico Casa directorate. Its purpose was the propagation of anarchist ideology and revolutionary theories to the working class of the area. One of its more spirited and controversial organizing efforts took place among the employees of the American-owned Texas Oil Company of Mexico. Only a small number of its workers were unionized, however, and those who openly acknowledged affiliation with the radicals were dismissed.[6]

As a part of their effort to influence the development of the Mexican labor movement, the Tampico Casa and Germinal sponsored the Second National Labor Congress, which convened on October 13, 1917, the anniversary of Ferrer Guardia's execution. Invitations were extended to all the remaining syndicates and anarchist organizing groups in Mexico.[7] The majority of the syndicates still allowed to exist in the central area of the country were dominated by the government and Luis Morones. He attended the Tampico congress with a host of cohorts, claiming to represent the working class of Mexico City and the "reorganized" workers of the state of Hidalgo. A head count revealed that Morones' supporters slightly outnumbered the anarchosyndicalists in attendance.

Morones, aided by Ricardo Trevino, who quit the IWW-affiliated Tampico Petroleum Workers shortly before the meeting got under way in order to support Morones, engaged in an extensive debate over the contents of the congress report with the principal leader of the Tampico labor groups, Jorge D. Borrán, a Spanish anarchist. Borrán wanted the usual anarchist antipolitical declaration calling for "revolutionary syndicalism, rationalist education and popular libraries (*bibliotecas populares*), and common ownership of private property." Morones, with the Federal District and Hidalgo delegations supporting him, narrowly defeated Borrán and the Tampico delegates on

every vote. The result was a 10-point resolution that recognized the
workers' need for better working, health, and educational conditions;
that stated their right to whatever form of political expression they
deemed convenient; and that called for the formation of a central
committee (Comité Central) to direct a new Mexican "regional" labor
organization, the General Confederation of Labor (Confederación
General Obrera). The committee's headquarters were to be located in
Torreón, but, because of the deep divisions within the congress, the
committee never received sufficient support from its constituents and
the project was abandoned six months later.[8] Following the convention, the Carranza government expelled Borrán from the country.[9]
The anarchosyndicalists were outvoted in a major organized labor
assembly for the first time since the creation of the Casa. They would
never again successfully challenge Luis Morones and his government-
supported followers in a fully attended national urban working-class
assembly. They had to create an alternative organization.

During and after the confrontation between the Casa anarchosyndicalist old guard and the Carranza government, newer syndicate
leaders, led by Luis Morones and fearing the ultimate defeat of organized labor, stressed the success of earlier cooperation with the government and suggested its continuation. In the discouraging urban
labor vacuum of late 1917, most of the less ideologically oriented
syndicates, leaders, and rank-and-file that had rushed to join the Casa
in 1915 and 1916 were now looking to Morones for leadership in the
creation of a new labor organization.

In the spring of 1918, Morones and his followers, with government
support, arranged a fourth labor convention. The gathering was held
in Saltillo between May 1 and 12. About one hundred syndicate delegates from across the nation attended. The represented syndicates had
a total national membership of only 38,000. Some anarchosyndicalists attended, and Jacinto Huitrón was a member of the directing
Junta, but they were a distinct minority. After many heated debates,
which led to the withdrawal of Huitrón and other leftists, the congress
created the Confederación Regional Obrera Mexicana (CROM). Despite the convention's declared allegiance to the "principles of the
Casa," and the presence of some anarchosyndicalist members in
CROM, many workers refused to join it. The anarchist concept of a
"Mexican region" within a revolutionary international working-class
movement lived on in name only. Morones and two of his closest associates, Ricardo Trevino and J. Marcos Tristán, were elected to the
three-member Central Committee (Comité Central) of the new Confederation. The threesome soon left Saltillo to attend the meeting of
the Samuel Gompers–led American Federation of Labor (AFL) in
Saint Paul, Minnesota, where declarations of mutual support and ad-

miration were exchanged.[10] Mexican anarchosyndicalists and nationalists were outraged, and by the end of 1918 CROM membership had dwindled to only a little more than seven thousand. In April 1919, *Luz* published a fourteen-point critique of Morones and the CROM.[11]

The General Confederation of Workers (CGT)

In the spring of 1919, Luz, Cultura Racional of Aguascalientes, and the Hermanos Rojos of Villa Cecilia near Tampico all expressed a growing sense of urgency for the establishment of a "libertarian" alternative to CROM.[12] But no purely anarchosyndicalist convention could be held as long as the hostile Carranza regime was in power. Luz did create a Mexico City–based workers' organizing group, the Central Workers Corps (Cuerpo Central de Trabajadores), in 1919, which was later renamed the Communist Federation of the Mexican Proletariat (Federación Comunista del Proletariado Mexicano). Its declared objective was to serve as an antipolitical opposition against the Labor party of the CROM and to oppose the new Communist party.[13] But these activities, like those of the Communists, had to be low key.

In 1920, Obregón, a leader more sympathetic toward organized labor, toppled Carranza after a brief struggle. Although he favored Morones and the CROM, the anarchosyndicalists enjoyed a far less intimidating milieu than that which had prevailed since August 1916.

From February 15 to February 22, 1921, an anarchosyndicalist convention was held in Mexico City designed to create a new regional (Mexican) labor organization. It was sponsored by the Communist Federation of the Mexican Proletariat. Fifty representatives from thirty syndicates in the Federal District and twenty from the states attended. They created the CGT. Some of the more important CGT syndicates were a consolidated textile factory workers' group, the Federación de Obreros de Hilados y Tejidos del Estado de México y del Distrito Federal; the streetcar conductors, plant workers, and right-of-way maintenance employees from the Mexico City Transit Company, the Empleados y Obreros de Tráfico de la Compañia de Tranvías and the Sindicato de Vía Permanente de la Compañia de Tranvías; some telephone workers, the Obreros y Empleados de Telefonos "Ericsson"; textile factory workers, the Obreros Progresistas de Santa Rosa (Orizaba); tobacco factory employees, Tabaqueros (Veracruz); the Obreros de Artes Gráficas Comerciales del D.F.; the Obreros y Obreras del Palacio de Hierro; the *canteros* from Coyoacán; and various other groups, largely from Veracruz, Orizaba, Puebla, the state of México, the Federal District, Tampico, and Jalisco. Many were former Casa groups. The newcomers included the Industrial Workers of the World.

José Refugio Rodríguez represented a contingent of the IWW in Mexico City, and Michael Paley was the delegate from an IWW unit, the Industrial Petroleum Workers, in Tampico.[14]

In its constitution the CGT accepted "libertarian communism" (*comunismo libertario*), "rationalist education for the working class" (*el sistema racionalista para la instrucción del pueblo trabajador*), "class struggle" (*lucha de clases*), and "direct action" (*la acción directa, que implica la exclusión de toda clase de política*) as fundamental principles because they were necessary for "the complete emancipation of the workers and peasants" (*obreros y campesinos*).[15]

Some of the CGT founders were long-time leaders of Mexican anarchosyndicalism, among them Rafael Quintero and Jacinto Huitrón. They were joined by younger but equally aggressive adherents. Typical of these men was the executive committee of the Communist Federation which presided over the first CGT convention. It was composed of Albert Araoz de Léon, José C. Valadés, and Manuel Díaz Ramírez. The latter two members later became rival interpretors of Mexican working-class history, Valadés offering an anti-Marxist radical perspective and Díaz Ramírez the Stalinist viewpoint. The foundling CGT suffered no lack of brainpower or leadership.

The convention passed several significant resolutions, calling for immediate agrarian land reform and creation of *campesino* organizing committees. The agrarian program would be pressed by the CGT throughout its history, but with little success. One of the declarations observed that the workers of the United States, Panama, Cuba, and Santo Domingo, among others, were victims of a "White Terror" (*terror blanco*) carried out by the "American Capitalists." The CGT protested the deportation of six of its foreign-born organizers—Sebastián San Vicente, Frank Seaman, Natalia Michaelova, Michael Paley, José Rubio, "Fort Mayer" [*sic*], and José Allen. Another resolution denounced the Pan American Federation of Labor (Confederación Panamericana del Trabajo) as an attempt by the American government and the AFL to manipulate the working class of the Western Hemisphere. This was also an attack on Morones and the CROM, which had established close ties with Gompers and the AFL. The CGT, like the PLM before it and unlike the Casa, was deeply aware of and concerned with Yankee imperialism. Consistent with the "popular front" sentiments of anarchists in other countries in 1921, the Communist party was welcomed into CGT membership.[16] The CGT affiliated with the Moscow-led International and sent Díaz Ramírez to Moscow as its representative[17]—a mission and experience that would forever reshape his ideology. The CGT even accepted the principle of a "Dictatorship of the Proletariat," although it was given an anarchosyndicalist definition. The "dictatorship" was not to be controlled by a political cadre or group claiming to represent the proletariat; rather, it was described as "the working class organized into, and ruling through, councils of workers, *campesinos*, and soldiers." The new Communist party was in attendance at the convention and apparently suffered through it all without complaint. The CGT inaugural conclave signed all its proclamations "Health and Libertarian Communism" (Salud y Comunismo Libertario).

The anarchosyndicalist leadership of the CGT soon came into open conflict with the Communist party. The occasion was the First National Workers Congress of the CGT (Primero Congreso Obrero Nacional de la CGT) held in Mexico City from September 4 to September 11, 1921. Debates and ideological disputes during the convention resulted in balloting won by the anarchosyndicalist directorate. Finally, the delegates approved an anarchosyndicalist motion to ask the membership of the syndicates to decide in an election if the CGT should drop or retain its affiliation with the Moscow-based Third International. This action was taken in the context of the repression of Russian anarchists carried out by the Bolsheviks. The Communist party delegation walked out of the CGT convention in protest.[18] The withdrawal of the small Communist party gave the CGT unity, but its anti-Marxism also meant that some of the most active and brilliant of Mexico's young radicals would look elsewhere for identification. The CGT had begun to isolate itself from Mexico's future.

An anarchosyndicalist control group, the Libertarian Syndicalist Center (Centro Sindicalista Libertario, CSL), emerged from the September convention with unchallengeable power over the organization. Patterned after La Social of the nineteenth century, the *obreros intelectuales* of the Artes Gráficas, and Luz and Lucha of the Casa, the CSL was the organizing and propaganda nucleus of the CGT. It carried the responsibility of ideological direction and organizational impetus. Special subcommittees were formed by the CSL for such duties as the recruitment of new syndicates and to petition for the release of CGT "political prisoners" held without trial by the government. Among the CSL's members were Quintero, Valadés, Araiza, Salazar, Aguirre, and a number of other former Casa leaders. The CSL published the official CGT newspaper, *Verbo Rojo*, under the direction of Araiza. The usual European writers—Bakunin, Proudhon, Kropotkin, Lorenzo, Malatesta, and Reclus—provided the essays on political theory for *Verbo Rojo*, while the Mexicans contributed their views regarding contemporary conditions and CGT strategies for their own country. An occasional essay by Ricardo Flores Magón, imprisoned at Leavenworth, Kansas, appeared. To the CGT-CSL his continued struggle for anarchist communism was heroic and he was venerated as a revolutionary martyr.[19]

On May 13, 1922, Huitrón, Quintero, and Alejandro Montoya called a special meeting of the CSL at which Rosendo Salazar and José G.

Escobedo were expelled from the CGT directorate for their collaboration with the political movement led by Adolfo de la Huerta in his
quest for the presidency of Mexico and for past political activities
about which they had been warned. The expelled members defended
themselves valiantly and the decisive vote was not taken until 6:00
A.M. on May 14.[20] The CGT intended to remain divorced from "politics" although a number of its radical members individually and in
secrecy assisted de la Huerta's efforts among the workers.

The twelve-year history of the CGT as an anarchosyndicalist group
was spotted with violence, especially during its militant first six years.
These incidents were usually precipitated by the omnipresent, over-
zealous authorities, but occasionally the CGT resorted to drastic measures in pursuit of its goals. The 1922 CGT May Day commemoration
was one example. A march to the American Consulate was held in
order to articulate demands for the release of Ricardo Flores Magón
and Librado Rivera from the federal penitentiary at Leavenworth.
When the crowd was parading through downtown Mexico City on its
way back to the CGT's headquarters, it passed the Knights of Columbus (Caballeros de Colón) center. The ultraconservative Caballeros
were waiting on the balcony and at the windows. An exchange of cat-
calls and insults was followed by a sniper's gunshot and the instant
death of a CGT marcher's young son. Dozens in the crowd of about
one thousand, many of which were combat veterans of the Red Battalions, drew pistols and charged the building, scaled the walls, and
broke down the front door. They sacked the interior of the building
and "Rojos" pursued "Cristeros" through the narrow streets of the
older downtown section of Mexico City.[21] The police were discreet in
their delayed presence.

Four months later violence erupted at an old trouble spot, the textile factory of San Ildefonso in San Angel on the southwestern edge
of Mexico City, so often the center of violent workers' organizing efforts in the nineteenth century. The plant was closed down by a wildcat strike called by the workers. They had no union at the time and
appealed to the highly placed government leaders of the CROM and
the Mexican Labor party (Partido Laborista Mexicano) of Morones
for help. To their dismay their plea was rejected, for the owners of the
San Idlefonso plant wielded considerable political influence at the local and national levels. When the CGT was approached for assistance
by the strikers, the CSL decided to give them all-out support. CGT
organizers and speakers arranged and addressed strike rallies and
helped set up picket lines. When these efforts failed to achieve any
beneficial results and strikebreakers began to enter the plant, a strike
of all CGT textile syndicates in the Federal District was called. In
their zeal, the workers at the nearby La Magdalena plant cut the power
cables to the factory before walking out in support of their San Ilde-

fonso counterparts. The textile plant operators of the San Angel–
Contreras area had defeated the workers before, however, and they
demonstrated their determination by declaring a lockout at the six
factories in the area.

The confrontation continued into October 1922 and was escalated
by the kidnapping of the textile syndicate leader (Federación Hiland-
era), Julio Márquez. On October 20 a CGT-led rally was held to protest
the Márquez disappearance. It culminated at the San Angel City Hall.
About five thousand persons were in the crowd when the mounted
police fired upon them and charged forward on horseback. One worker
was killed and dozens more were injured in the gunfire and panic
that ensued. The CGT blamed General Celestino Gasca—military
governor of the Federal District, a former member of the Casa, and
commander of the Red Battalions—for the attack. They also blamed
the national government and President Obregón for allowing a general climate of repression to develop that made the attack possible.
On October 22 posters appeared throughout the Federal District protesting the attack, blaming Gasca, and calling for a protest march
October 25 to the governor's palace. The CGT, under uncompromis-
ing CSL leadership, was completely isolated from the leftist revolutionaries like Gasca who held power and sided with the pragmatic
CROM.[22]

On October 25 thousand of workers gathered near CGT headquarters on Calle Uruguay in downtown Mexico City and marched from
there to the governor's palace. En route they were joined by about
three hundred independently organized but militant railroad workers
from the Nonoalco train yards. Huitrón, Araiza, and others delivered
speeches in front of the governor's palace describing the events of
October 20 in San Angel. The governor, who looked on impassively,
never accepted responsibility for what had transpired. The factories
reopened after a few days with the vast majority of employees now
members of the CGT, but it was a Pyrrhic victory.[23] Few concessions
were granted by the employers, and the government was more hostile
than ever to the CGT. Three years later, in 1925, the CROM would
attempt to penetrate the CGT textile workers' stronghold of San
Angel–Contreras, leading to street battles, gunfights, strikes, lockouts,
and government military-police intervention on behalf of the CROM
minority. The Centro Sindicalista Libertario had established its willingness to confront capital and government whatever the odds, but
the national situation was discouraging. Increasing numbers of workers found it more satisfying to enjoy the limited benefits provided
by the bloated, government-supported national CROM leaders and
their frequently militant local officers than to risk a precarious future
with the anarchosyndicalist CGT.

The CSL continued the radical but lonely course of the CGT during

1923. More violence was the result. On January 3 the shop workers for the Mexico City Transit Company went on strike. Three weeks later, when the dispute was not resolved, the CGT called a general strike of all transit employees, and company operations were completely closed down. The CGT and its powerful transit workers' syndicate, the Federation of Employees and Workers of the Transit Company of Mexico, were the organizers of the strike. The government and CROM opposed it. After company operations had closed down, a joint meeting of company management and the CROM leadership was held with the striking workers in an attempt to lure them back to work. Special cash incentives were used: double-time pay was offered for the first day back (Monday), and those who returned would also be paid for their Sunday holiday. Penalties were threatened for those who refused to meet the established deadline.[24]

The Centro Sindicalista Libertario's approach to the situation was aggressive and typical. The CGT called for a general strike of all its members in the Federal District in support of the transit workers. The CGT's numerical strength in the Federal District was considerable and growing, about forty thousand, but most industries and public services continued to operate. More importantly, the strike call intensified working-class unrest and the transit company remained inoperative. The CGT held strike meetings, and angry newcomers swelled the ranks of its transit workers' syndicate.

On February 1, 1923, an assembly of the striking transit workers was held at CGT headquarters. While the meeting was in progress, word was received that a CROM member was driving a streetcar toward downtown Mexico City along the route from Tacubaya on the city's western edge. The streetcar's route would cause it to pass directly in front of the CGT headquarters where hundreds of the transit company strikers and CGT members were gathered. The street was quickly closed by barricades and red-and-black *roji-negra* flags were hoisted. When the streetcar, carrying two armed soldiers as an escort, arrived on the scene, it could not pass.

The soldiers and the conductor disembarked and one soldier threatened the CGT members around him with his weapon. At that point José Salgado rushed the man, seized his rifle, and struck him over the head with it. The soldier fell to the ground and died there. The other soldier and the motorman then drew their weapons, but they had no chance. The armed CGT strikers shot them down. The omnipresent plainsclothes political police stationed outside CGT headquarters witnessed the beginning of the encounter and rushed to request reinforcements. About two hundred mounted riot police (precursors of the more recent *granaderos*) and some cavalry troops were dispatched to the scene in order to restore order. Some five hundred cavalry soldiers had been recently shifted to Mexico City by the government in order to contain the worker unrest.

En route the police and troops encountered a belligerent crowd of CGT telephone company workers and other transit strike supporters in front of the Ericsson Telephone Company offices. The police, swinging their clubs, charged the crowd with their horses, easily dispersing it and seizing its red-and-black flag. However, it was a different story when the contingent of galloping mounted police reached the CGT barricades on Calle Uruguay and attempted the same tactics. Accustomed to dealing with intimidated and unarmed civilians, they rode down the street directly into withering gunfire. Several were killed and wounded in the first few moments. An hour-long street battle then ensued with CGT gunmen firing from behind their barricades and from the windows and doorways of nearby buildings. At the conclusion of hostilities, the one hundred CGT members who had not escaped surrendered to the police and military reinforcements under the command of General de Brigada Arnulfo R. Gómez. They surrendered in return for a guarantee of safe conduct, but they were arrested and the building was sacked. Thirteen CGT members were wounded; five mounted riot police, two soldiers, and one CROM motorman were killed; and an unknown quantity of police and military personnel were wounded. On February 3 the government announced the expulsion from Mexico of four foreign-born CGT prisoners arrested at the scene. They were all Spaniards: Sebastián San Vicente, Alejandro Montoya, J. Pérez Gil, and Urbano Legaspi. All four had been prominent transit strike leaders.

The resort to arms within the context of the international anarchosyndicalist movement was a common tactic at the time. These tactics were put in vogue by contemporary Spanish anarchists who resorted to the use of *pistoleros* in retaliation against assassinations carried out by semiofficial, police-sponsored, right-wing terrorist groups and the police themselves in Spain. A moderated form of these tactics was adopted in Mexico where the Spaniards were numerous and active. On March 10 the CGT marched in protest against the assassination in Spain of the prominent anarchosyndicalist ideologue and writer Salvador Seguí (pseud., Noy del Sucre), who was shot down in a Barcelona street by unknown assailants.

Following the street battle in front of CGT headquarters, General Plutarcho Elías Calles, then minister of government (*secretario de gobernación*), decreed the strike ended and stated that the army would tolerate no more civil disobedience or strike activity. With one hundred members already in custody and facing serious prosecution, the CGT backed away and the strike ended. During the next few years the majority of transit company workers were affiliated with the

CROM. The release of the one hundred CGT prisoners by the national government was facilitated by Adolfo de la Huerta, the new leader of the military left wing and perhaps the second most powerful individual in Mexico. He pleaded the CGT prisoners' cause with President Obregón.[25]

The fact that the CGT suffered very little direct punitive action as a result of its tactics can be understood in light of three factors. First, its surrender during the seige came when its gunners enjoyed strong firing positions and could have embarrassed the government with heavy fighting and casualties. Second, the CGT's strike capitulation left the government, CROM, and the transit company victorious. And, finally, because de la Huerta was a strong challenger for the presidency and commanded the allegiance of a significant portion of the army, Obregón was trying to forestall his inclination to revolt and thus avoid civil war. That revolt came later the same year when Obregón selected Calles, a close confidant and friend, to succeed him in office. De la Huerta was defeated militarily, and the CGT, although it avoided overt support of the de la Huerta revolt and condemned it on January 3, 1924, found itself in dire straits confronted by an openly hostile and more powerful government.[26] That hostility was prophetically announced on March 10, 1923, when Calles' assistant, Undersecretary of Government Gilberto Valenzuela, ominously declared that *"acción directa"* was not necessarily a legitimate working-class tactic and that it had to conform to existing law.

During 1922 and 1923 the Veracruz-Orizaba area was a major center of CGT conflict with the government. In 1922 a massive anarchist-organized rent strike swept the city of Veracruz precipitating conflicts between groups that represented a cross section of society. The groups involved included the mass-based several-thousand-member renters' union and allied CGT syndicates, the CROM-affiliated labor unions whose hostile leadership and sympathetic rank-and-file were divided by the conflict, the property owners' association, and elements of the city, state, and national governments.

Socioeconomic conditions in Veracruz, while similar to the pattern of demographic growth, unemployment, and rising prices common to other cities in central Mexico, were extreme and contributed immensely to the strife that afflicted the city. The population had almost doubled in the metropolitan area from 29,164 to 58,225 in the previous twenty years, and new housing, with few exceptions, consisted of crowded, filth-ridden *vecindades*. Slightly more than 96 percent of the population were non-property-owning renters. The influx of *campesinos* to the city in search of opportunity increased the pressure on available housing and encouraged a continual upward spiral in rental fees. The owners of rental housing organized themselves in the Unión de Proprietaros and resorted to a special police force, the *policía privada de comercio*, to evict tenants whose unstable employment or inadequate wages rendered them unable to match the rising rent rates.[27]

The appearance in 1922 in Veracruz of a revolutionary union for the defense of tenant interests, however, was not only due to general conditions, but also because the city had a nucleus of experienced artisan and other working-class organized labor activists led by the anarchist tailor Herón Proal. Proal was born on October 17, 1881, in Tulancingo, Hidalgo, where his father, Victor, a Frenchman, and his mother, Amada Islas, from Mexico City, had settled. In 1897 Herón joined the Marine Corps, an experience that was useful in 1906 when he became a PLM revolutionary and learned his anarchism. When Madero became president, Proal settled down in Veracruz and opened a tailor shop.[28]

During the revolution the port city was the site of considerable labor unrest and in 1912 the Casa had created the Confederación de Sindicatos Obreros there. Led by Pedro Junco, it was "anticapitalist, antimilitarist, and anti-Catholic."[29] A sizeable number of artisans joined as individuals and some of them, including Proal, held positions in the directorate. But Veracruz was a key Constitutionalist stronghold during the civil war with Villa and Zapata and by 1916 some of the syndicate leaders in the city had close ties with the government. They failed to support the Mexico City and local *casas* in their fateful confrontation with the Carranza regime. Still, the militancy and loyalty to Casa principles of many workers in the port city caused the Federation of Federal District Syndicates to choose Veracruz in late 1916 as the site for the convening of the Congreso Preliminar Obrero, the first post-Casa attempt to reorganize the urban working-class movement at the national level. Proal served as president of the Congreso's executive committee.[30]

Working-class organizing continued in the city and in 1919 the Federación de Trabajadores del Puerto de Veracruz was founded. It later became the principle CGT affiliate in the port area and Proal was a member of its directorate. In January 1922, Proal and a group of CGT anarchists convened a series of public meetings to protest what were regarded as exorbitant increases in rental rates and alleged abusive behavior on the part of the property owners' private police force in the eviction of delinquent renters. Angry and increasingly larger crowds, including a contingent of prostitutes, attended the meetings while the authorities ignored the protestors' pleas for the redress of their grievances.

The renters' union was formally created on February 3, 1922, when a group of indignant members of the CROM Unión de Marineros y Fogoneros walked out of their union meeting after their leaders refused to support the developing rent strike. They joined Proal and his group in the street and formalized their alliance by inaugurating the Sindicato Revolucionario de Inquilinos. Proal was elected president of the new union.[31]

During the next months special groups of Inquilino syndicate members organized a growing rent strike and battled the private property owners' "police force" in the streets in order to prevent evictions. Simón Cáceres, the chief of the *policía privada* and owner of several apartment buildings, was Proal's principal protagonist during the struggle. As the size and violence of the renters' union contingents, which included men and women, young and old, increased, they gradually drove the *policía privada* from the streets.[32]

The local authorities, under pressure from the Unión de Proprietarios, were belatedly anxious to end the strike, but they had allowed it to get out of control before giving it their attention. Now, they could not gain the cooperation of governor Adalberto Tejada, who was one of the "socialist governors of the Gulf coast" and did not wish to alienate the great majority of Veracruz citizens who paid rents and sympathized with or participated in the mass demonstrations that periodically marched across the city in numbers that on several occasions exceeded ten thousand, an estimated 20 percent of the city's population. Tejada stalled action by a concerned President Obregón while the "socialist governors" pressed an embarrassed president to select Calles as the presidential successor instead of de la Huerta. Proal, surrounded in his living quarters and at the syndicate meeting hall by armed supporters, was inaccessible to the local authorities as long as they lacked military assistance.[33]

In the wake of the rent strike, mass demonstrations, and armed renters' "defense" groups, rental rates were stabilized and even reduced in wide areas of the city. By May, Proal and the Sindicato de Inquilinos sensed an even greater potential for their movement. Ursulo Galván was given the job of mobilizing the peasantry as the first step in creating an even more powerful mass-based "antipolitical" working-class organization.[34]

On May 9 the long-planned and largest demonstration yet held took place. Proal announced that the victory over the property owners was just the beginning. Now, the syndicate intended to bring about lowered and stabilized prices for essential foodstuffs and clothing. On the same day federal troops finally moved into the city but took no action. At that point the syndicate's new campaign was delayed by a conflict in the directorate between the "antipolitical" anarchist majority and several members of the new Mexican Communist party, who insisted that the movement should participate in both local and national political campaigns. The result of the dissension was the departure of the Communists and Proal's public declaration on June 30 that the renters' syndicate would remain "revolutionary, antipolitical, and *genuinely* communist."[35]

By July 5 the Inquilinos were ready to begin the campaign to stabilize and reduce food and clothing prices. A demonstration involving several thousand participants began under threatening skies that soon unleashed a deluge. As the rain fell the crowd broke up and Proal, his associates, and guards made their way back to the syndicate's headquarters. As night fell troops closed off the area, surrounded the building, and began to close in. The syndicate personnel were taken by surprise. An intense but uneven gunfight ensued.

The following day the local newspaper, *El Dictamen*, long sympathetic to the property owners' cause, reported one policeman and several union members killed, with five soldiers and ten unionists wounded. Proal was taken prisoner, incarcerated in Mexico City, and sent into exile. In 1924, after Obregón left office, and again in 1926, the greatly reduced Sindicato de Inquilinos reported its own estimate, buttressed by "independent assessments," of "over 150 dead," and 141 arrested and temporarily held for "sedition and murder." The estimate of wounded was not given. Most observers reported casualties approximately half-way between the *El Dictamen* report and the syndicate's claim.[36] Galván went on to lead the famous Liga de Comunidades Agrarias y Sindicatos del Estado de Veracruz, founded in March 1923. He soon rejected anarchism, became an avowed Marxist, and enjoyed the support of governor Tejada.[37]

During the second half of 1923 the scene of CGT action shifted to the Orizaba area. On June 20, Enrique Flores Magón addressed striking textile workers at Orizaba and urged them to use violence in their struggle.[38] The factory owners of Orizaba and Veracruz attempted a lockout, and the result was a CGT-and-CROM-supported general strike. Strikes, sabotage, lockouts, and then internicine labor conflicts spread over the industrialized areas of the state and endured for months. The CROM and CGT factions fought over jurisdictions, strike settlements, and ideology.[39]

On September 15 the CGT joined the anarchosyndicalist International Workingmen's Association (Asociación Internacional de Trabajadores, AIT) and announced plans for its third national congress. The congress met in January 1924.[40] The high point came with the release of a research report on textile factory closings in the Federal District. The owners claimed that short-term shutdowns were necessary because of shortages of materials caused by the Veracruz general strike. Prepared by José C. Valadés, the CGT report began a battle that would last eight months. It claimed that some factories had stockpiles of materials sufficient for three months and recommended that, in the context of gross mismanagement by the industrialists, the workers be given control of the factories. The CGT national congress adopted the report. The lockouts continued.[41]

On March 3, CGT representatives met with the textile factory owners of the Federal District and declared that the plants should remain open or the workers would take them over. The owners asked for additional time in order to prepare a response, and the meeting was adjourned. On March 8, General Manuel Pérez Treviño asserted that the cause of the textile manufacturers was "just," and the next day the government of the Federal District dispatched troops to guard the textile factories against worker takeovers. The dispute boiled through the spring and early summer with serious strikes and occasional violence. Finally, the CGT textile syndicate leaders Otilo Wences and Ciro Mendoza were invited to government-sponsored arbitration along with two representatives of the industrialists. The disputes were settled and the textile factories of the Federal District experienced relative peace until CROM textile worker organizers challenged CGT hegemony almost a year later.[42]

The Calles administration came into office in late 1924 and worked more openly than ever with the CROM and against the CGT. On December 2, Morones was appointed secretary of industry, commerce, and labor (*secretario de industria, comercio, y trabajo*). Morones' prestige and the government's open support of the CROM made it attractive to many workers and employers. During December 1924 important labor legislation was approved by the government which greatly enhanced the position of the CROM and undermined the CGT. The two bills approved that month with the support of Morones and Calles provided that only a union with majority representation among the workers in a given enterprise could be recognized. The new laws were popular with the workers because they provided for mandatory collective bargaining in all labor disputes and guaranteed the employment security of strikers.[43] The larger and officially sanctioned CROM benefited nicely from the new laws. During the two years 1925–1926 the CROM's claimed membership increased from 1,200,000 to 2,000,000. In reality it was probably more like 100,000, nearly twice as large as the CGT.[44] CGT bargaining and strike activity for dissident minorities or at a facility simply declared to have a CROM majority was now in violation of federal statutes. On January 28, 1925, Morones and his department of government, the Secretaría de Industria, Comercio, y Trabajo, named the officials who were to serve in the various states and the Federal District as labor dispute investigators, conciliators, and arbitrators. Almost all thirty-two of the appointees were CROM members. Created by law, the government's new commissions for labor relations, the Juntas de Conciliación y Arbitraje, were dominated by Morones' office. They became extremely important, consistently rendering decisions favorable to CROM in labor disputes and usually remaining hostile to and always aloof from the CGT.[45] During 1925 the CGT confronted a combined CROM-government assault in the Federal District that threatened its very existence.[46]

The trouble began with a series of jurisdictional disputes that culminated in physical assaults and, finally, the sniper killing of a female CROM member during the May Day celebrations.[47] Amid charges that some of its most prominent syndicate leaders were responsible, the CGT convened its fourth national congress from May 4 to May 10. The declarations of the congress intensified the situation. Two new campaigns were announced: First, the CGT declared in favor of the six-hour work day in order to eliminate unemployment. Second, it reasserted long-standing Mexican anarchist support for the agrarian movement and demanded full and immediate hacienda land redistribution to the *campesinaje*. Furthermore, it criticised the government for inactivity. Earlier in the year CGT regional groups had declared their support for the far-reaching agrarian reform plan advocated by a former Casa member and Zapatista, Congressional Deputy Antonio Díaz Soto y Gama. The Mexican Congress rejected Díaz Soto y Gama's measure. Luis León, secretary of development and agriculture, responded angrily to the proposal of the CGT "reds," declaring that it would "require a new revolution." He claimed that the Calles regime was doing everything possible within the law to carry out land reform. The CGT congress in its other pronouncements called for "*escuelas racionalistas*" and "*acción directa*" and rejected the legitimacy, honesty, and authority of the labor Juntas de Conciliación dominated by Morones. A direct confrontation was impending.[48]

On July 7 the owners of the La Abeja, La Magdalena, and La Hormiga textile plants in the CGT-permeated San Angel–Contreras region of the Federal District officially asked the local Junta de Conciliación to consider "readjusted salaries." The Junta de Conciliación's decision was not favorable to the CGT workers at these plants and it provoked the powerful CGT-affiliated Federación General Obrera del Ramo Textil to announce that it would "not recognize the authority of the Federal District Junta de Conciliación y Arbitraje." On July 14 the national government filed charges in court against the CGT for holding an illegal strike at La Hormiga, for preventing nonunion and CROM workers from entering La Magdalena, and for convening illegal workers' meetings inside La Magdalena.[49]

On July 20 a wave of violence swept the textile factory area of San Angel–Contreras. Gangs of CROM members, some carrying guns (*pistoleros*), attacked CGT workers in the streets outside the plants and at least one CGT worker, a female, was killed. The street battles were fought between the CGT "Rojos" and what they called CROM supporters, "Amarillos" (Yellows). In August the Junta de Conciliación declared that workers at any factory where a majority of their numbers were not organized could not be represented by any union. This was a blow to the CGT, which held the vast majority of unionized workers in the San Angel–Contreras textile plants, as well as the Federal District, but confronted a constant turnover of workers in the factories and thus often fell below the requisite 50 percent. The Junta ruling backfired when the CGT and the owners of the San Antonio de Abad textile plant in Mexico City averted a strike by agreeing to eliminate all workers who refused to join the union.[50]

In September the CGT once again declared its refusal to recognize the Junta de Conciliación. That agency of the Secretaría de Industria, Comercio, y Trabajo replied in kind and declared the CGT an outlaw organization and all its strikes illegal. The dispute continued in October when the CGT refused to attend a Morones-sponsored conclave of the textile industry under the aegis of his secretariat. The CGT statement said it "did not collaborate with politicians." In November more violence broke out at La Magdalena between gun-toting CGT and CROM members when the latter were admitted to employment by the owners of the plant. The CGT called a "general strike" of its textile workers to reinforce its demands that the CROM members be ejected. A violent strike ensued with more fighting between the two centrals.

The turning point in the impasse came on December 17 when, with CGT picket lines holding fast outside the factories, the government sent the mounted police into the fray. The picket lines were broken up and scattered. The CGT protested and staged sporadic work stoppages throughout the Federal District, but to no avail. In January 1926, fifty CGT members were fired at La Magdalena and government troops were posted at the factory to protect CROM workers and the physical plant. The owners of La Abeja, suffering property damage and ever lower productivity during the strife, closed down that plant a few days later leaving three hundred unemployed. The CGT vigorously protested and the plant reopened with some increase in CROM personnel.

When it was all over, the San Angel–Contreras textile struggle had led to very marginal shifts in the balance of syndicate power. The CROM gained a few positions but revealed an incredible depth of corruption. The textile workers' union remained one of CGT's strongest affiliates, relatively large and militant but on the defensive. In territories farther removed from the Mexico City area and the CGT's center of strength, the CROM had its way much more easily.[51]

Throughout the four years of the Calles regime, CGT headquarters and member syndicates suffered bombings, fires, burglaries, and assaults, and its personnel experienced frequent arrests. Only the continued aggressive spirit and posture of the Centro Sindicalista Libertario kept the CGT's national membership steady at about sixty thousand,[52] but it was on the defensive and dues collections were insufficient to support a permanent office staff. Perhaps the CGT's persistent defense paid dividends. Whatever the reason, there was a reduction of intraunion violence in 1926 as the CROM turned from intrusions into CGT territories to the organization of nonunionized sectors of the urban work force.[53] At the grass roots levels, there was an abundance of sincere, dedicated CROM labor organizers.

The CGT remained undaunted in the face of adversity. In mid-July 1926 its fifth Mexican regional congress was held. Some of the strongest, most militant, and oldest anarchosyndicalist syndicates represented at the conclave were the textile workers, the transit company workers, the Obreros y Obreras del Palacio de Hierro, the bakers, and the telephone company workers. All these groups had long-standing records of revolutionary labor activities, some of them dating back to the earliest Casa strikes. Prominent long-time anarchosyndicalist leaders still on the scene were Rafael Quintero and Rodolfo Aguirre, who had signed the fateful Casa-Constitutionalist pact at Veracruz during the revolution, and Luis Araiza, who was prominent during the general strikes of 1916. With Valadés and Araoz de León assisting in the conduct of the convention, the assembly unanimously declared the CGT's ultimate goal to be anarchist communism (*comunismo anarquista*). It continued affiliation with the anarchosyndicalist AIT headquartered in Berlin. It created special committees to work for the release by national and state governments of what it claimed were CGT "political prisoners." The convention issued yet another call for agrarian reform and announced the creation of special *campesino* organizing committees. Finally, it vowed "to decisively and faithfully follow the path toward social revolution and anarchist communism taken by Mikhail Bakunin" and ordered its affiliates to indoctrinate the rank-and-file accordingly.[54]

During 1927 the CGT's main efforts involved strike support for its militant petroleum workers' syndicate in Tampico and for the striking independent Confederation of Railway Societies, which at the height of its effort in February became the better known Confederation of Transportation and Communications Workers (Confederación de Transportes y Comunicaciones). On February 9 the CGT called for a "general strike" of its workers in the Federal District in order to support the railwaymen. The railroad workers had assisted earlier CGT strikes, including the violent textile strike of 1922 and the equally intense transit strike of 1923. The "general strike" heightened the intensity of emotions on all sides but did nothing to resolve the conflict. The strike continued for another month. The Tampico petroleum strike quickly deepened with the dispatch of troops to the scene by

President Calles, "to protect" company property. The soldiers were involved in shooting incidents and the strikers retaliated with sabotage. One scholar has observed that troops were used largely because it was a CGT syndicate on strike.[55]

In 1928 the CGT, despite continued anarchosyndicalist rhetoric and affiliation with the AIT, began to show signs of discouragement and wear and tear in its revolutionary zeal. Despite a wave of CGT- and CROM-sponsored strikes during the spring highlighted by the paralysis of the Río Blanco textile plant for over four months and a serious CGT strike in August at the Ericsson Telephone Company, the most significant events from the standpoint of anarchosyndicalism during the year was the beginning of a CGT shift toward accommodation with the government and the collapse of the CROM.

The latter event came about at the end of 1928 after a lengthy and sometimes bitter feud between Morones and his CROM supporters on one side and Obregón and his followers on the other. The differences between presidential-aspirant Morones and Obregón were aggravated in 1927 when a group of pro-Obregón trade unionists met in Saltillo and considered, among other things, strategies to unseat Morones as the leader of the CROM. Following Obregón's assassination by a religious fanatic on July 17, 1928, some of his upset followers claimed that Morones was at least "intellectually and morally responsible" for the killing because of the climate of rancor and hate generated during their clash. This criticism destroyed what little chance Morones may have had to gain the presidency.

In a gesture of protest against the criticism, Morones on July 21, just four days after the assassination, resigned his post as secretary of industry, commerce, and labor. Two other CROM and Labor party supporters, Gasca and Eduardo Moneda, also left their high government posts in protest. Morones' resignation was a strategic error. It eroded his prestige and removed him from the inner circles of government power. It ultimately placed him in an adversary position with the incumbent administration and led to the destruction of the CROM. By August newspapers in the Federal District were criticising the CROM for the first time, and their workers, formerly constituted in CROM syndicates, withdrew.[56]

Morones came into conflict with President Calles when Emilio Portes Gil was selected to serve as interim president. Morones opposed the choice and continued an incredible series of blunders that left strongman Calles to choose between his former ally Morones and the candidate supported by his new and personally created National Revolutionary party. In retrospect, Calles' decision seems to have been the only logical alternative. He chose not to risk the disruption of his party and the political control and stability it represented. He supported Portes Gil.

In December 1928, when Calles' position was known, CROM syndicates, beginning with those whose leaders were most opposed to Morones, began a massive exodus from the organization. By mid 1929 the CROM, which was created on a foundation of government support, had disintegrated. Its political and numerical hegemony over Mexico's working class was broken. Most of CROM's deserting units became independent or formed their own local unions while awaiting developments and soliciting government support. Some of the more radical former CROM syndicates joined the CGT, swelling its ranks by another twenty thousand members to a total slightly over eighty thousand. President Portes Gil, who denied claims that he was intent on breaking Morones and the CROM, did nothing to stop the collapse of the enormous labor confederation. Indeed the CGT, the CROM's historic rival, experienced less government harassment than at any previous time in its history.[57]

In 1929 the CGT seemed to lose its sense of direction. The great majority of its eighty thousand members were resident in the Federal District, and the leadership enjoyed its closest and most harmonious period of governmental relations. In view of the obviously increasing power and stability of the government, many of the CGT's older leaders were now in agreement with the newer, formerly CROM, members that *acción directa*, anarchy, and revolutionary syndicalism were unrealistic. The capitulation by some of the leadership of their anarcho-syndicalist position was understandable in the context of the CGT's long and discouraging repression. That discouragement, and also old age, had already caused a number of former CGT-CSL leaders to give up the fight in a manner similar to the defeat of the Casa. The sense of defeat was facilitated by the presence of the former CROM leaders, who preached the virtues of cooperating with the government. From 1929 to 1931 the CGT went through a two-year identity crisis, a time of dissension and flux. Quintero, López Dónez, Arce, and Valadés were now absent. When that time span ended, the bulk of the CGT leadership, despite the opposition of the Tampico affiliates, was ready for the first time to cooperate fully with the government.[58]

In the meantime the government was taking steps that would ensure its control over the Mexican working class. Under President Portes Gil, a new labor code (Código Federal de Trabajo) was prepared which greatly increased government intervention into the working-class movement and into labor-management relations. Under its provisions, the regime of President Pascual Ortiz Rubio reported that during the period July 1, 1929, to June 30, 1930, 402 labor conflicts were intervened, "always to protect the interests of the workers. . . . The Junta Federal de Conciliación y Arbitraje has come to function normally . . . establishing equilibrium and harmony among the important sectors of production and always separating itself from political influence and union sectarianism. . . . there has been a notable decrease in [the number and intensity of] industrial strikes." The report also mentioned that private enterprise paid 136,278.29 pesos to support the Junta Federal de Conciliación y Arbitraje.[59]

During 1929–1931 the Ortiz Rubio government prepared an expanded labor code which, among other things, delegated to the government the power to recognize unions, to approve all strikes, and to negotiate binding settlements with the parties concerned. Ortiz Rubio explained: "As president I understood the importance of this law that was demanded as an urgent national necessity. I gave instructions that the secretary of industry, commerce, and labor should make a careful revision of all previous efforts. The new code [*proyecto*] was elaborated by a commission presided over by the secretary."[60]

At first the CGT and several other labor organizations were opposed to the new code. At a meeting held in the presidential palace the emerging labor leader Vicente Lombardo Toledano read a protest which the CGT endorsed. But on July 20, 1931, the Mexican Chamber of Deputies passed the new code and several CGT syndicate leaders, including Wolstano Pineda, Ciro Mendoza, and Luis Araiza, accepted the verdict. On that date, the CGT began breaking up. Enrique Rangel, Rosendo Salazar, and Jacinto Huitrón were among those who led dissident and rival factions. A crucial blow to the hopes for the CGT came when the powerful Federación Obrera del Ramo de Lana withdrew in the midst of the wrangling.[61] Perhaps the cynicism revealed in the comments of a former CGT leader interviewed in 1933 by Marjorie Ruth Clark best explains the thinking of those in charge during the demise of July 1931. Clark reported the conversation in part as follows: "When asked how the workers liked the new collaboration with the government, he replied, 'The masses are confused, of course, by the changes they see, but that is not important; when the leaders are anarchists they are anarchist; when the leaders are "governmental" they are governmental, too.' "[62]

Within a year the CGT had divided into at least four major parts.[63] Some of the dissidents, such as Salazar, had already given up on anarchosyndicalism as "unrealistic." One of them, Jacinto Huitrón, had not. An original member of the Grupo Luz which had founded the Casa, he remained faithful to the teachings of Juan Francisco Moncaleano and to the cause. For the remainder of his life, into the late 1960's, he led the Mexican Anarchist Federation (Federación Anarquista Mexicana, FAM). The FAM was the only significant anarchosyndicalist survival of the CGT, but it was small, composed of only individual members. It depended upon dues contributions to print the FAM newspaper, *Regeneración* (*segunda época*), which was published for over thirty years as a weekly and bimonthly. It had a limited circulation, and thus its consistent opposition to the cooperation of the leadership of organized labor wih the government had minimal effect on the Mexican working class.[64] Other small groups, such as the Grupo Cultural Ricardo Flores Magón and Tierra y Libertad, have experienced remarkable longevity, but their impact, too, in the government-dominated era since the demise of the CGT has not been significant.[65]

11. Conclusion

The Mexican anarchist movement was the product of several contributing elements: (a) the influx of outside anarchist immigrants, such as Rhodakanaty, Ferrés, Moncaleano, Tudó, and others who were largely from Spain; (b) the wide circulation of literature that propagated the ideology of Proudhon, Bakunin, Lorenzo, Kropotkin, and their Mexican counterparts; (c) governmental corruption and sociopolitical instability, which gave revolutionaries the opportunity to organize; (d) generally insufferable socioeconomic conditions endured by the Mexican laboring classes, both urban and rural, which created the extreme degree of societal alienation necessary for a mass of humanity to support revolutionary ideals; (e) the social mores of the increasingly landless Mexican peasantry, which, in its resistance to the metropoli and the intrusion of alien culture, already supported social banditry, and whose values were already identical to those expressed by the agrarian anarchism espoused by Rhodakanaty, Zalacosta, Santa Fe, and Díaz Soto y Gama; and (f) the process of industrialization in Mexico, which intensified preexisting social imbalances that had created support for urban crowds and *tumultos* in the preindustrial era.

Industrialization meant larger urban slums and threatened the artisan class with proletariatization. The artisans, with their Spanish guild traditions, reacted in self-defense by organizing for radical social change. In the mid-1870's tailors and hat makers, under assault from the rapidly growing textile industry, were the most militant artisan group. During the 1910 revolutionary era the *tipógrafos* and *canteros* were suffering from the overwhelming impact of the Linotype machine and modern cement industry, and they joined the hat makers and tailors in militancy. The artisans, although always in the minority, provided the anarchists and the urban working class with necessary leadership.

It is only natural for the artisan, a man steeped in individualism, to advocate a political ideal which demanded protection for him from the encroachments of an increasingly more powerful government, a government controlled by others and readily influenced by capitalist doctrines. The artisans identified with an ideal which sought to preserve the small workshop and handmade product and demanded better working conditions in the factories into which they were being forced by the modernized production techniques with which they could not compete. Cooperativism reflected these needs. It was an understandable response to the threat of the factory system from men who had always worked with their hands and prided themselves on their craftsmanship and independence. Anarchosyndicalism reflected their later reaction to the established and still growing factory production system.

It was to be expected that the government would react negatively to anarchosyndicalism and the more extreme forms of cooperativism, which were in reality attempts to create a society based upon worker-controlled productivity free of government and "capitalist exploitation." Government intervention by force and by strict regulations during the Porfiriato, the later stages of the revolution, and after the revolution first prevented the cooperatives from becoming a system of independent collectives and then prevented the anarchosyndicalists from gaining control of national industry. The artisans and anarchists were defeated in both phases. During the later stages of the nineteenth century the cooperatives were little more than mere artisan shops, the members of which enjoyed such typical mutual aid benefits as disability payments. In the postrevolutionary era the CROM and its successor, the Confederation of Mexican Workers (Confederación de Trabajadores Mexicanos), established government political control over the organized urban working class within a capitalist economy.

But the anarchists brought important changes to the Mexican working classes during the period 1860–1931. While not successful in their program, their goals—as expressed by the platforms of La Social, La Internacional, the Casa del Obrero Mundial, and the CGT—politicized the Mexican working class to a considerable extent. They called for the establishment of a "universal socialist republic, one and indivisible." Initial steps toward these ends were taken; the Congreso affiliated with the anarchist international, and, later, during the revolution, the Casa del Obrero was a self-described "regional" labor confederation. The Congreso, Casa, and CGT all supported the notion of an international open trade system after the workers had seized power. The CGT called itself communist-anarchist, and its national congress voted to seize the textile industry of Mexico City, Puebla, and Orizaba during the 1920's. Both the Casa and CGT were capable of limited but crippling general strikes. Between 1860 and 1931 hundreds of thousands of Mexican workers spanning three generations formally joined the Congreso, Casa, and CGT—organizations allied with an international movement based in Europe and dedicated to the ultimate overthrow of government and capitalism.

The Mexican anarchist movement demanded the long-range abolition of the salary system. In the meantime, raises in agricultural and industrial wages were to be procured by means of the strike. Short-run victories were achieved in a few cases, especially during the revolution when conditions were unusually favorable. Working-class tactics significantly changed during the period 1860–1926. Several long and torturous strikes were carried out during the nineteenth century, and at the end of the century Mexico's first general strike took place in Puebla. Mexican workers demonstrated, through their use of this weapon during and after the revolution, that they had come to regard the general strike as their most powerful tool against the employers. It was a dramatic step toward self-respect and confidence for the Mexican working classes because these strikes represented the declaration of a newly assumed right to question the authority of the previously all-powerful *patrón*. The anarchists cannot claim sole credit for the conduct of these strikes, but their role in them, as the principal urban-labor organizers and agitators, was a prominent one.

One endeavor in which the anarchists enjoyed an open victory was in the field of female workers' rights. The success enjoyed by Rhoda-kanaty and La Social in 1876, when Carmen Huerta was originally seated in the national Congreso over the objections of Juan de Mata Rivera, was a singular victory. There was no previous episode in Mexican working-class history in which a woman was permitted to play such an important role. Following that occasion, Mexican women played a significant part in the urban-labor movement, and large numbers of them employed in the textile mills were organized. Huerta even occupied the national chairmanship of the Congreso. Ironically, labor gains made during the revolution and 1920's made the employment of women less attractive to the factory operators, and the female presence in the plants greatly diminished thereafter.

The anarchists hoped to achieve an equalitarian, classless society organized into voluntary associations for the urban workers at the factory level and for the *campesinos* at the level of the *municipio libre*. The need for government, an institution which they saw as a vehicle by which the ruling class exercised its power over the people, would be negated by the nonexploitative nature of their new classless society. Thus, they called for the "neutralization of the exploitive power enjoyed by capital over labor" and the gradual leveling and redistribution of private property.

They wanted to reorganize society around industrial and agrarian *falanges*, the latter to be formed in conjunction with territorial banks which would regulate labor and the sale of products. This was to be in conjunction with the "liquidation of urban [capitalist] interests" in the countryside under the aegis of an agrarian law which would provide for the measuring and demarcation of lands in order to redistribute them. The military was to be replaced by working-class militia, the autonomous municipalities would become sovereign over the entire program in their own localities, and, ultimately, the national government would be dissolved.

The reasons for their failure during the early Díaz period are complex but clear. The Díaz regime consolidated a strong hold on the country and provided it with political tranquility and rapid economic growth for the first time. Antagonistic provincial elites and urban and rural working-class dissenters were dealt with by force. The revolutionary working-class movement was vulnerable because the industrialization process was not sufficiently advanced to create a massive urban labor force. The number of factory workers remained relatively small in contrast to the overall population, and those workers who were organized into the Círculo after 1870, and later into the affiliates of the Congreso, lacked organizational experience. They suffered chronic disunity. Their divisions and relatively small numbers reduced them to a point of weakness in the face of the armed might of the government.

The nineteenth-century cooperatives were failures due to lack of organizational experience and their economic isolation. The number of supporters that could expect to utilize them was far too limited to provide continued growth. The reason for their scarcity of number is found in the fact that Mexico was still a preindustrial, underdeveloped country. The immaturity of the Mexican economy and the lack of preparedness of the anarchist movement were all too obvious to such leaders as Rhodakanaty, Velatti, González, and Muñuzuri. They lamented the continued omnipresence of mutualist societies, the weakness of the cooperatives, and the development of government-dominated unions administered by *"charros."*

The tradition of government management of the labor movement began with Romero and Cano in the 1860's and early 1870's. It continued with Carlos Olaguibel in the late 1870's and 1880's. In the twentieth century, Mendoza of the GCOL, Luis Morones, and some contemporary union leaders are representative of this tendency. *Charrismo* was yet another factor in a milieu that left most of the Mexican masses disorganized and incapable of decisive action. Villanueva, Ferrés, López Dónez, Quintero, and the CGT-CSL leadership complained of the same problem.

The agrarian movement was forcibly beaten back during the reign of Juárez, when it first gained momentum, and later even more severely by the Díaz-led repression of the later nineteenth century. Scattered over the countryside, the agrarians suffered the fatal malady of disunity. Poorly equipped, they were unable to adequately defend themselves following their uncoordinated uprisings and land seizures. These conditions would also plague and defeat Zapata.

In the early twentieth century much of the disorganized structure of the nineteenth-century anarchist urban labor associations, and even their political strategy, was corrected by the formation of the Casa del Obrero Mundial and by the program of the Magonistas. The Díaz regime, because of its early successes, acted something like a filter against the direct transmission of the Mexican anarchist tradition.[1]

As a result, the twentieth-century Mexican anarchists turned, not to their nineteenth-century predecessors, but to Proudhon, Bakunin, and Kropotkin. The movement was once again stimulated by the presence of Spanish anarchists.[2] The first powerful anarchist organization developed around the Liberal party led by the Flores Magón brothers. Ricardo Flores Magón first read Kropotkin at an early age and testified to the strong impression that he had received. Later, as a student in Mexico City, he again read the Russian's work. He began to openly espouse anarchist political doctrine in 1906. Between 1900 and 1910, Magón and the Liberal party were the only serious challenge to the Díaz regime and they became a symbol of resistance. The first divergence of the twentieth-century anarchist movement from its nineteenth-century antecedent was a national revolutionary political force which advocated the overthrow and dismantling of the national government, the decentralization of political power, the collectivist organization of the urban economy, and the establishment of agrarian communes. The Liberal party led a series of unsuccessful agrarian village seizures and raids near the northern frontier. Magonista organizers entered Cananea and helped to lead the famous and violent rebellion there that revealed seething working-class unrest that surfaced again soon afterward at Río Blanco. Those rebellions rang the death knell of the government.

The Casa del Obrero Mundial developed during the turmoil of the Mexican Revolution. In the industrial areas the local branch of the Casa del Obrero represented a refuge where newly arrived former *campesinos* could communicate with fellow workers who had already united in common interest. Like their nineteenth-century precursors, these former agrarian workers found themselves alienated and alone in a new, hostile, urban environment which attacked their strong sense of community and destroyed tradition. The anarchist ideology of individual freedom, coupled with syndicalist social promises, was undoubtedly a strong inducement to the still-peasant mentality which had traditionally held these values inviolate in the agrarian *comunidad*.

As it gained strength, anarchosyndicalism unleashed a powerful force which the Obregón-Carranza Constitutionalists used to advantage against Villa and Zapata during the revolution. In one of those ironies of war, the Red Battalions of the Casa del Obrero were sent into battle more than once against the ideological heirs of Chávez López, the revolutionaries led by Zapata. Ideological differences on both sides were frequently vague, and, despite Zapata's peasant anarchistlike program, most members of the Casa del Obrero felt that he was limited to a too-narrow agrarian perspective. Also, their anticlericalism was enraged by the deep religious convictions shown by Zapata's *campesino* followers.[3]

The Casa del Obrero was enticed into an alliance with Obregón and Carranza with the promise that it would be the only union in Mexico, free to organize as it pleased in return for its continued support for the Constitutionalists.[4] The sincerity of this bargain must be doubted on both sides in view of the Casa del Obrero's revolutionary syndicalist objectives and the immediate suppression by the government during the general strike of 1916 after Zapata and Villa were no longer a strategic threat. The armed workers of the Casa del Obrero were subdued at the height of the general strike of July 30 to August 2, 1916, by isolated actions in town after town by the army, which made it a practice to initiate its attacks with surprise raids on the anarchist union's meeting halls and armories. Recognition of the union was officially withdrawn by the government and many of its leaders were arrested.[5]

The Casa was formally dissolved and many of its disillusioned members then entered the government-supported Confederación Regional Obrera Mexicana. The CROM had few anarchist tendencies and was dominated by the governments of Obregón and Calles. In 1928 the largest anarchist publication in Latin America, *La Protesta* of Buenos Aires, announced that the CROM, because of its collaboration with the Mexican government, could not be considered "*anarquista.*"[6] Many of the disgruntled former members of the Casa del Obrero joined the rival to the CROM, the CGT, which affiliated with the anarchist AIT.[7] The CGT survived the 1920's despite the continued success and government support of the CROM, but it was plagued by a lack of funds and internal divisions. After the passage of the Ley del Trabajo in 1931, it ceased to be a serious force.

Revitalized, during the decline of the Díaz regime, Mexican anarchism came into open conflict with the government during and after the revolution. In the years since that confrontation, the active reformism of the Obregón, Calles, and Lázaro Cárdenas regimes has relegated Mexican anarchism to a historical legacy, and the largest agrarian and urban labor organizations are controlled by the national government. In spite of increased national productivity, the Mexican working classes continue to experience a legacy of mass poverty. Their past struggles and present conditions indicate future unrest.

Notes

1. The Origins of Mexican Anarchism

1. Peter Alekseevich Kropotkin, *Mutual Aid*, pp. XIII–XIV.
2. For an excellent discussion of these points, see George Woodcock, *Anarchism*, pp. 201–202.
3. Kropotkin, *Mutual Aid*, p. 293.
4. Paul Avrich, *The Russian Anarchists*, pp. 28–32.
5. Kropotkin, *Mutual Aid*, p. 296.
6. Ibid., pp. 298–299.
7. Ibid., pp. 299–300.
8. Woodcock, *Anarchism*, pp. 21, 318–325.
9. *Boletín de Información C.N.T.-A.I.T.-F.A.I.*, no. 193, February 27, 1934; cited in John Brademas, "Revolution and Social Revolution: The Anarcho-Syndicalist Movement in Spain, 1930–1937" (Ph.D. diss.), p. 343.
10. Avrich, *Russian Anarchists*, pp. 19, 45, 55, 154–156; and Woodcock, *Anarchism*, p. 426.
11. For works which describe at length the ineffectiveness of agrarian militias with anarchistlike organization, see Antonio Díaz Soto y Gama, *La Revolución agraria del sur y Emiliano Zapata su caudillo*, p. 293; Robert E. Quirk, *The Mexican Revolution, 1914–1915*, p. 325; John Womack, *Zapata and the Mexican Revolution*, p. 435; and almost any volume of a large body of literature on the Spanish Civil War.
12. Ignacio Altamirano, *Paisajes y leyendas: Tradiciones y costumbres de Mexico*, pp. 184–185.
13. *El Socialista*, January 23, 1873.
14. For example, see Gastón García Cantú, *El socialismo en México, siglo XIX*, p. 515.
15. Juan de Dios Bojórquez, *La inmigración española en México*, p. 5.

2. The Proselytizer

1. "Pequeña biografía de Plotino C. Rhodakanaty," *La Paz*, March 17, 1873; cited in José C. Valadés, "Precursores del socialismo anti-autoritario en México," *La Protesta* (Buenos Aires), May 22, 1928.
2. "Pequeña biografía."
3. Plotino C. Rhodakanaty, *Cartilla socialista o sea el catecismo elemental de la escuela de Carlos Fourier–El falansterio*, ed. José C. Valadés, p. 16.
4. For other examples of his belief in the innate goodness of man and of man's corruption by private property and environmental conditions, see Rhodakanaty, "Estudios de filosofía social," *El Socialista*, Feb-

ruary 26, May 9, 1883. Also idem, articles in *El Socialista*, April 22, July 4, August 15, 1880.

5. Valadés, "Precursores del socialismo."
6. *El Obrero Internacional*, September 7, 1874.
7. Rhodakanaty, *Neopanteísmo, consideración sobre el hombre y la naturaleza.*
8. Valadés, "Precursores del socialismo."
9. Rhodakanaty, "Lo que queremos," *El Hijo del Trabajo*, April 28, 1878.
10. Rhodakanaty, "El programa social," *El Socialista*, April 16, 1876.
11. Rhodakanaty, article in *El Socialista*, May 28, 1876; italics added.
12. For some excellent samples of this contempt for the bourgeois intellectual, see articles by José María González in *El Hijo del Trabajo*, July 14, 28, 1878.
13. *El Hijo del Trabajo*, May 22, 1881; also see almost any edition of *El Hijo del Trabajo* between 1876 and 1883.
14. Rhodakanaty, "El programa social."
15. Editorial, *El Hijo del Trabajo*, May 9, 1876.
16. Rhodakanaty, "La organización del trabajo," *El Socialista*, February 27, 1876. For a discussion of this aspect of Proudhon's thought, see J. Hampden Jackson, *Marx, Proudhon and European Socialism*, p. 133.
17. Ibid.
18. For the best analysis of Proudhon's serial principle, see George Woodcock, *Pierre Joseph Proudhon*, p. 78.
19. Rhodakanaty, *Medula panteística del sistema filosófico de Spinoza.* This essay also can be found as a series of articles with the same title in *El Socialista*, March 27, 31, April 10, 1885. The same theme is used by Rhodakanaty in articles entitled "Estudios de filosofía social," *El Socialista*, February 26, May 9, 1883.
20. Emetrio Valverde y Téllez, *Crítica filosófica o estudio bibliográfico y crítico de las obras de filosofía*, p. 432.
21. Rhodakanaty, "Peligros para el porvenir," *El Socialista*, March 12, 1867; "La asociación," *El Socialista*, March 26, 1876; "Lo que queremos"; and "Viva socialismo," *El Hijo del Trabajo*, March 17, 1878.
22. For example, see Rhodakanaty, article in *El Socialista*, May 28, 1876; see also *El Hijo del Trabajo*, May 9, 1876.
23. Rhodakanaty, "El programa social."
24. Rhodakanaty, article in *El Socialista*, May 28, 1876. For Kropotkin's view, see Kropotkin, *Mutual Aid*, p. 362.
25. Rhodakanaty, "Peligros para el porvenir."
26. Text of Rhodakanaty speech commemorating the reinauguration of La Social in *El Socialista*, May 14, 1876.
27. Rhodakanaty, article in *El Hijo del Trabajo*, April 28, 1878.
28. Víctor Alba, *Las ideas sociales contemporáneas en México*, p. 102. Alba provides an example of this tendency toward oversimplification by classifying Rhodakanaty as a disciple of Fourier.
29. See Rhodakanaty, "La organización del trabajo," and "Lo que queremos."
30. For their close similarity of viewpoints on the issue of wealth distribution, see Proudhon, *What Is Property?*, pp. 121–140; and Rhoda-

kanaty, article in "El programa social," *El Hijo del Trabajo*, April 28, 1878, "Viva socialismo," and article in *El Socialista*, May 28, 1876.

31. Rhodakanaty, "Peligros para el porvenir." For a discussion of this stage in Proudhon's thought, see Alan Ritter, *The Political Thought of Pierre Joseph Proudhon*, pp. 86–90.

32. See *El Craneoscopio, periódico Frenológico y Científico*, April 16 to June 10, 1874.

33. Rhodakanaty, *El Craneoscopio*, April 16, 22, 29, 1874.

34. Ibid., May 5, 1874, special supplement.

35. Rhodakanaty, articles in *El Socialista*, May 14, 28, 1876; and the text of a speech delivered by Rhodakanaty at the reinauguration of La Social on May 7, 1876, in *El Hijo del Trabajo*, May 9, 1876. See also *El Craneoscopio*, April 29, May 5, 1874.

36. Rhodakanaty, *El Craneoscopio*, April 16 to June 10, 1874. See also Rhodakanaty, *Medula panteística*.

37. For a complete exposition of his thought on this matter, see Rhodakanaty, *Cartilla socialista*, p. 16; and his articles in *El Socialista*, especially "Estudios de filosofía social."

38. Rhodakanaty, "Peligros para el porvenir," and article in *El Socialista*, May 28, 1876.

39. Rhodakanaty, *Medula panteística*. This was an extract of *Neopanteísmo*, originally published in 1864 and from which virtually all revolutionary ideas had been edited.

3. The Organizers

1. For a brief description of La Social and insight into its ideology, see *El Hijo del Trabajo*, May 9, 1876.

2. "Pequeña biografía."

3. Letter, Rhodakanaty to Zalacosta, March 21, 1870; cited by Dieter Koniecki, interview, Mexico City, August 16, 1968.

4. José C. Valadés, "Sobre los orígenes del movimiento obrero en México," *La Protesta* (Buenos Aires), June 1927, p. 72.

5. *El Obrero Internacional*, September 7, 1874; and *El Socialista*, August 25, 1872.

6. *La Internacional*, July 21, 1878.

7. Valadés, "Precursores del socialismo," p. 411.

8. Manuel Díaz Ramírez, *Apuntes históricos del movimiento obrero y campesino de México, 1844–1880*, p. 77.

9. Moisés González Navarro, *El porfiriato: La vida social*, p. 433.

10. Díaz Ramírez, *Apuntes históricos*, pp. 31–32; and Valadés, "Precursores del socialismo," p. 411.

11. Díaz Ramírez, *Apuntes históricos*, pp. 31–32.

12. *Diario del Imperio*, June 19, 1865. This special police force was intended to number 182 men, with district forces of 8 or 9 men each in the neighboring towns of Tlalnepantla, Texcoco, San Cristóbal, Tlalpán, Santa Fe, and Río Frío.

13. "Pequeña biografía."
14. Díaz Ramírez, *Apuntes históricos*, p. 32.
15. Rhodakanaty, "Lo que queremos," *El Hijo del Trabajo*, April 28, 1878.
16. Juan Hernández Luna, "Movimiento anarco-fourierista entre el imperio y la reforma," *Cuadernos de Orientación Política*, no. 4 (April 1956), pp. 19–20. Also interviews with José C. Valadés, Oaxtepec, November 6, 1969, and Mexico City, August 13, 1971. The majority of historical works, in referring to this school, call it the Escuela Libre de Chalco. However, this was only a general name used by anarchists in the nineteenth century to describe the type of school which they dedicated to the education of the workers.
17. The intention was to organize the *campesinos* on the hacienda near Texcoco on which he worked.
18. Chávez López was just beginning to master the art of writing.
19. Letter, Rhodakanaty to Zalacosta, September 3, 1865; cited by Koniecki, interview.
20. Letter, Rhodakanaty to Zalacosta, Mexico City, November 1868, Archivo Judicial del Estado de Querétaro.
21. Díaz Ramírez, *Apuntes históricos*, p. 35.
22. Letter, Gen. Rafael Cuéllar, Jefe Político de Chalco, to Sebastián Lerdo de Tejada, Minister de Gobernación, Río Frío, March 10, 1868, Archivo General de la Nación, Ramo de Gobernación, Tranquilidad Pública (hereinafter cited as AGN, Tranquilidad Pública), legajo 1546.
23. Letter, Antonio Flores, Prefect of Texcoco, to Lerdo, Texcoco, March 7, 1868, ibid.
24. Letters, Cuéllar to Lerdo, Ayotla, March 7, 1868, and Lerdo to Cuéllar, Mexico City, March 9, 1868, ibid.
25. Letters, R. T. García to Lerdo, Chalco, March 14, 19, 1868, ibid.
26. Letter, Flores to Lerdo, Texcoco, June 17, 1868, ibid.
27. Report of Judge José María Almarás (with affidavits from witnesses in support of Flores' charges), August 18, 1868, ibid.
28. Ibid.
29. Letter, Ignacio L. Vallarta to Cuéllar, Mexico City, June 22, 1868, ibid.
30. Letter, Ignacio Mejía to Cuéllar, Mexico City, June 25, 1868, ibid. See also letter, Vallarta to Cuéllar, Mexico City, June 28, 1868, ibid.
31. Flores et al., undated document, ibid.
32. The government of the state of México to the Ministro de Gobernación, Toluca, communication no. 208, October 14, 1868, ibid.
33. Letter, Chávez López to Zalacosta, January 13, 1869, Archivo Judicial del Estado de Querétaro.
34. Letter, Chávez López to Zalacosta, April 18, 1869, ibid.
35. For the most extensive discussion available of the agrarian movement in the nineteenth century, see Jesús Silva Herzog, *El agrarismo Mexicano y la reforma agraria*, p. 627; and Díaz Soto y Gama, *La revolución agraria*, p. 293. However, neither of these works offers an attempt to measure the development of agrarian ideology during the period.

36. Bibliothèque Nationale, Paris, no. 205, fol. 3f; cited by Charles C. Gibson, *The Aztecs under Spanish Rule*, pp. 141–142.
37. Gibson, *The Aztecs*, pp. 290–291.
38. The Ramo de Tierras, AGN, and the Archivo 6 de Enero 1916 of the Mexican Agrarian Commission contain the records of numerous land disputes, in which legal action was initiated in the courts, between the indigenous villages of Chalco province and the haciendas of the area, beginning in 1570 and extending until 1807.
39. Gibson, *The Aztecs*, pp. 407–409. See also the Ramo de Tierras, AGN, Chalco.
40. Venustiano Carranza tried to capitalize on this sentiment during his address to the 1916–1917 constitutional convention in Querétaro. See *Diario de los debates del Congreso Constituyente, 1916–1917*, 1:266.
41. For a description of the land-acquisition process in the colonial period, see François Chevalier, *Land and Society in Colonial Mexico*, p. 334. For an excellent discussion of hacienda expansion in nineteenth-century Morelos, see Womack, *Zapata and the Mexican Revolution*, pp. 37–66.
42. Gibson, *The Aztecs*, pp. 139–142.
43. Antonio García Cubas, *Diccionario geográfico histórico de los Estados Unidos Mexicanos*, 2:431. The district of Chalco was comprised of the eight major municipalities of Chalco, Amecameca, Ayotzingo, Cuautzingo, Ixtapaluca, Ozumba, Tlalmanalco, and Xuchitepec; and of seven lesser *municipios*, Atlautla, Ayapango, Cocotitlan, Ecatzingo, Temantla, Tenango, and Tepetlixpa. The district of Chalco was, and is, bordered on the north by the district of Texcoco, on the west by the Federal District, on the east by Puebla and on the south by Morelos.
44. Ibid.
45. Ramo de Gobernación, AGN, legajo 1786, "Tierras," expediente 22, June 19, 1866. This legajo should not be confused with the Ramo de Tierras.
46. Ibid., expediente 19, February 23, 1866.
47. Ibid., expedientes 21 and 24, May 9, 1866.
48. Eric R. Wolf, *Peasant Wars of the Twentieth Century*, pp. 294–295.
49. Julio Chávez López, "Manifiesto a todos los oprimidos y pobres de México y del universo," Chalco, April 20, 1869; text from Juan Hernández Luna, "Movimiento anarco-fourierista entre el imperio y la reforma," *Cuadernos de Orientación Política*, no. 4 (April 1956), pp. 25–26.
50. Díaz Ramírez, *Apuntes históricos*, p. 36.
51. Ibid.; see also Díaz Soto y Gama, *La revolución agraria*, p. 29; and Hernández Luna, "Movimiento anarco-fourierista."
52. Díaz Ramírez, *Apuntes históricos*, p. 36.
53. Ibid., pp. 36–37.
54. Unfortunately, a great deal of material and information about the Escuela del Rayo y del Socialismo and, presumably, the activities of

Rhodakanaty, Zalacosta, Chávez López, Gómez, and others involved with the school were lost when the building and records were destroyed in a fire.
55. Chávez López, "Manifiesto," from Hernández Luna, "Movimiento anarco-fourierista," p. 24.
56. *Diario de los debates*, 1:266.
57. Letter, Rhodakanaty to Zalacosta, November 1868, Archivo Judicial del Estado de Querétaro.
58. Letters, Chávez López to Zalacosta, January 13, April 18, 1869, ibid.

4. The Anarchists and the Origins of the Urban Labor Movement

1. Chester Lyle Gutherie, "Riots in Seventeenth-Century Mexico City: A Study of Social and Economic Conditions," in *Greater America*, ed. Adele Ogden and Engel Sluiter, pp. 243–254; see also Noel Stowe, "The Tumulto of 1624: Turmoil at Mexico City" (Ph.D. diss.), pp. 58, 382, 383.
2. Romeo Flores Caballero, "Etapas del desarrollo industrial," in *La economía mexicana en la época de Juárez*, ed. Luis González et al., pp. 114–116.
3. *El Socialista*, January 23, 1873.
4. Valadés, "Precursores del socialismo," p. 411; and Díaz Ramírez, *Apuntes históricos*, p. 32.
5. Díaz Ramírez, *Apuntes históricos*, p. 32.
6. *El Hijo del Trabajo*, February 17, 1878.
7. Alfonso López Aparicio, *El movimiento obrero en México*, p. 107; and *El Socialista*, August 25, 1872.
8. Díaz Ramírez, *Apuntes históricos*, pp. 33–34; and Lino Medina Salazar, "Albores del movimiento obrero en México," *Historia y Sociedad* 4 (1965): 60.
9. Díaz Ramírez, *Apuntes históricos*, pp. 33–34; and Medina Salazar, "Albores del movimiento obrero en México," p. 60.
10. *El Hijo del Trabajo*, May 9, July 9, 1876.
11. Letter, Juan Cano to Benito Juárez, May 23, 1870, documento 8164, Archivo Juárez, Biblioteca Nacional de México.
12. Quoted in Díaz Ramírez, *Apuntes históricos*, pp. 37–38.
13. "Manifiesto de La Social," *El Socialista*, May 9, 1876.
14. *El Socialista*, July 9, 1871; March 1, 1874.
15. Ibid., September 29, 1872.
16. Ibid.; and José María González, "Nuestra opinión," *El Hijo del Trabajo*, August 5, 1877; and "Ante un cadáver o ante una fiera," *El Hijo del Trabajo*, March 31, 1878.
17. *El Socialista*, September 29, 1872.
18. Ibid., March 16, 1873.
19. *El Hijo del Trabajo*, December 17, 1876.
20. *El Socialista*, October 15, November 12, 1871.
21. Ibid., September 29, 1872.
22. Ibid., November 23, 1873.

23. Ibid., August 4, 1872.

24. For a thorough discussion of the prolonged economic difficulties experienced by the operators of the Real del Monte in the first half of the nineteenth century, see Robert W. Randall, *Real del Monte*, p. 257.

25. *El Socialista*, August 18, 1872; also see the articles by Ricardo Velatti in *El Obrero Internacional*, November 3, December 1, 1874.

26. *El Obrero Internacional*, October 6, 13, 1874.

27. Ibid., August 31, 1874.

28. Ibid.

29. José María González, "Las sociedades mutualistas," *El Hijo del Trabajo*, August 6, 1876.

30. This is what happened between 1934 and 1939 in the Levant and Old Aragon in Spain; see Hugh Thomas, "Agrarian Anarchist Collectives in the Spanish Civil War," in *A Century of Conflict, 1850–1950*, ed. Martin Gilbert, pp. 245–263.

31. Ricardo Velatti, article in *El Obrero Internacional*, November 11, 1874.

32. Rosendo Rojas Coria, *Tratado de cooperativismo mexicano*, pp. 125, 186. The book, Fernando Garrido's *Historia de las asociaciones obreras en Europa* (Barcelona, May 28, 1864), is available in the Biblioteca Arus, Barcelona. Garrido was one of Spain's leading "libertarian socialist" intellectuals at the time.

33. *El Socialista*, September 21, 1873.

34. José Muñuzuri, article in *El Hijo del Trabajo*, August 20, 1876.

35. *El Obrero Internacional*, October 27, 1874.

36. *El Hijo del Trabajo*, May 1, 22, July 2, August 27, 1876.

37. The first recorded reference to a national workers' congress can be found in "Los obreros de San Luis Potosí," *El Socialista*, October 15, 1871. This need was discussed repeatedly in the pages of *El Hijo del Trabajo* in 1876, *El Obrero Internacional* in 1874, and *El Socialista* during the period extending from late in 1875 throughout 1876.

38. *El Socialista*, February 27, 1876.

39. Ibid., March 5, 1876.

40. José C. Valadés, "El 50 aniversario del Primer Congreso Obrero en América," *La Protesta*, April 1926.

41. *El Socialista*, March 21, 1876.

42. For example, see ibid., June 11, 1876.

43. "Manifiesto," ibid., April 23, 1876.

44. *El Hijo del Trabajo*, May 9, 1876.

45. *El Socialista*, May 7, 1876; and *El Hijo del Trabajo*, May 9, 1876.

46. "We are all men beneath the same heaven and entitled to the same justice and dignity in our work" (Valadés, "El 50 Aniversario").

47. *El Hijo del Trabajo*, May 22, 1876; also see article by Juana la Progresista.

48. Ibid., December 20, 1879; May 16, 1880.

49. *El Socialista*, June 11, 1876.

50. For example, see articles by Juan Villareal and José María González in *El Hijo del Trabajo*, December 24, 1876.

51. *El Socialista*, June 25, 1876.
52. See numerous articles extolling the virtues of Díaz and the plan of Tuxtepec in *El Hijo del Trabajo* during 1876.
53. *El Socialista*, June 25, 1876.
54. *El Hijo del Trabajo*, December 14, 1876.
55. See ibid., December 2, 9, 1877; and numerous articles in ibid., *La Internacional*, and *El Socialista* throughout the two-year period.
56. *El Hijo del Trabajo*, February 3, 17, 1878.
57. Ibid., April 6, 13, 1879.
58. Ibid.
59. Ibid., May 16, 1880.
60. Ibid., April 25, May 16, 1880.
61. Ibid. García de la Cadena had a long and impressive record of support for both the urban labor and the agrarian movements. For details, see Trinidad García de la Cadena, General de la Brigada, expediente 15-395, Archivo Histórico de la Defensa Nacional (AHDN).
62. *El Socialista*, December 18, 1879; *El Hijo del Trabajo*, December 14, 20, 1879.
63. "Manifiesto de La Social."
64. *La Internacional*, August 25, October 6, 1878.
65. *El Socialista*, September 26, 1882.
66. For examples, see their proclamations in any issue of *La Internacional*.

5. Nineteenth-Century Anarchism and the Agrarian Movement

1. In recent years a number of works have explored the complexity of nineteenth-century Mexican agrarian uprisings. See Friedrich Katz, "Labor Conditions on Haciendas in Porfirian Mexico: Some Trends and Tendencies," *Hispanic American Historical Review* 54 (February 1974): 1–47; John H. Coatsworth, "Railroads and the Concentration of Landownership in the Early Porfiriato," ibid., pp. 48–71; and Jean Meyer, *Problemas campesinos y revueltas agrarias (1821–1910)*, p. 235.
2. Colin Maclachlan, "The Crisis of Order in New Spain: A New Departure in the Administration of Justice," in *Mexican History Edition, The North Dakota Quarterly*, ed. John M. Hart, pp. 7–21.
3. Enrique Semo and Gloria Pedrero, "La vida en una hacienda-aserradero mexicana a principios del siglo XIX," *Investigación Económica*, pp. 129–161. This wage pattern apparently did not hold in areas of the south (see Katz, "Labor Conditions," pp. 18–23). An example of long-standing village land disputes can be found in the *legajos* for Anenecuilco and Ayala in the Archivo Seis de Enero of the National Agrarian Commission. The pre- and post-Zapata fighting between these two *ejidos* dates from "*tiempos inmemorables.*"
4. Norman Cohn, *The Pursuit of the Millennium*, pp. 228, 230.
5. An intensive historical analysis, "The Mexican Agrarian Movement, 1810–1910," is under research. For a useful overview of most of these episodes, see Meyer, *Problemas campesinos*. An important

study of the *campesino*'s struggle is Arturo Warman, *Y venimos a contradecir*, p. 351.

6. Eric J. Hobsbawn, *Primitive Rebels*, p. 84.
7. For discussions of the Río Verde uprisings, see Valentín Gama, "La propiedad en México: La reforma agraria," *Revista Mexicana de Ingeniería y Arquitectura*, nos. 6, 8, 9, 10 (1931); also Silva Herzog, *El agrarismo mexicano*, pp. 62–63.
8. For the most extensive discussion of the agrarian movement in the nineteenth century, see Silva Herzog, *El agrarismo Mexicano*.
9. The principal periodicals involved were *El Socialista, El Hijo del Trabajo, El Obrero Internacional*, and *La Internacional*.
10. José María González, "El pueblo esclavo," *El Hijo del Trabajo*, October 14, 1877.
11. For example, see González, "Miseria," ibid., January 20, 1878.
12. González, in a speech to the Sociedad Mutua del Ramo de Sombrerería, reported in *El Socialista*, November 17, 1879.
13. González, articles in *El Hijo del Trabajo*, July 30, 1876.
14. González, "A la sociedad de artesanos de Oaxaca," ibid., October 7, 1877.
15. González, "Las sociedades mutualistas," ibid., August 6, 1876.
16. Ibid.
17. For examples, see *La Internacional*, July 28, 1878; González, "También son hombres," *El Hijo del Trabajo*, September 23, 1877; and González and others in the series entitled "La cuestion indígena," which was carried by *El Hijo del Trabajo* throughout 1877–1878.
18. González, "¡Apeo y deslinde de terrenos! ¡Abajo la usurpación!" *El Hijo del Trabajo*, November 4, 1877.
19. González, "La cuestion indígena (Hacienda de las Bocas)," ibid., December 2, 1877.
20. *La Internacional*, August 25, 1878.
21. Report from Juan Othón, Señor Secretario de la Prefectura Superior Política del Departmento de San Luis Potosí, January 1864, cited by González in "La cuestion indígena (Hacienda de las Bocas)." See also Jan Bazant, *Cinco haciendas mexicanas*, pp. 121–122.
22. González, article in *El Hijo del Trabajo*, January 27, 1878.
23. This was probably done in 1876, although no record of the exact date of the event exists.
24. González, "La cuestion indígena (Hacienda de las Bocas)."
25. Communique from Joaquín Flores to Commandant F. Rodríquez, according to *La Internacional* reporter Moctezuma and telegraphed to *La Internacional* on July 20, 1878. It was published in *La Internacional*, July 21, 1878.
26. Editorial, ibid., July 28, 1878.
27. For examples, see González, "¡Apeo y deslinde de terrenos! ¡Abajo la usurpación!"; and "¡De rodillas, miserables!" *El Hijo del Trabajo*, August 12, 1877.
28. *La Internacional*, August 25, October 6, 1878.
29. Ibid., July 14, 1878.
30. Coatsworth, "Railroads," pp. 56–65.

31. Ibid.; Díaz Soto y Gama, *La revolución agraria*, pp. 43–47; Díaz Ramírez, *Apuntes históricos*, pp. 63–66; Meyer, *Problemas campesinos*, pp. 21–24; and interview, Valadés, Oaxtepec, November 6, 1969.

32. Interview, Valadés, Oaxtepec, November 6, 1969; see also Díaz Soto y Gama, *La revolución agraria*, pp. 52–53.

33. Alberto Santa Fe, "La Ley del Pueblo," *La Revolución Social* (Puebla), December 18, 1879; and *El Socialista*, August 4, 1878.

34. Alba, *Las ideas sociales contemporáneas en México*, p. 103.

35. *El Socialista*, April 11, 1883.

36. Santa Fe had worked with Rhodakanaty, González, and Zalacosta on the staffs of *El Hijo del Trabajo* and *La Internacional*.

37. Letters, Santa Fe to the Editor, *El Hijo del Trabajo*, June 15, November 23, 1879.

38. Santa Fe, "La Ley del Pueblo."

39. Letters, Santa Fe to the Editor, *El Hijo del Trabajo*, June 15, November 23, 1879; and *El Socialista*, January 15, 1880.

40. *La Revolución Social* (Puebla), October 17, 24, 1878; see also Díaz Soto y Gama, *La revolución agraria*, pp. 50–53.

41. Letters, Santa Fe to the Editor, *El Hijo del Trabajo*, June 15, November 23, 1879.

42. *El Socialista*, August 29, 1886.

43. "Don Miguel Negrete," *El Hijo del Trabajo*, October 10, 1880.

44. Miguel Negrete, article in *El Socialista*, June 9, 1879.

45. See "Don Miguel Negrete"; and *El Hijo del Ahuizote*, November 2, 1890.

46. Negrete, article in *El Socialista*.

47. Ibid.; see also letters, Gen. González Ortega to Negrete, New York, September 10, 1866, and Silvestre Aranda to Benito Juárez, Chihuahua, April 22, 1866, Archivo Juárez, Biblioteca Nacional de México.

48. *Diario del Imperio*, June 14, 1865.

49. Letters, Gen. Francisco Naranjo to Negrete, Villa Aldama, Nuevo León, January 27, February 6, 7, 1866; also, Gen. Juan N. Sáenz to Negrete, February 6, 7, 1866 (point of dispatch unknown), Archivo Juárez, Biblioteca Nacional de México.

50. Letters, Cuéllar to Lerdo, Ayotla, March 7, 1868, AGN, Tranquilidad Pública, legajo 1546; and Lerdo to Cuéllar, Mexico City, March 9, 1868, ibid.; and five letters, Negrete to Col. Pedro Villegas, Santa Ana, Puebla, February 14, 1869; also letter, Negrete to Lt. Col. Melitrón Galarza, February 14, 1869, Chiautla, Puebla, Archivo Juárez, Biblioteca Nacional de México.

51. "Don Miguel Negrete."

52. Ibid.

53. Miguel Negrete, "Municipio Libre," *El Hijo del Trabajo*, May 23, 1880.

54. Letter, Negrete to Porfirio Díaz, January 30, 1893, Archivo Histórico de la Defensa Nacional, expediente X/111.2/15-709, primer tomo, documento 499.

55. Díaz Ramírez, *Apuntes históricos*, p. 73.

56. Tiburcio Montiel, "Comunismo," *El Socialista*, July 31, 1878.

57. Díaz Soto y Gama, *La revolución agraria*, p. 43.
58. Montiel, "Comunismo."
59. Rafael Ramos Pedrueza, *La lucha de clases a través de la historia de México*, 2:412.
60. Díaz Ramírez, *Apuntes históricos*, p. 73.
61. González Navarro, *El porfiriato*, p. 244.
62. For data on land distribution and the size of haciendas before the revolution of 1910, see Womack, *Zapata*, pp. 391–392; Gildardo Magaña, *Emiliano Zapata y el agrarismo en México*, 1:39; and Domingo Díez, *Dos conferencias sobre el estado de Morelos*, p. 56.
63. Professor John Womack, in his perceptive *Zapata and the Mexican Revolution* (p. 405), makes the claim of "originality" for Zapata's Plan de Ayala and Agrarian Law. Díaz Soto y Gama, however, has argued the case for the precursors, with the claim that the Plan de Ayala offered the people nothing more than what the nineteenth-century agrarians had proposed in the face of insurmountable odds (*La revolución agraria*, pp. 49–50).
64. For the closest comparison, see Santa Fe, "Ley del Pueblo."
65. Womack, *Zapata*, p. 393.

6. Decline and Perseverance

1. *El Socialista*, February 1, 1880.
2. Ibid., January 8, 1880.
3. Ibid., April 29, 1880.
4. Ibid., February 8, 1880.
5. "Protesta," proclamation in *El Hijo del Trabajo*, May 16, 1880.
6. *El Socialista*, January 8, April 29, 1880.
7. "Protesta."
8. *El Socialista*, September 26, 1882.
9. González, "El círculo de obreros," *El Socialista*, February 17, March 10, 1878.
10. Letter, Santa Fe, to the editor, *El Hijo del Trabajo*, May 11, 1879.
11. Montiel, "Comunismo." See also Díaz Ramírez, *Apuntes históricos*, p. 73.
12. Interview, Valadés, Oaxtepec, November 6, 1969.
13. Their abilities in this context are attested to in several instances. For example, see Ramo de Gobernación, AGN, Rurales report no. 54, 1881.
14. There are several secondary sources available which describe the extension by the Díaz government of its control over the agrarian population. The best of these are Silva Herzog, *El agrarismo mexicano*, pp. 104–147; and González Navarro, *El porfiriato*, pp. 239-259.
15. *El Hijo del Trabajo*, July 6, 1879.
16. For a general description of government suppression, see López Aparicio, *El movimiento obrero*, p. 112.

17. The best example of editorial outrage was signed with a pseudonym: Luigi, "La revolución es necesaria," *El Hijo del Trabajo*, December 28, 1879.
18. *El Socialista*, November 26, 1880.
19. *El Hijo del Trabajo*, March 6, 1881.
20. "El círculo de obreros," *El Hijo del Trabajo*, March 19, 1882.
21. "Obituario al Gran Círculo," *El Socialista*, November 2, 1883; also see Ramos Pedrueza, *La lucha de las clases*, p. 412.
22. *El Socialista*, January 15, 1880.
23. Nathan Ganz: "What We Will and What We Will Not," and "War against the Authorities by Various Methods and Means," *El Socialista*, January 10, 1881. For details of the convention, see Woodcock, *Anarchism*, p. 258.
24. *El Socialista*, December 7, 1884; italics added.
25. For a biographical essay and a description of the labor career of Pedro Ordóñez, see *El Socialista*, June 30, 1881.
26. Gen. Carlos Pacheco, Secretario de Fomento, *Memoria presentada al Congreso de la Unión por el secretario de Estado y del despacho de Fomento, Colonización, Industria y Comercio de la República Mexicana* [hereafter cited as *Memoria de Fomento*]: *Corresponde a los años trascurridos de enero de 1883 a junio de 1885*, pp. 195–212.
27. Manuel Fernández Leal, Secretario de Fomento, *Memoria de Fomento: Corresponde a los años transcurridos de 1892 a 1896*, pp. 13–16.
28. *El Socialista*, June 28, 1885.
29. López Aparicio, *El movimiento obrero*, p. 115.
30. *El Socialista*, July 5, 1884.
31. Ibid., May 31, 1885.
32. Bojórquez, *La inmigración española*, p. 5.
33. Rojas Coria, *Tratado de cooperativismo mexicano*, pp. 214–230, 235.
34. Ibid., pp. 240–241.
35. Letter, Gen. González Ortega to Negrete, New York, September 10, 1866, Archivo Juárez, Biblioteca Nacional de Mexico. For additional information regarding one of their conspiracies against Juárez, see letter, Silvestre Aranda to Juárez, Chihuahua, April 22, 1866, ibid.
36. García de la Cadena supported Díaz against both Juárez and Lerdo de Tejada. See Trinidad García de la Cadena, General de Brigada, expediente 15-395, documentos 5, 6, 153, 154, 165–173, AHDN.
37. The esteem in which García de la Cadena was held is indicated by the following: "It [the ceremony] was presided over by General García de la Cadena for whom the working class has nothing but praise" (*El Socialista*, March 24, 1879).
38. Trinidad García de la Cadena, article in *El Socialista*, June 2, 1879.
39. *El Siglo XIX*, November 3, 1866.
40. Negrete, "El Plan de Loma Alta," Loma Alta, Puebla, June 26, 1886, expediente X/111.2/15-709, tomo II, documento 00342, AHDN.
41. See the reports of Hinojosa for July, August, September, October, 1886, expediente X/111.2/15-709, tomo II, ibid.
42. Luis Carballeda, Reports, Mexico City, October 20, 1886, expediente X/111.2/15-709, tomo II, documentos 00359, 00360, ibid.

43. Román Suastegui a Pedro Hinojosa, Ministro de Guerra y Marina, Zacatecas, October 19, 1886, expediente 15-395, documento 204; Hinojosa, Directive to capture García de la Cadena, Mexico City, October 20, 1886, expediente 15-395, documento 214; Gen. Carlos Lueso, Reports concerning the death of García de la Cadena, Zacatecas, November 11, October 25, 1886, expediente 15-395, documentos 218, 220; Hinojosa, Report, Mexico City, November 16, 1886, documento 219, ibid.

7. The Resurgence

1. Moisés González Navarro, *Las huelgas textiles en el porfiriato*, pp. 36–40.
2. Ibid., pp. 40–48.
3. López Aparicio, *El movimiento obrero en México*, p. 115.
4. Alfredo Chavero, *Segunda Conferencia Internacional de América, ciudad de México, 1901–1902, La Comisión de Extradición y Protección contra el Anarquismo*, p. 181.
5. Ibid., pp. 187–188, 215.
6. Fernando Rosenzweig, "El desarrollo económico de México de 1877 a 1911," *Trimestre Económico* 37 (July–September 1965): 418.
7. John H. Coatsworth, "The Mexican Economy, 1810–1910," unpublished manuscript, University of Chicago, 1975; and Seminario de la Historia Moderna de México, *Estadísticas económicas del porfiriato: Fuerza de trabajo y actividad económica por sectores*, p. 25. The Coatsworth study contains a re-evaluation of Rosenzweig's data, including the identification of erroneous 1877 crop statistics.
8. González Navarro, *El porfiriato*, p. 210. For an incisive analysis of Porfirian agricultural development, see John H. Coatsworth, "Anotaciones sobre la producción de alimentos durante el porfiriato," *Historia Mexicana* 102 (October–December 1976): 167–187.
9. James Wilkie, *The Mexican Revolution*, p. 189.
10. For sugar and other crop data, see Seminario, *Estadísticas económicas*, pp. 68–82.
11. See Ward Barrett, *The Sugar Hacienda of the Marqueses del Valle*, p. 147. Barrett dispels the notion among scholars that the hacienda was not run as a business in search of cash profits. The origin of this misunderstanding was George McCutchen McBride's literal acceptance of the claim by Andrés Molina Enríquez that "*La hacienda no es negocio.*" Molina Enríquez could have said that the hacienda, beset by Mexico's incessant internal turmoil and the fluctuations of both domestic and foreign prices, was a difficult business. See McBride, *The Land Systems of Mexico*, pp. 38–40; and Molina Enríquez, *Los grandes problemas nacionales*, p. 347.
12. Seminario, *Estadísticas económicas*, pp. 68–82. For a useful study of the impact of *latifundia* upon village life, see Paul Friedrich, *Agrarian Revolt in a Mexican Village*, pp. 43–50.
13. Rosenzweig, "El desarrollo económico," p. 444.

14. Enrique Florescano and María de Rosario Lanzagorta, "Política económica," in *La economía mexicana en la época de Juárez*, ed. Luis González et al., p. 83.

15. It is noteworthy that these ideas, e.g., the elimination of urban capitalists from rural landownership, the redistribution of agrarian lands, agrarian development banks, etc., expressed thirty years after their popularity in the 1870's by Andrés Molina Enríquez in his monumental *Los grandes problemas nacionales*, were applauded by some observers, and later even scholars, as original, imaginative, and brilliant proposals.

16. Interviews, Rosendo Salazar, Tlalnepantla, August 10, 1969; and Gen. Celestino Gasca, Mexico City, August 19, 1969.

17. Ricardo Flores Magón's background is well known. Two useful sources in English that treat this period of his life are Juan Gómez Quiñones, *Sembradores: Ricardo Flores Magón y El Partido Liberal Mexicano*, pp. 1–18; and James D. Cockcroft, *Intellectual Precursors of the Mexican Revolution, 1900–1913*, pp. 86–87. For reference to Ricardo's early anarchism, see Cockcroft, *Intellectual Precursors*, pp. 72, 80.

18. Gómez Quiñones, *Sembradores*, p. 23; and Cockcroft, *Intellectual Precursors*, pp. 117–120.

19. Gómez Quiñones, *Sembradores*, p. 25.

20. Cockcroft, *Intellectual Precursors*, p. 124.

21. "El informe secreto de la Pinkerton," *El Democrata*, September 4, 1924.

22. Cockcroft, *Intellectual Precursors*, p. 137.

23. Ibid., pp. 119–121.

24. Rosendo Salazar, *Historia de las luchas proletarias de México, 1923 a 1936*, 1:63, 72, 74.

25. "Como juzgan los revolucionarios a sus camaradas," in *Documentos históricos de la Revolución Mexicana*, vol. 10, *Actividades políticas y revolucionarias de los hermanos Flores Magón*, ed. Josefina E. de Fabela, pp. 86–88.

26. Rodney D. Anderson, *Outcasts in Their Own Land*, p. 99; and Cockcroft, *Intellectual Precursors*, p. 124.

27. Armando Bartra, "Ricardo Flores Magón en el cincuentenario de su muerte," *Supplemento de Siempre*, December 6, 1972; see also Fabela, *Documentos*, 10:36–40, 78, 89–90, 99; and Vol. 11, *Precursores de la Revolución Mexicana, 1906–1910*, p. 53.

28. "El informe secreto," *El Democrata*, September 4, 1924. The PLM's base of working-class support, its anarchism, and the techniques used by Furlong to frustrate its revolutionary plans were revealed in an interview by the detective who gained employment within the Junta's offices. His identity was confirmed by the reporter through Enrique Flores Magón, who remembered him all too well. See also Thomas Furlong, *Fifty Years a Detective*.

29. Luis Araiza, *Historia del movimiento obrero mexicano*, 2:43, 49.

30. Letter, Esteban Baca Calderón, Cananea, Sonora, to Antonio I. Villareal, Saint Louis, April 6, 1906, in Manuel González Ramírez, ed.,

Fuentes para la historia de la Revolución Mexicana, vol. 3, *La huelga de Cananea*, p. 9.

31. Ibid., p. 45; and Esteban Baca Calderón, *Juicio sobre la guerra del yanqui y génesis de la huelga de Cananea*, pp. 19–33.

32. Jesús González Monroy, "El porfirismo y la oposición," unpublished; quoted in Bartra, "Ricardo Flores Magón."

33. Cockcroft, *Intellectual Precursors*, p. 135.

34. William Dirk Raat, "The Diplomacy of Suppression: Los Revoltosos, Mexico and the United States, 1906–1911," *Hispanic American Historical Review* 56 (November 1976): 529–550.

35. Cockcroft, *Intellectual Precursors*, pp. 136–137.

36. "Programa del Partido Liberal y manifiesto a la nación," in Fabela, *Documentos*, 10:41–68.

37. Cockcroft, *Intellectual Precursors*, pp. 124, 146–149; Gómez Quiñones, *Sembradores*, pp. 31–32; and Bartra, "Ricardo Flores Magón."

38. Dawn Keremitsis, *La industrial textil mexicana en el siglo XIX*, p. 113.

39. González Navarro, *Las huelgas textiles*, p. 226.

40. González Navarro, *El porfiriato*, p. 326.

41. "Delegados a la Primera y Unica Convención de Obreros e Industriales del Ramo Textil Verificada en agosto de 1912," *La Revolución Social* (Mexico City), November 18, 1922.

42. Araiza, *Historia*, 2:99.

43. "Delegados a la Primera y Unica Convención de Obreros e Industriales del Ramo Textil Verificada en agosto de 1912."

44. Araiza, *Historia*, 2:99–100; and Rodney D. Anderson, "Díaz y la crisis laboral de 1906," *Historia Mexicana* 19 (April–July 1970): 516.

45. Araiza, *Historia*, 2:100–101.

46. Anderson, "Díaz y la crisis," p. 520.

47. Araiza, *Historia*, 2:101–102.

48. Ibid., pp. 103, 109–110; and González Navarro, *Las huelgas textiles*, pp. 51–61, 72.

49. González Navarro, *El porfiriato*, p. 324.

50. Ibid., p. 326.

51. Ibid., pp. 326–327; and Araiza, *Historia*, 2:105.

52. González Navarro, *El porfiriato*, p. 331; and Araiza, *Historia*, 2:110–111.

53. Araiza, *Historia*, 2:114–115, 117; and González Navarro, *Las huelgas textiles*, pp. 79–80.

54. González Navarro, *Las huelgas textiles*, p. 80.

55. Araiza, *Historia*, 2:115; and González Navarro, *Las huelgas textiles*, p. 80.

56. Jacinto Huitrón, *Orígenes e historia del movimiento obrero en México*, p. 118; and Araiza, *Historia*, 2:121.

57. González Navarro, *El porfiriato*, p. 334. For a version which estimates far smaller workers' casualty counts at Río Blanco and rejects the contention that the *rurales* were involved or executed, see Anderson, *Outcasts in Their Own Land*, pp. 166–169.

58. *El Imparcial*, January 9, 1907.

59. Ibid., January 11, 13, 23, February 14, 23, April 17, May 30, June 1, 3, 5, 1907; and *El País*, May 29, 1907; cited in González Navarro, *Las huelgas textiles*, p. 409.

60. *Charrismo* is a Mexicanism for "working-class leaders" who, in the view of their critics, actually serve capital or the government rather than the workers.

61. *El Imparcial*, January 8, May 28, 29, 1908; cited in González Navarro, *Las huelgas textiles*, p. 409. For reference to unrest in the wake of Río Blanco, see Anderson, *Outcasts in Their Own Land*, p. 194.

62. *El Imparcial*, April 23, 25, May 13, 14, 1909; cited in González Navarro, *Las huelgas textiles*, p. 409.

63. *El Imparcial*, July 25, 26, 1910; *El País*, July 24, 27, 1910; cited in González Navarro, *Las huelgas textiles*, p. 409.

64. Cockcroft, *Intellectual Precursors*, p. 151; and Gómez Quiñones, *Sembradores*, pp. 32–33.

65. Cockcroft, *Intellectual Precursors*, pp. 152–153; and Bartra, "Ricardo Flores Magón."

66. Raat, "The Diplomacy of Suppression," p. 546; and Colin M. Maclachlan, "The Making of a Chicano Radical: The Federal Trials of Ricardo Flores Magón," unpublished manuscript, Tulane University, 1975, pp. 4–11.

67. Gómez Quiñones, *Sembradores*, pp. 33, 35–36.

68. Ibid., p. 46; and Cockcroft, *Intellectual Precursors*, pp. 179–183. For additional information on the life and activities of Praxedis Guerrero, see his *Praxedis Guerrero: Artículos literarios y de combate*.

69. Bartra, "Ricardo Flores Magón"; and Cockcroft, *Intellectual Precursors*, pp. 177–183.

70. The termination of silver purchases by foreign governments and its reduced value helped precipitate lowered real wages. For data, see Seminario, *Estadísticas económicas*, p. 447. For an interpretation, see David M. Pletcher, "The Fall of Silver in Mexico, 1870–1910, and Its Effects on American Investments," *Journal of Economic History* 18 (March 1958): 38.

8. Anarchism, the Working Class, and the Opening Phases of the Revolution

1. "Libertad, A.I.T., F.A.I., C.N.T.: Tres postulados, tres banderas del proletariado español con repercuciones universales. Proletariados de todo el mundo. La revolución social de España es vuestra revolución," *Regeneración* (Mexico), May 1, 1937; and Amadeo Ferrés, "Hacia el porvenir," *El Tipógrafo Mexicano*, July 1, 1912.

2. Agustín Segura, "La influencia de Amadeo Ferrés," *El Tipógrafo Mexicano*, December 27, 1911; and Fernando Córdova Pérez, "El Movimiento anarquista en México (1911–1921)" (Licenciado Thesis), pp. 1–8. See also Ramón Eduardo Ruiz, *Labor and the Ambivalent Revolutionaries*, p. 27.

3. Ferrés, "Hacia el porvenir."
4. Ferrés, "¡Compañeros, Saludemos!" *El Tipógrafo Mexicano*, November 10, 1911.
5. Ferrés, "El despertar del obrero mexicano," *El Tipógrafo Mexicano*, December 27, 1911.
6. Ferrés, "Hacia el porvenir," "¡Compañeros, Saludemos!" and "El despertar del obrero mexicano."
7. Ferrés, "¡Compañeros, Saludemos!" and "El despertar del obrero mexicano."
8. José López Dónez, "La significación de la imprenta," *El Tipógrafo Mexicano*, June 1, 1912; and Segura, "La influencia de Amadeo Ferrés."
9. Anastacio S. Marín, "Luchemos por la reinvindicación del proletariado," *El Tipógrafo Mexicano*, August 1, 1912.
10. López Dónez, "La significación de la imprenta."
11. Rafael Quintero, "19 de mayo de 1912," *El Tipógrafo Mexicano*, June 1, 1912.
12. Ferrés, "El despertar del obrero mexicano"; and Córdova Pérez, "Movimiento," p. 2.
13. Ferrés, "Hacia el porvenir"; Marín, "Nuestro llamamiento en favor de la lucha reinvindicadora ha merecido la atención de los tipógrafos," *El Tipógrafo Mexicano*, December 27, 1911; Segura, "La influencia de Amadeo Ferrés"; and "Extracto de la sesión del 5 de noviembre de 1911," *El Tipógrafo Mexicano*, December 1, 1911.
14. "Corte de caja," *El Tipógrafo Mexicano*, December 27, 1911.
15. *El Tipógrafo Mexicano*, November 10, 1911.
16. "Extracto de la sesión del 5 de noviembre de 1911"; see also letter, Manuel Arriola, Guatemala, to the Secretary, Confederación Tipográfica Mexicana, *El Tipógrafo Mexicano*, December 27, 1911.
17. "Extracto de la sesión del 5 de noviembre de 1911"; see also *El Tipógrafo Mexicano*, December 1, 27, 1911, December 1, 1912.
18. *El Tipógrafo Mexicano*, December 1, 1912; and "La voz del oprimidio," ibid., August 1, 1912.
19. Severino Rodríguez Villafuerte, "Discurso," ibid., July 1, 1912.
20. Córdova Pérez, "Movimiento," p. 25.
21. Ibid., p. 27.
22. "Extracto de la sesión del 29 de noviembre de 1911," *El Tipógrafo Mexicano*, July 1, 1912.
23. *El Tipógrafo Mexicano*, December 1, 1911; "Extracto de la sesión del 29 de noviembre de 1911"; "Extracto de la sesión del 8 de mayo de 1912," ibid., July 1, 1912; and "Extracto de la sesión del 15 de noviembre de 1912," ibid., December 1, 1912.
24. López Dónez, "Las huelgas," ibid., May 1, 1913.
25. *El Tipógrafo Mexicano*, December 1, 1911.
26. Córdova Pérez, "Movimiento," pp. 41–43; and Araiza, *Historia*, 3:12.
27. Córdova Pérez, "Movimiento," pp. 36–37; Rosendo Salazar and José G. Escobedo, *Las pugnas de la gleba, 1907–1922*, 1:40–41; and Araiza, *Historia*, 3:12–17.
28. Huitrón, *Orígenes e historia*, p. 198.

29. Araiza, *Historia*, 3:12–13; and Córdova Pérez, "Movimiento," pp. 36–39.
30. Huitrón, *Orígenes e historia*, pp. 199–206.
31. *Luz*, July 17, 1918; and Córdova Pérez, "Movimiento," pp. 40–41.
32. Huitrón, *Orígenes e historia*, pp. 210–212; and Córdova Pérez, "Movimiento," p. 15.
33. Córdova Pérez, "Movimiento," pp. 42–43.
34. Araiza, *Historia*, 3:17–29.
35. Córdova Pérez, "Movimiento," pp. 57–58.
36. "Luz," *Luz*, April 1, 1913.
37. "La Gran Confederación del Trabajo," *El Obrero Liberal*, February 1, 1913; and "La Gran Liga Obrera y la sesión tormentosa de la Confederación," ibid.
38. "Un boicot, un jurado y una manifestación," *Lucha*, February 5, 1913; and Huitrón, *Orígenes e historia*, p. 227.
39. Lorenzo Camacho Escamilla, "Ingenioso primer jurado sindical," *Gaceta Obrera*, no. 6 (June 1962), p. 26.
40. "Un boicot, un jurado y una manifestación"; and Huitrón, *Orígenes e historia*, p. 227.
41. "Confederación Internacional del Trabajo," *Lucha*, February 5, 1913; and Córdova Pérez, "Movimiento," pp. 57, 81–82. For a discussion of the government's promanagement position, see Ruiz, *Labor*, p. 30.
42. Hilario Carrillo, "¡Aparteos vampiros!" *Lucha*, May 1, 1913.
43. Rafael Pérez Taylor, *El socialismo en México*, p. 59.
44. Timoteo García, "Protesta," *Lucha*, May 1, 1913.
45. Córdova Pérez, "Movimento," pp. 65–71.
46. Araiza, *Historia*, 3:35–41; Rosendo Salazar, *La Casa del Obrero Mundial*, pp. 35–38; Salazar and Escobedo, *Las pugnas*, 1:63–67; and Huitrón, *Orígenes e historia*, pp. 229–234.
47. Huitrón, *Orígenes e historia*, p. 230; and Córdova Pérez, "Movimiento," p. 83.
48. Córdova Pérez, "Movimiento," p. 84. For a careful assessment of the politics of the Huerta regime, see Michael Meyer, *Huerta: A Political Portrait*.
49. "Calendario Laico. Efemérides. Septiembre," *Luz*, May 1, 1918; and Jacinto Huitrón, "El movimiento sindical en México," *Regeneración*, September 15, 1942.
50. "A todos los sastres de México," *El Sindicalista*, October 10, 1913.
51. Huitrón, *Orígenes e historia*, pp. 235–236; "Horario de asambleas," *El Sindicalista*, October 10, 1913; Pérez Taylor, *Socialismo*, p. 84; and "Calendario Laico. Efemérides. Septiembre."
52. Huitrón, *Orígenes e historia*, pp. 236–237; Araiza, *Historia*, 3:43–44; and Salazar and Escobedo, *Las pugnas*, 1:64–70.
53. Salazar and Escobedo, *Las pugnas*, 1:69–72.
54. Araiza, *Historia*, 3:44–48; Córdova Pérez, "Movimiento," pp. 98–103; see also Higinio C. García, "Actitud del sindicato de tipógrafos," *El Sindicalista*, October 10, 1913.
55. Córdova Pérez, "Movimiento," pp. 101–105.
56. Huitrón, *Orígenes e historia*, p. 240.
57. Pérez Taylor, *Socialismo*, pp. 15–16.

58. Epigmenio H. Ocampo, "Valor y serenidad," *El Sindicalista*, September 30, 1913.
59. Antonio Díaz Soto y Gama, "Educación racional, lucha reinvindicadora," ibid.
60. "La declaración de principios de la Casa del Obrero Mundial," cited by Huitrón, *Orígenes e historia*, p. 250.
61. Díaz Soto y Gama, "Educación racional, lucha reinvindicadora."
62. Santiago R. de la Vega, "La paradoja triste," *El Sindicalista*, November 20, 1913.
63. "El himno del porvenir," ibid., October 10, 1913.
64. Córdova Pérez, "Movimiento," p. 106.
65. Salazar and Escobedo, *Las pugnas*, 1:76–77.
66. "Los últimos mitines que se han celebrado en la Casa del Obrero Mundial," *Emancipación Obrera*, May 15, 1914.
67. Araiza, *Historia*, 3:48–49; and Salazar and Escobedo, *Las pugnas*, 1:80.

9. The Casa del Obrero Mundial and the Constitutionalists

1. Salazar and Escobedo, *Las pugnas*, 1:83–85; and Araiza, *Historia*, 3:49.
2. "Calendario Laico. Efemérides. Septiembre"; and Córdova Pérez, "Movimiento," pp. 131–132.
3. "Quedará constituido el sindicato de costureras," *Nueva Patria*, October 13, 1914; "Sindicato de Carpinteros," ibid., October 13, 1914; "Calendario Laico. Efemérides. Septiembre"; and "Movimiento obrero," *Ideas*, November 22, 1914.
4. Córdova Pérez, "Movimiento," p. 134.
5. Ibid.
6. Ibid., pp. 141–142.
7. "¡Proletarios, Salud!" *Tinta Roja*, October 24, 1914.
8. Jacinto Huitrón, "Organización," *La Vanguardia*, June 1, 1915; interviews, Salazar and Gasca; and *Excelsior*, January 28, 1926.
9. Salazar and Escobedo, *Las pugnas*, 1:91–93; and Huitrón, *Orígenes e historia*, pp. 257–260.
10. Interviews, Salazar and Gasca.
11. Ibid.; and Ruiz, *Labor*, p. 50.
12. Interviews, Salazar and Gasca.
13. Huitrón, *Orígenes e historia*, p. 267; Salazar and Escobedo, *Las pugnas*, 1:93; and Córdova Pérez, "Movimiento," pp. 146–147.
14. Salazar and Escobedo, *Las pugnas*, 1:93–95.
15. Ibid., 1:95–101; and Araiza, *Historia*, 3:63–66.
16. Interviews, Salazar and Gasca; also Gasca, *Un fragmento vivo de las luchas del movimiento obrero nacional*, pp. 18–19; Salazar and Escobedo, *Las pugnas*, 1:95–101; Araiza, *Historia*, 3:67–79; and Huitrón, "Organización" and *Orígenes e historia*, pp. 259–264. For further discussions, see Ruiz, *Labor*, pp. 47–52; and Barry Carr, *El movimiento obrero y la política en México, 1910–1929*, 1:84–85, 91.

17. Araiza, *Historia*, 3:79–103; Salazar and Escobedo, *Las pugnas*, 1:107–109; and Salazar, *La Casa del Obrero Mundial*, pp. 161–173.
18. Salazar and Escobedo, *Las pugnas*, 1:116–117; Ruiz, *Labor*, pp. 52–54; and Carr, *El movimiento obrero*, 1:90.
19. Interviews, Salazar and Gasca.
20. Guillermo Palacios, "La salida de los batallones tercero y cuarto rojo y la fundación de la Casa del Obrero Mundial de Morelia, Michoacán," *Crom*, June 1, 1930; and Huitrón, *Orígenes e historia*, pp. 279–289.
21. "La Casa del Obrero Mundial en Mérida," *La Vanguardia*, June 2, 1915; and Córdova Pérez, "Movimiento," pp. 156–157.
22. Huitrón, "Organización."
23. Carlos M. Rincón, "La Casa del Obrero Mundial de México es el alma de la revolución constitucionalista: El alma mundial de la revolución," *Pluma Roja*, August 30, 1915.
24. Roberto de la Cerda Silva, *El movimiento obrero en México*, p. 116; Huitrón, *Cinquentenario de la Casa del Obrero, 1912–1962*, and *Orígenes e historia*, p. 289; and Salazar and Escobedo, *Las pugnas*, 1:134.
25. "Por que la carne cuesta cara," *La Vanguardia*, June 2, 1915; and "Crítica situación de la ex-capital," ibid., June 3, 1915.
26. Leonardo P. Castro, "Nuestros mejores auxiliares," *Ariete*, November 7, 1915.
27. Adalberto Concha, "Maquinaciones del alto comercio de México para aumentar el costo de la vida del pueblo," *Acción Mundial*, February 5, 1916; and idem, "Cargos concretos al alto comercio sobre el costo de la vida," ibid., February 12, 1916.
28. Huitrón, *Orígenes e historia*, pp. 279–289; and Cerda Silva, *Movimiento obrero*, pp. 115–116.
29. Castro, "Nuestros mejores auxiliares"; "Nuevos sindicatos," *Ariete*, October 24, 1915; "Movimiento obrero local: Sindicato de zapateros," ibid., November 21, 1915; "Movimiento obrero local: Las obreras se sindican," ibid.; "Movimiento obrero local: Sindicato de costureras," ibid., December 12, 1915; and Huitrón, *Orígenes e historia*, p. 291.
30. Castro, "Nuestros mejores auxiliares."
31. Araiza, *Historia*, 3:106–107.
32. Juan Tudó, "Desde la Atalaya," *Ariete*, October 31, 1915; Castro, "La infancia de la Casa del Obrero Mundial," ibid., October 24, 1915; and Rosendo Medina, "Destruyamos los viejos moldes," ibid., December 12, 1915.
33. "Movimiento obrero local: Huelga de panaderos," ibid., November 7, 1915.
34. "Nuevos sindicatos."
35. "Movimiento obrero local: Los compañeros tejedores," ibid., December 12, 1915.
36. "Movimiento obrero local: Sindicato de carpinteros y similares," ibid., December 12, 1915.
37. "Movimiento obrero local: Sindicato de botoneras," ibid., December 12, 1915; "Movimiento obrero local: La huelga de la perfeccionada,"

ibid., December 19, 1915; and "Movimiento obrero local: Sindicato de peluqueros," ibid., December 19, 1915.

38. Interview, Antonio Matta Reyes, Tacubaya, July 8, 1975; and Salazar and Escobedo, *Las pugnas*, 1:167–169.

39. Araiza, *Historia*, 3:106–109, 120–125; Salazar and Escobedo, *Las pugnas*, 1:147–153; and Huitrón, *Orígenes e historia*, pp. 292–293. For an analysis of the conflict between the Casa and the government, see Ruiz, *Labor*, pp. 52–58.

40. Huitrón, "La Casa del Obrero y la revolución social," *Regeneración*, August 12, 1943; and Salazar and Escobedo, *Las pugnas*, 1:165–166.

41. Huitrón, *Orígenes e historia*, p. 294; Araiza, *Historia*, 3:129–135; Salazar and Escobedo, *Las pugnas*, 1:170–177; and Carr, *El movimiento obrero*, 1:97.

42. Huitrón, *Orígenes e historia*, pp. 294, 297; Araiza, *Historia*, 3:135–137; and Salazar and Escobedo, *Las pugnas*, 1:177–180.

43. "La huelga general de obreros del Distrito Federal," *Acción Mundial*, May 22, 1916; "La huelga, su orígen, su desarrollo, sus consecuencias," ibid.; Dr. Atl, "Los obreros y la revolución: La huelga actual," ibid.; Salazar and Escobedo, *Las pugnas*, 1:184–187; Huitrón, "La Casa del Obrero y la revolución social," and *Orígenes e historia*, pp. 294–295.

44. Dr. Atl, "Los obreros y la revolución: La huelga actual."

45. Araiza, *Historia*, 3:138–140.

46. Salazar, *La Casa del Obrero Mundial*, pp. 217–222.

47. Salazar and Escobedo, *Las pugnas*, 1:181–184; Huitrón, *Orígenes e historia*, p. 295; and Araiza, *Historia*, 3:138–140.

48. Slight variances in this organization's name can be noted, depending on the date and the source consulted. The Federación de Sindicatos Obreros was the most common usage; see Huitrón, *Orígenes e historia*, p. 295.

49. Araiza, *Historia*, 3:140–143.

50. Ibid., 3:143–144.

51. Ibid., 3:148–156, 175–177; and interview, Salazar.

52. Another version of the Casa's defeat holds that Luis Morones and other leaders of a new Casa faction—who supported him and who hoped to work with Obregón in order to eventually gain control of the urban labor movement for themselves—encouraged the general strike of July 31–August 2, 1916. They hoped to discredit and eliminate the independent anarchosyndicalist leadership of the Casa. Knowing the strike was hopeless, they remained in the background, betrayed it, and capitalized upon its failure to gain the objective of their ambition (interview, Salazar; also see Araiza, *Historia*, 3:178).

53. "El caso del compañero Ernesto H. Velasco," *El Rebelde*, October 20, 1917; and Araiza, *Historia*, 3:161–175.

54. "La muerte de José Barragán Hernández unirá a los trabajadores," *Luz*, October 17, 1917; Araiza, *Historia*, 3:178–184; and Salazar and Escobedo, *Las pugnas*, 1:211–223.

10. The Aftermath of August 1916: Continued Activity

1. Tudó, "Desde la Atalaya: Grito de sordos y llamamiento a la libertad," *Luz*, October 24, 1917.
2. Ibid., August 29, 1917.
3. Ibid.; and "Orientaciones para la celebración del 1º de mayo," ibid., April 17, 1918.
4. López Dónez, "En linea recta," ibid., August 14, 1918; idem, "Nuevo Paladín," ibid., January 15, 1919; "Acracia," *El Azote*, June 11, 1917; and Córdova Pérez, "Movimiento," pp. 183–186, 193.
5. "A nuestros lectores," *Tribuna Roja* (Tampico), September 18, 1915.
6. "De Texas con Germinal," *Germinal*, February 7, 1918.
7. "La Casa del Obrero Mundial de Tampico a los organizaciones obreras de la región mexicana, Salud," *Luz*, September 5, 1917.
8. Araiza, *Historia*, 3:187–192; Córdova Pérez, "Movimiento," pp. 204–206; and Salazar and Escobedo, *Las pugnas*, 1:243–249.
9. Huitrón, *Orígenes e historia*, p. 300.
10. Salazar and Escobedo, *Las pugnas*, 2:7–25, 33–46.
11. "Se impone la organización de la verdadera confederación," *Luz*, April 16, 1919; Huitrón, *Orígenes e historia*, p. 300; and Jorge Basurto, *El proletariado industrial en México (1850–1930)*, p. 203.
12. *El Pequeño Grande*, April 6, 1919; and Córdova Pérez, "Movimiento," pp. 206–207.
13. Huitrón, "En el XXIII aniversario de la CGT," *Regeneración*, February 15, 1944.
14. Araiza, *Historia*, 4:56–66.
15. Ibid.; Salazar and Escobedo, *Las pugnas*, 2:116–118; and Huitrón, *Orígenes e historia*, pp. 306–307.
16. "Comienza el terror blanco en México," *Bandera Roja*, June 5, 1921; *El Trabajador*, May 8, 15, October 15, 1921; and Araiza, *Historia*, 4:56–66. For a description of the CGT program and its agrarianism, see Ruiz, *Labor*, pp. 98–99.
17. *El Trabajador*, November 1, 1921; and Araiza, *Historia*, 4:67–69.
18. "La Confederación General de Trabajadores y la Internacional de Sindicatos Rojos," *Nuestros Ideales*, June 2, 1922; Salazar and Escobedo, *Las pugnas*, 2:124–128; and Araiza, *Historia*, 4:70–73, 78.
19. Araiza, *Historia*, 4:74–84.
20. Huitrón, *Orígenes e historia*, pp. 307–308.
21. Miguel T. Ochoa, "Asesinos," *Nueva Solidaridad Obrera*, May 15, 1922; Araiza, *Historia*, 4:87–91; and Salazar and Escobedo, *Las pugnas*, 2:149–157.
22. "El zarpazo de la fiera," *Nuestra Palabra*, October 18, 1923.
23. Araiza, *Historia*, 4:91–101; and Salazar and Escobedo, *Las pugnas*, 2:107–210.
24. *Nuestra Palabra*, August 2, October 11, 1923.
25. Araiza, *Historia*, 4:108–122; and Marjorie Ruth Clark, *Organized Labor in Mexico*, pp. 100, 114.
26. Salazar, *Historia de las luchas*, 1:116.

27. Octavio García Mundo, *El movimiento inquilinario de Veracruz, 1922,* pp. 19–35.
28. Ibid., p. 53.
29. Ibid.; and Salazar and Escobedo, *Las pugnas,* 1:36–38.
30. García Mundo, *El movimiento inquilinario,* pp. 13–15, 54, 56.
31. Ibid., pp. 72–76.
32. Ibid., pp. 83–88, 122.
33. Ibid., pp. 109–128.
34. Ibid., pp. 92–93.
35. *El Dictamen* (Veracruz), June 30, 1922; and García Mundo, *El movimiento inquilinario,* pp. 129–132, 153.
36. García Mundo, *El movimiento inquilinario,* pp. 129–131, 159–171.
37. Heather Fowler, "Los orígenes de las organizaciones campesinas en Veracruz: Raíces políticas y sociales," *Historia Mexicana* 85 (July–September 1972): 66, 70, 73.
38. Salazar, *Historia de las luchas,* 1:72, 74, 78.
39. "¡Los traidores sobran en el mundo!" *Nuestra Palabra,* August 30, 1923.
40. "Nos reafirmamos en la idea antipolítica," *Nuestra Palabra,* December 13, 1923; Salazar, *Historia de las luchas,* 1:72, 74, 78, 101; and Araiza, *Historia,* 4:123–124.
41. Salazar, *Historia de las luchas,* 1:119.
42. Ibid., 1:125.
43. Araiza, *Historia,* 4:124–128; and Cerda Silva, *El movimiento obrero,* p. 137.
44. Cerda Silva, *El movimiento obrero,* pp. 137–143. For an assessment which doubts CROM membership claims, see Jean Meyer, "Los obreros en la Revolución Mexicana: Los Batallones Rojos," *Historia Mexicana* 81 (July–September 1971): 28. For a version which accepts CROM figures, see Carr, *Movimiento obrero,* 2:5–20.
45. Salazar, *Historia de las luchas,* 1:173.
46. "Quienes desean unirse a la C.R.O.M.," *Nuestra Palabra,* February 19, 1925.
47. Salazar, *Historia de las luchas,* 1:187–188.
48. Ibid., 1:191–192, 196–197, 199, 204, 207–210.
49. Ibid., 1:196.
50. Ibid., 1:197, 199, 204.
51. Ibid., 1:207–210.
52. Cerda Silva, *El movimiento obrero,* p. 140.
53. Salazar, *Historia de las luchas,* 1:215–235.
54. Araiza, *Historia,* 4:128–138.
55. Clark, *Organized Labor,* pp. 114–119; and Salazar, *Historia de las luchas,* 1:261, 265.
56. For an in-depth analysis of Morones' demise, see Carr, *Movimiento obrero,* 2:115–176. For pro-CGT contemporary accounts, see "La Confederación General de Trabajadores," *¡Avante!* July 15, 1928; E. Leal, "El fracaso de los políticos y la idea anarquista," ibid., February 1, 1929; and "¡Votalos, pero no votes!" ibid., June 15, 1928.

57. Araiza, *Historia*, 4:138–156; Salazar, *Historia de las luchas*, 1:290–291, 306–307, 329; and Clark, *Organized Labor*, pp. 138, 140.
58. Librado Rivera, "Las farsas electorales," *¡Avante!* January 30, 1930; "El VII Congreso de la C.G.T.," ibid., July 10, 1929; Araiza, *Historia*, 4:157–189; and Clark, *Organized Labor*, pp. 140, 147, 195, 233, 268.
59. Luis G. Franco, *Glosa del perioda de gobierno del C. General e Ingeniera Pascual Ortíz Rubio, 1930–31–32*, p. 32.
60. Ibid., p. 40.
61. Salazar, *Historia de las luchas*, 2:15–18, 40–42, 47, 62.
62. Clark, *Organized Labor*, p. 274.
63. Ibid., pp. 140, 147, 195, 233, 268; and Araiza, *Historia*, 4:197–199.
64. "La C.G.T. no es filial a la A.I.T.," *Regeneración*, no. 1 (April 1937); and "¡No abdicamos nuestra ideología revolucionaria!" *Regeneración*, November 15, 1954.
65. "A todos los grupos e individualidades anarquistas de la región mexicana," *Tribuna Obrera*, August 1934; and *El Tornillo*, June 28, 1937.

11. Conclusion

1. It is interesting to note that many nineteenth-century ideas—e.g., the elimination of urban capitalists from rural landownership, the redistribution of agrarian lands, agrarian development banks, etc.—when explained by Molina Enríquez thirty years later in his monumental *Los grandes problemas nacionales* were applauded by some observers, and later even scholars, as original, imaginative, and brilliant proposals.
2. Interviews, Salazar and Gasca.
3. Ibid.
4. Ibid.; also Salazar and Escobedo, *Las pugnas*, 1:93–103.
5. Interviews, Salazar and Gasca; also, Salazar and Escobedo, *Las pugnas*, 1:200–213.
6. *La Protesta*, May 23, 1929.
7. Letter, Valadés, Mexico City, to the Secretary, Asociación Internacional de Trabajadores, Berlin, December 27, 1923, International Institute of Social History, Nettlau Archive, Amsterdam.

Bibliographic Note

Studies on Anarchism

The best introductions to the subject of anarchism are George Woodcock's *Anarchism: A History of Libertarian Ideas and Movements* and Daniel Guerin's *Anarchism: From Theory to Practice*. Other useful works in the field include *The Anarchists*, by James Joll, and *The Anarchists*, by Irving L. Horowitz. The Horowitz version offers the reader a diverse collection of anarchist essays. A seminal approach by Paul Avrich in *The Russian Anarchists* has resulted in a valuable methodological contribution to the study of anarchism in one country. He successfully relates developments within Russia to Western Europe. The older classics by Max Nomad, *Rebels and Renegades* and *Apostles of the Revolution*, are excellent studies.

Essential for an understanding of the movement are the works contributed from the anarchist leadership itself. Among these are essays by three men who profoundly affected Mexican anarchism: Kropotkin, Bakunin, and Proudhon. The most important of these works is Kropotkin's *Mutual Aid: A Factor of Evolution*, which gave anarchism historical justification at a critical phase in the movement's growth. Proudhon's *What Is Property?* was a landmark effort and had tremendous influence in nineteenth-century Mexico. Also useful are *Fields, Factories and Workshops* and *The Conquest of Bread*, by Kropotkin, and a collection of Bakunin's essays edited by G. P. Maximoff, entitled *The Political Philosophy of Bakunin*.

Studies on Mexico

There are several social histories of Mexico that will provide an understanding of nineteenth-century Mexican social realities and knowledge of either the urban labor or the agrarian movements. The best study is Moisés González Navarro's monumental *El porfiriato: La vida social* from the Historia Moderna de México series edited by Daniel Cosio Villegas. This book contains a wealth of material regarding the overall Mexican social scene between 1876 and 1910, including social unrest. Unfortunately, the footnotes are indecipherable.

A work of importance is *Estadísticas económicas del porfiriato: Fuerza de trabajo y actividad por sectores*, compiled by the Seminario de la Historia Moderna de México, with an introduction by Fernando Rosenzweig. This study offers a wealth of economic data which prepares the basis of an explanation for not only the resurgence of Mexican anarchism, but also the causation of lower-class alienation and an analysis of the coming of the Mexican Revolution.

Four indispensable contributions are Francisco R. Calderón, *La república restaurada: La vida económica*; Luis González y González et al., *La re-*

pública restaurada: La vida social; two volumes by Luis Nicolau d'Olwer et al., *El porfiriato: La vida económica*; and two volumes by Daniel Cosio Villegas, *El porfiriato: La política interior*—all part of the Historia Moderna de México series.

Interpretations which discuss the social setting and the labor and agrarian movements are Jesús Silva Herzog, *El agrarismo mexicano y la reforma agraria*; Luis Chávez Orozco's brief *Prehistoria del socialismo en México*; and *El movimiento obrero en México* by Alfonso López Aparicio. Two works which contain information regarding anarchism and the critical years of the labor and agrarian movements are *El nacimiento, 1876–1884*, vol. 1 of *El porfirismo: Historia de un régimen*, by José C. Valadés; and *Apuntes históricos del movimiento obrero y campesino de México, 1844–1880*, by Manuel Díaz Ramírez. The latter book, despite its polemical aspects, was the first attempt to analyze the nineteenth-century Mexican agrarian and urban labor movements. For an examination of the Porfirian regime's management of organized labor, see David Walker's master's thesis, "The Mexican Industrial Revolution and Its Problems: Porfirian Labor Policy and Economic Dependency, 1876–1910."

An important recent contribution is *El socialismo en México, siglo XIX*, by Gastón García Cantú. The first section of this book is a well-written conceptualization of nineteenth-century Mexican socialism in contemporary Marxian terms. The author tries to convince us that Marx had a heavy impact upon Mexican socialism in the 1860's and 1870's. Mexicans in that early period were indeed interested in "socialism," but it was the Spanish *"antiautoritario"* variety that reached them first. Marxism remained a secondary force within Mexican socialism until the success of the Russian Revolution provided a model for Mexican revolutionaries. The appendices enhance this volume with 150 pages of valuable documents. The footnotes are better than average for works dealing with pre-twentieth-century Mexican social history. This volume, when read with a degree of critical enthusiasm, is a valuable asset to any scholar interested in the development of mass movements in Mexico.

The series of articles by José Valadés in *La Protesta*, the anarchist magazine published in Buenos Aires during the 1920's, pioneered the study of nineteenth-century Mexican working-class movements. They are indispensable. Among these essential essays are "Sobre los orígenes del movimiento obrero en México," June 1927; "Noticia para la bibliografía anarquista en México," June 1927; and "Precursores del socialismo antiautoritario en México," May 22, 1928. These early studies by Valadés, although far from complete, laid the basis for Díaz Ramírez' work. His bibliography contains several works no longer available, some of which are of little value, but it is a landmark effort. The most complete collections of *La Protesta* are available at the International Institute of Social History in Amsterdam and in the private library of Dieter Koniecki of Mexico City.

The revolutionary precursor period, 1900–1910, has been treated most imaginatively by James D. Cockcroft in his wide-ranging and thought-provoking *Intellectual Precursors of the Mexican Revolution, 1900–1913*. A study which doubts most claims for revolutionary ideology in the pre-1910 working class is Rodney D. Anderson's *Outcasts in Their Own Land:*

Mexican Industrial Workers, 1906–1911. The basis for an understanding of the precursors, Flores Magonistas, and the prerevolutionary working-class crisis has been prepared by excellent documentary collections, which include Isidro and Josefina Fabela, *Documentos de la revolución mexicana*; and Manuel González Ramírez, *Fuentes para la historia de la revolución mexicana* and *Epistolario y textos de Ricardo Flores Magón.* Moisés González Navarro provides an essential understanding of an important segment of the prerevolutionary labor movement with *Las huelgas textiles en el porfiriato.*

The revolutionary and postrevolutionary periods have been treated by countless authors. Four books written by former anarchosyndicalist members of the Casa del Obrero Mundial are essential for an understanding of the working-class movement, despite the authors' personal and emotional involvement. They are Luis Araiza, *Historia del movimiento obrero mexicano*; Jacinto Huitrón, *Orígenes e historia del movimiento obrero en México*; and Rosendo Salazar, *Las pugnas de la gleba, 1907–1922* and *Historia de las luchas proletarios de México, 1923 a 1936.* Two works by professional historians are Barry Carr's *El movimiento obrero y la política en México, 1910–1929* and Ramón Eduardo Ruiz' *Labor and the Ambivalent Revolutionaries: Mexico, 1911–1923.*

With the background information available in these works, the scholar will be equipped to recognize greater significance in Mexico's working-class newspapers. This study was partially based upon a thorough examination of these newspapers, spanning a period of more than sixty-six years with respect to the anarchist, urban labor, and agrarian movements. One important area remains to be developed—additional details are needed regarding workers' associations of the nineteenth century, the revolution, and their strike activities. Unfortunately, very few data are presently available in this regard because the archives of the Congreso, the Gran Círculo, La Social, the Liberal party, the Casa del Obrero Mundial, and the Confederación General de Trabajadores are still missing and the working-class press provides only limited coverage. When the archive of the new Centro de Estudios Históricos del Movimiento Obrero Mexicano has reached maturity, perhaps new light will be shed by the additional data that will then be available.

Bibliography

Unpublished

Archival Material

Archivo del Centro de Estudios Históricos del Movimiento Obrero, Mexico City.
Archivo de Transportes y Comunicaciones, Mexico City.
Archivo General de la Nación, Mexico City.
Archivo General [Judicial] del Estado de Querétaro, Querétaro.
Archivo Histórico de la Defensa Nacional, Mexico City.
Archivo Juárez, Biblioteca Nacional de México, Mexico City.
Archivo Seis de Enero de la Comisión Agraria de México, Mexico City.
Bancroft Library, Silvestre Terrazas Collection, University of California, Berkeley.
Biblioteca Arus, Barcelona.
Biblioteca del Colegio de México, Mexico City.
Biblioteca del Museo de Antropología de México, Mexico City.
Hermeroteca Nacional de México, Mexico City.
International Institute of Social History (IISH), Nettlau Archive, Amsterdam.
Latin American Collection, University of Texas, Austin.
University of the Americas Library, General Porfirio Díaz Collection, Cholula.

Manuscripts

Albro, Ward Sloan, III. "Ricardo Flores Magón and the Liberal Party: An Inquiry into the Origins of the Mexican Revolution of 1910." Ph.D. dissertation, University of Arizona, 1967.
Anderson, Rodney D. "Mexican Industrial Workers and the State, 1900–1911." Paper, Southwestern Labor History Conference, April 1975, Stockton, California.
Brademas, John. "Revolution and Social Revolution: The Anarcho-Syndicalist Movement in Spain, 1930–1937." Ph.D. dissertation, Oxford University, 1956.
Coatsworth, John H. "The Impact of Railroads on the Development of Mexico, 1877–1910." Ph.D. dissertation, University of Wisconsin, 1972.
———, "The Mexican Economy, 1810–1910." University of Chicago, 1975.
Córdova Pérez, Fernando. "El movimiento anarquista en México (1911–1921)." Licenciado thesis, Facultad de Ciencias Políticas y Sociales, UNAM, Mexico City, 1971.

Cronshaw, Francine. "An Inquiry into the Cananea Strike of 1906." University of Houston, 1975.

Gómez-Quiñones, Juan. "Social Change and Intellectual Discontent: The Growth of Mexican Nationalism, 1890–1911." Ph.D. dissertation, University of California at Los Angeles, 1972.

Hollander, Fred. "Ricardo Flores Magón and the Formation of Popular Mexican Nationalism." University of California at Los Angeles, 1967.

Maclachlan, Colin. "The Making of a Chicano Radical: The Federal Trials of Ricardo Flores Magón." Tulane University, 1975.

Meyer, Elizabeth Howell. "The Mexican Liberal Party, 1903–1909." Ph.D. dissertation, University of Virginia, 1971.

Niemeyer, E. V., Jr. "The Mexican Constitutional Convention of 1916–1917: The Constitutionalizing of a Revolutionary Ideology." Master's thesis, University of Texas at Austin, 1951.

Stowe, Noel. "The Tumulto of 1624: Turmoil at Mexico City." Ph.D. dissertation, University of Southern California, 1970.

Walker, David. "The Dynamics of Development: Mexico, 1877–1910." University of Houston, 1975.

———. "The Mexican Industrial Revolution and Its Problems: Porfirian Labor Policy and Economic Dependency, 1876–1910." Master's thesis, University of Houston, 1976.

Wasserman, Mark. "Oligarchy and Foreign Enterprise in Porfirian Chihuahua." Ph.D. dissertation, University of Chicago, 1975.

Published

Books and Articles

Agetro, Leafar [pseud. Rafael C. Ortega]. *Las luchas proletarias en Veracruz: Historia y autocrítica.* Jalapa, Ver.: Editorial "Barricada," 1942.

Aguilera Gómez, Manuel. *La reforma agraria en el desarrollo económico de México.* Mexico City: Instituto Mexicano de Investigaciones Económicas, 1969.

Aguirre Beltrán, Gonzalo. *El senorio de Cuauhtochco, luchas agrarias en México durante el virreinato.* Mexico City: Ediciones Frente Cultural, 1940.

Alba, Víctor. *Historia del movimiento obrero en América Latina.* Mexico City: Libreros Mexicanos Unidos, 1964.

———. *Las ideas sociales contemporáneas en México.* Mexico City: Fondo de Cultura Económica, 1960.

Alexander, Robert J. *Organized Labor in Latin America.* New York: Free Press, 1965.

Altamirano, Ignacio. *Paisajes y leyendas: Tradiciones y costumbres de México.* Mexico City: Antigua Librería de Robredo, 1949.

Anaya Ibarra, Pedro María. *Precursores de la revolución mexicana.* Mexico City: Secretaría de Educación Pública, 1955.

Anderson, Alexander Dwight. *The Tehuantepec Inter-Ocean Railroad*. New York: A. S. Barnes and Co., 1880.

Anderson, Rodney D. "Díaz y la crisis laboral de 1906." *Historia Mexicana* 19 (April–July 1970): 513–535.

————. "Mexican Workers and the Politics of Revolution, 1906–1911." *Hispanic American Historical Review* 54 (February 1974): 94–113.

————. *Outcasts in Their Own Land: Mexican Industrial Workers, 1906–1911*. DeKalb: Northern Illinois University Press, 1976.

Anuario estadístico de los estados unidos mexicanos. Mexico City, 1893, 1896, 1898, 1902, 1905, 1909.

Araiza, Luis. *Historia del movimiento obrero mexicano*. 5 vols. Mexico City, 1964–1966.

Arenas Guzmán, Diego. *Prensa y tribunas revolucionarias*. Mexico City: Compañia Editora Mexicana, 1916.

Avrich, Paul. *The Russian Anarchists*. Princeton: Princeton University Press, 1967.

Baca Calderón, Esteban. *Juicio sobre la guerra del yanqui y génesis de la huelga de Cananea*. Mexico City: Ediciones del Sindicato Mexicano de Electricistas, 1956.

Bakunin, Mikhail. *The Political Philosophy of Bakunin*, ed. G. P. Maximoff. London: Free Press of Glencoe, Collier-Macmillan, 1953.

Barrera Fuentes, Florencio. *Historia de la revolución mexicana: La etapa precursora*. Mexico City: Biblioteca del Instituto de Estudios Históricos de la Revolución Mexicana, 1955.

Barrett, Ward. *The Sugar Hacienda of the Marqueses del Valle*. Minneapolis: University of Minnesota Press, 1970.

Basurto, Jorge. *El proletariado industrial en México (1850–1930)*. Mexico City: Instituto de Investigaciones Sociales, UNAM, 1975.

Bazant, Jan. *Los bienes de la iglesia en México (1856–1875)*. Mexico City: El Colegio de México, 1971.

————. *Cinco haciendas mexicanas: Tres siglos de vida rural en San Luis Potosí (1600–1910)*. Mexico City: El Colegio de México, 1975.

————. "La desamortización de los bienes corporativas en 1856." *Historia Mexicana* 16 (October–December 1966): 193–212.

Bernstein, Marvin D. *The Mexican Mining Industry, 1890–1950*. Albany: The State University of New York, 1966.

Blaisdell, Lowell L. *The Desert Revolution: Baja California, 1911*. Madison: University of Wisconsin Press, 1962.

Blanquel, Eduardo. "El anarco-magonismo." *Historia Mexicana* 13 (January–March 1964): 394–427.

Bojórquez, Juan de Dios. *La inmigración española en México*. Mexico City: Edición Especial de Crisol, 1932.

Branch, H. M. *The Mexican Constitution of 1917 Compared with the Constitution of 1857*. Supplement to the *Annals of the American Academy of Political and Social Science, Philadelphia*. May 1917.

Bullejos, José. *El movimiento obrero mundial*. Mexico City: Centro de Estudios y Documentación Sociales, 1964.

Bustamante, Luis F. *El anarquismo científico*. Mexico City, 1916.

————. *La defensa de "El Ebano."* Tampico: Imprenta "El Constitucional," 1915.

————. *De El Ebano a Torreón.* Monterrey: Tip. El Constitucional, 1915.

Buve, R. Th. J. "Protesta de obreros y campesinos durante el porfiriato: Unas consideraciones sobre su desarrollo e interrelaciones en el este de México central." *Boletín de Estudios Latinoamericanos* 13 (1972): 1–25.

Calderón, Francisco R. *La república restaurada: La vida económica.* La Historia Moderna de México Series. Mexico City: Editorial Hermes, n.d.

Carr, Barry. *El movimiento obrero y la política en México, 1910–1929.* 2 vols. Mexico City: SepSetentas, 1976.

Cerdo Silva, Roberto de la. *El movimiento obrero en México.* Mexico City: Instituto de Investigaciones Sociales, UNAM, 1961.

Chavero, Alfredo. *Segunda Conferencia Internacional de América, ciudad de México, 1901–1902, La Comisión de Extradición y Protección contra el Anarquismo.* Mexico City: Tip. de la Oficina Impresora de Estampillas, 1902.

Chávez López, Julio. "Manifiesto a todos los oprimidios y pobres de México y del universo," Chalco, April 20, 1869. Text in "Movimiento anarco-fourierista entre el imperio y la reforma," by Juan Hernández Luna. *Cuadernos de Orientación Política,* no. 4 (April 1956), pp. 25–26.

Chávez Orozco, Luis. *La agonía del artesanado mexicano.* Mexico City, 1958.

————. *Documentos para la historia económica de México.* 10 vols. Mexico City: Publicaciones de la Secretaría de la Economía Nacional, 1933–1936.

————. *Historia económica y social de México: Ensayo de interpretación.* Mexico City: Ediciones Botas, 1938.

————. *Prehistoria del socialismo en México.* Mexico City: Publicaciones del Departamento de Bibliotecas de la Secretaría de Educación Pública, 1936.

————. *Revolución industrial, revolución política.* Mexico City: D.A.P.P., 1937.

Chevalier, François. *Land and Society in Colonial Mexico: The Great Hacienda.* Berkeley: University of California Press, 1963.

Clark, Marjorie Ruth. *Organized Labor in Mexico.* Chapel Hill: University of North Carolina Press, 1934.

Coatsworth, John H. "Anotaciones sobre la producción de alimentos durante el porfiriato." *Historia Mexicana* 102 (October–December 1976): 167–187.

————. "Railroads and the Concentration of Landownership in the Early Porfiriato." *Hispanic American Historical Review* 54 (February 1974): 48–71.

Cockcroft, James D. *Intellectual Precursors of the Mexican Revolution, 1900–1913.* Austin: University of Texas Press, 1968.

Cohn, Norman. *The Pursuit of the Millennium: Revolutionary Messianism in Medieval and Reformation Europe and Its Bearing on Modern Totalitarian Movements.* New York: Harper Torchbooks, 1961.

"Colonel William C. Green and the Cananea Copper Bubble." *Bulletin of the Business Historical Society*, December 1952, pp. 179–198.

Cosio Villegas, Daniel. *El porfiriato: La política interior.* 2 vols. La Historia Moderna de México Series. Mexico City: Editorial Hermes, 1973.

Creelman, James. Interview with Porfirio Díaz. *Pearsons Magazine* 19, no. 3 (March 1908): 241–277.

Cue Canovas, Agustín. *Historia social y económica de México, 1521–1854.* Mexico City: Editorial América, 1946.

———. *Ricardo Flores Magón: La Baja California y los Estados Unidos.* Mexico City: Libro Mex, 1957.

Cumberland, Charles C. *Mexican Revolution: Genesis under Madero.* Austin: University of Texas Press, 1952.

———. *Mexican Revolution: The Constitutionalist Years.* Austin: University of Texas Press, 1972.

———. "Precursors of the Mexican Revolution of 1910." *Hispanic American Historical Review* 22 (May 1942): 344.

Davies, Keith A. "Tendencías demográficas urbanos durante el siglo XIX en México." In *Ensayos sobre el desarrollo urbano de México*, ed. Edward E. Calnek et al., pp. 131–174. Mexico City: Secretaría de Educación Pública, 1974.

Diario de los debates del Congreso Constituyente, 1916–1917. 2 vols. Mexico City: Imp. de la Cámara de Diputados, 1922.

Díaz Ramírez, Manuel. *Apuntes históricos del movimiento obrero y campesino de México, 1844–1880.* Mexico City: Fondo de Cultura Popular, 1938.

Díaz Soto y Gama, Antonio. *La revolución agraria del sur y Emiliano Zapata su caudillo.* Mexico City: Privately published, 1961; reprinted, Mexico City: Ediciones "El Caballito," 1976.

Díez, Domingo. *Dos conferencias sobre el estado de Morelos.* Vol. 1 of "Memorias de la Asociación de Ingenieros y Arquitectos de México," covering conferences held on the state of Morelos, 1917 and 1919. Mexico City: Impr. "Victoria," 1919.

Fabela, Isidro, and Josefina Fabela, eds. *Documentos de la revolución mexicana.* 11 vols. Mexico City: Editorial Jus, 1960–1966.

Fernández Leal, Manuel, Secretario de Fomento. *Memoria de Fomento: Corresponde a los años transcurridos de 1892 a 1896.* Mexico City: Secretaría de Fomento, 1897.

Flores Caballero, Romeo. "Etapas de desarrollo industrial." In *La economía mexicana en la época de Juárez*, ed. Luis González et al., pp. 103–126. Mexico City: Secretaría de Industria y Comercio, 1972.

Flores Magón, Enrique. "Apuntes históricos para mis memorias." *Todo*, April 2, May 28, June 18, July 16, August 13, 20, November 26, 1953.

———. "Los genuinos precursores." *Todo*, November 22, 1945.

———. "La vida de los Flores Magón." *Todo*, January 2–June 19, 1934.

Flores Magón, Ricardo. *Antología*, ed. Gonzalo Aguirre Beltrán. Mexico City: Universidad Nacional Autónoma de México, 1970.

————. *Epistolario revolucionario e íntimo.* 3 vols. Mexico City: Grupo
Cultural "Ricardo Flores Magón," 1925.
————. *Semilla libertaria.* 2 vols. Mexico City: Grupo Cultural "Ricardo
Flores Magón," 1923.
————. *Tribuna roja.* Mexico City: Grupo Cultural "Ricardo Flores
Magón," 1925.
Florescano, Enrique, and María de Rosario Lanzagorta. "Política econó-
mica." In *La economía mexicana en la época de Juárez,* ed. Luis
González et al. Mexico City: Secretaría de Industria y Comercio,
1972.
Fowler, Heather. "Los orígenes de las organizaciones campesinas en Vera-
cruz: Raíces políticas y sociales." *Historia Mexicana* 85 (July–
September 1972): 52–76.
Franco, Luis G. *Glosa del período de gobierno del C. General e Ingeniera
Pascual Ortíz Rubio, 1930–31–32.* Mexico City: Secretaría de In-
dustria, Comercio y Trabajo, 1945.
Frank, Andre G. "Not Feudalism, Capitalism." *Monthly Review* 15, no. 8
(December 1963): 468–478.
Friedrich, Paul. *Agrarian Revolt in a Mexican Village.* Englewood Cliffs,
N.J.: Prentice-Hall, 1970.
Fuentes Díaz, Vicente. *Los partidos políticos en México. Tomo I, 1810–
1911.* Mexico City: Privately published, 1954.
Furlong, Thomas. *Fifty Years a Detective.* St. Louis: C. E. Barnett, 1912.
Gama, Valentín. "La propiedad en México: La reforma agraria." *Revista
Mexicana de Ingeniería y Arquitectura,* nos. 6, 8, 9, 10 (1931).
García, Genaro, and Carlos Pereyra. *Documentos inéditos o muy raros para
la historia de México.* Mexico City: Viuda de C. Bouret, 1907.
García Cantú, Gastón. *El socialismo en México, siglo XIX.* Mexico City:
Ediciones Era, 1969.
García Cubas, Antonio. *Diccionario geográfico histórico de los estados
unidos mexicanos.* 3 vols. Mexico City: Antigua Imprenta de Mur-
guía, 1888.
García Granados, Ricardo. *Historia de México desde la restauración de la
república en 1867, hasta la caída de Huerta.* Mexico City: Editorial
Jus, 1956.
García Mundo, Octavio. *El movimiento inquilinario de Veracruz, 1922.*
Mexico City: SepSetentas, 1976.
Gasca, General Celestino. *Un fragmento vivo de las luchas del movimiento
obrero nacional.* Mexico City: Privately printed, 1942.
Gibson, Charles C. *The Aztecs under Spanish Rule.* Stanford: Stanford
University Press, 1964.
Gómez, Marte R. *La reforma agraria en las filas villistas, años 1913 a 1915
y 1920.* Mexico City: Instituto Nacional de Estudios Históricos de
la Revolución Mexicana, 1966.
Gómez Quiñones, Juan. *Sembradores: Ricardo Flores Magón y el partido
liberal mexicano: A Eulogy and Critique.* Los Angeles: Atzlán Pub-
lications, University of California at Los Angeles, 1973.
González, José María. *Del artesanado al socialismo.* Mexico City: SepSetentas, 1974.

González Navarro, Moisés. "La huelga de Río Blanco." *Historia Mexicana* 6 (April–June 1957): 510–533.
————. *Las huelgas textiles en el porfiriato.* Puebla: Editorial José Cajica, 1971.
————. "Las huelgas textiles en el porfiriato," *Historia Mexicana* 6 (October–December 1956): 201–216.
————. "La ideología de la revolución mexicana." *Historia Mexicana* 1 (April–June 1961): 628–636.
————. *El porfiriato: La vida social.* La Historia Moderna de México Series. Mexico City: Editorial Hermes, 1957.
González Ramírez, Manuel, ed. *Epistolario y textos de Ricardo Flores Magón.* Mexico City: Fondo de Cultura Económica, 1964.
————, ed. *Fuentes para la historia de la revolución mexicana.* 4 vols. Mexico City: Fondo de Cultura Económica, 1954–1957.
González y González, Luis, et al. *La república restaurada: La vida social.* La Historia Moderna de México Series. Mexico City: Editorial Hermes, n.d.
Guerin, Daniel. *Anarchism: From Theory to Practice.* New York: Monthly Review Press, 1970.
Guerrero, Praxedis. *Praxedis Guerrero: Artículos literarios y de combate.* Mexico City: Grupo Cultural "Ricardo Flores Magón," 1924.
Gutherie, Chester Lyle. "Riots in Seventeenth-Century Mexico City: A Study of Social and Economic Conditions." In *Greater America: Essays in Honor of Herbert Eugene Bolton*, ed. Adele Ogden and Engel Sluiter. Berkeley: University of California Press, 1945.
Hart, John M. "Agrarian Precursors of the Mexican Revolution: The Development of an Ideology." *The Americas* 29 (October 1972): 131–150.
————. "Miguel Negrete: La epopeya de un revolucionario." *Historia Mexicana* 24 (July–September 1974): 70–93.
————. "Nineteenth Century Urban Labor Precursors of the Mexican Revolution: The Development of an Ideology." *The Americas* 30 (January 1974): 297–318.
Hernández, Ana María. *La mujer mexicana en la industria textil.* Mexico City: [Tip. Moderna], 1940.
Hernández Luna, Juan. "Movimiento anarco-fourierista entre el imperio y la reforma." *Cuadernos de Orientación Política*, no. 4 (April 1956), pp. 19–20.
————. "Los precursores intelectuales de la revolución mexicana." *Filosofía y Letras* 30, nos. 57–59 (January–December 1955): 279–317.
Hobsbawm, Eric. *Primitive Rebels: Studies in Archaic Forms of Social Movement in the 19th and 20th Centuries.* Manchester: University Press, 1959.
————, and George Rudé. *Captain Swing: A Social History of the Great English Agricultural Uprising of 1830.* New York: Pantheon Books, 1968.
Horowitz, Irving L. *The Anarchists.* New York: Dell Publishing Co., 1964.
Huitrón, Jacinto. *Cinquentenario de la Casa del Obrero, 1912–1962.* Mexico City, 1962.

————. *Orígenes e historia del movimiento obrero en México.* Mexico City: Editores Mexicanos Unidos, 1975.

Jackson, J. Hampden. *Marx, Proudhon and European Socialism.* London: English University Press, 1957.

Jellinek, Frank. *The Paris Commune.* New York: Grosset and Dunlop, 1965.

Joll, James. *The Anarchists.* New York: Grossets Universal Library, 1964.

Katz, Friedrich. "Labor Conditions on Haciendas in Porfirian Mexico: Some Trends and Tendencies." *Hispanic American Historical Review* 54 (February 1974): 1–47.

Keremitsis, Dawn. *La industria textil mexicana en el siglo XIX.* Mexico City: SepSetentas, 1973.

Krimerman, Leonard I., and Lewis Perry. *Patterns of Anarchy.* New York: Anchor Books, 1966.

Kropotkin, Peter Alekseevich. *The Conquest of Bread.* London: Chapman and Hall, 1906.

————. *The Essential Kropotkin.* Ed. Emile Capouya and Keitha Tompkins. New York: Liveright, 1975.

————. *Ethics: Origin and Development.* New York: Tudor, 1947.

————. *Fields, Factories and Workshops.* London: Hutchinson and Co., 1899.

————. *Memoirs of a Revolutionist.* Boston and New York: Houghton Mifflin Co., 1930.

————. *Mutual Aid: A Factor of Evolution.* Boston: Extending Horizon Books, 1955.

————. *The State: Its Historic Role.* London: "Freedom Office," 1898.

Lefebre, Georges. *The Coming of the French Revolution.* Princeton: Princeton University Press, 1947.

Lombardo Toledano, Vicente. *La libertad sindical en México.* Mexico City: Talleres Linotipográficos "La Lucha," 1926.

López Aparicio, Alfonso. *El movimiento obrero en México.* Mexico City: Editorial Jus, 1958.

McBride, George McCutchen. *The Land Systems of Mexico.* New York: Octagon Books, 1923.

Maclachlan, Colin. "The Crisis of Order in New Spain: A New Departure in the Administration of Justice." In *Mexican History Edition, The North Dakota Quarterly*, ed. John M. Hart. Grand Forks: University of North Dakota Press, 1972.

Magaña, General Gildardo. *Emiliano Zapata y el agrarismo en México.* 5 vols. Mexico City: Editorial Ruta, 1951.

Mancisidor, José. *Hidalgo y la cuestión agraria.* Mexico City: Taller Autográfico, 1944.

Medina Salazar, Lino. "Albores del movimiento obrero en México." *Historia y Sociedad*, Winter 1965.

Meyer, Jean. "Los obreros en la revolución mexicana: Los Batallones Rojos." *Historia Mexicana* 81 (July–September 1971): 1–37.

————. *Problemas campesinos y revueltas agrarias (1821–1910).* Mexico City, 1973.

Meyer, Michael. *Huerta: A Political Portrait*. Lincoln: University of Nebraska Press, 1972.

The Mexican Year Book. London: McCorquodale and Co., 1911.

Molina Enríquez, Andres. *Los grandes problemas nacionales*. Mexico City: Ed. del Instituto Nacional de la Juventud Mexicana, 1964.

Moreno Toscano, Alejandra, and Enrique Florescano. "El sector externo y la organización espacial regional de Mexico, 1521–1910." In *Proceedings of the IV International Congress of Mexican Studies*. Santa Monica, Calif., October 17–21, 1973.

Nettlau, Max. *Michael Bakunin*. 3 vols. London: Privately printed, 1896–1900.

Neymet, Marcela de. "El movimiento obrero y la revolución mexicana." *Historia y Sociedad*, Spring 1967.

Nicolau d'Olwer, Luis, et al. *El porfiriato: La vida económica*. 2 vols. La Historia Moderna de México Series. Mexico City: Editorial Hermes, 1965.

Niemeyer, E. V., Jr. *Revolution at Querétaro: The Mexican Constitutional Convention of 1916–1917*. Austin: University of Texas Press, 1974.

Nomad, Max. *Apostles of the Revolution*. Boston: Little, Brown, 1939.

———. *Rebels and Renegades*. New York: Macmillan Co., 1932.

Pacheco, General Carlos, Secretario de Fomento. *Memoria presentada al Congreso de la Unión por el secretario de Estado y del despacho de Fomento, Colonización, Industria y Comercio de la República Mexicana: Corresponde a los años transcurridos de enero de 1883 a junio de 1885*. Mexico City: Secretaría de Fomento, 1887.

Padua, Candido Donato. *Movimiento revolucionario 1906 en Veracruz*. Tlalpan, Mex., 1941.

Pérez Taylor, Rafael. *El socialismo en México*. Mexico City, 1913; reprinted, Mexico City: Centro de Estudios Históricos del Movimiento Obrero Mexicano, 1976.

Pérez y Hernández, José María. *Estadística de la República Mejicana*. Mexico City, 1862.

Phipps, Helen. *Some Aspects of the Agrarian Question in Mexico: A Historical Study*. *University of Texas Bulletin*, no. 2515. Austin, April 15, 1925.

Pletcher, David M. "The Fall of Silver in Mexico, 1870–1910, and Its Effects on American Investments." *Journal of Economic History* 18 (March 1958): 33–55.

———. *Rails, Mines and Progress: Seven American Promoters in Mexico, 1867–1911*. Ithaca: Cornell University Press, 1958.

Poblete Troncoso, Moisés, and Ben G. Burnett. *The Rise of the Latin American Labor Movement*. New York: Bookman Associates, 1960.

Powell. T. G. *El liberalismo y el campesinado en el centro de México, 1850 a 1876*. Mexico City: SepSetentas, 1974.

Proudhon, Pierre Joseph. *What Is Property?* New York: H. Fertig, 1966.

Pyziur, Eugene. *The Doctrine of Anarchism of M. A. Bakunin*. Milwaukee: Gateway, 1955.

Quirk, Robert E. *The Mexican Revolution, 1914–1915: The Convention of Aguascalientes*. Bloomington: University of Indiana Press, 1960.

Quiroz, Eleuterio. "Plan político y eminentemente social," Río Verde, San Luis Potosí, March 13, 1849. In "La propriedad en México: La reforma agraria," by Valentín Gama. *Revista Mexicana de Ingenería y Arquitectura*, nos. 6, 8, 9, 10 (1931).

Ramos Pedrueza, Rafael. *La lucha de clases a través de la historia de México.* 2 vols. Mexico City: Talleres Gráficos de la Nación, 1936, 1941.

Randall, Robert W. *Real del Monte: A British Mining Venture in Mexico.* Austin: University of Texas Press, 1972.

Rebelión y plan de los indios huaxtecos de Tantoyuca. Mexico City, 1856.

Rhodakanaty, Plotino C. *Cartilla socialista o sea el catecismo elemental de la escuela de Carlos Fourier–El falansterio.* Ed. José C. Valadés. Mexico City: Published by the editor, 1968.

———. *Neopanteísmo, consideración sobre el hombre y la naturaleza.* Mexico City: Imp. de Rivera, 1864.

Rodea, Marcelo N. *Historia del movimiento obrero ferrocarrilero en México (1890–1943).* Mexico City, 1943.

Rojas Coria, Rosendo. *Tratado de cooperativismo mexicano.* Mexico City: Fondo de Cultura Económica, 1952.

Rosenzweig, Fernando. "El desarrollo económico de México de 1877 a 1911." *Trimestre Económico* 37 (July–September 1965): 405–454.

———, et al. *El porfiriato: La vida económica.* 2 vols. Historia Moderna de México Series. Mexico City: Editorial Hermes, 1965.

Rudé, George. *The Crowd in the French Revolution.* Oxford: Clarendon Press, 1959.

Ruiz, Ramón Eduardo. *Labor and the Ambivalent Revolutionaries: Mexico, 1911–1923.* Baltimore: Johns Hopkins University Press, 1976.

Salazar, Rosendo. *Al rojo libertario.* Orizaba: Talleres Gráficos de la "Casa del Obrero Mundial," 1915.

———. *La carta del trabajo de la revolución mexicana: Fundamentos de una evolución.* Mexico City: Libro Mex Editores, 1960.

———. *La Casa del Obrero Mundial.* Mexico City: Costa-Amic, Editor, 1962.

———. *Hacia el porvenir.* Mexico City: Editores Avante, 1916.

———. *Historia de las luchas proletarias de México, 1923 a 1936.* 2 vols. Mexico City: Editorial Avante, 1938.

———. *México en pensamiento y en acción.* Mexico City: Editorial Avante, 1926.

———. *Los primeros de mayo en México.* Mexico City: Costa-Amic, Editor, 1965.

———, and José G. Escobedo. *Las pugnas de la gleba, 1907–1922.* 2 vols. Mexico City: Editorial Avante, 1923.

Santillán, Diego Abad de. *Ricardo Flores Magón, el apóstol de la revolución social mexicana.* Mexico City: Grupo Cultural "Ricardo Flores Magón," 1925.

Segunda conferencia internacional América, México, 1901–1902. Mexico City, 1903.

Seminario de la Historia Moderna de México. *Estadísticas económicas del*

porfiriato: Fuerza de trabajo y actividad por sectores. Mexico City: El Colegio de México, 1965.
Semo, Enrique, and Gloria Pedrero. "La vida en una hacienda-aserradero mexicana a principios del siglo XIX." *Investigación Económica,* January–March 1973, pp. 129–161.
Shulgovski, Anatoli. *México en la encrucijada de su historia.* Mexico City: Ediciones de Cultura Popular, 1968.
Silva Herzog, Jesús. *El agrarismo mexicano y la reforma agraria.* Mexico City: Fondo de Cultura Económica, 1959.
———. *Breve historia de la revolución mexicana.* 2 vols. Mexico City: Fondo de Cultura Económica, 1960.
———. *Trayectória ideológica de la revolución mexicana, 1910–1917.* Mexico City: Cuadernos Americanos, 1963.
Soboul, Albert. *The Sans Culottes.* New York: Anchor Books, 1972.
Tannenbaum, Frank. *Peace by Revolution—An Interpretation of Mexico.* New York: Columbia University Press, 1933.
Thomas, Hugh. "Agrarian Anarchist Collectives in the Spanish Civil War." In *A Century of Conflict, 1850–1950: Essays for A. J. P. Taylor,* ed. Martin Gilbert. New York: Atheneum, 1967.
Turner, Ethel Duffy. *Ricardo Flores Magón y el partido liberal mexicano.* Morelia: Editorial "Erandi," del Gobierno del Estado, 1960.
Turner, John Kenneth. *Barbarous Mexico.* Chicago, 1910; 2d ed., Austin: University of Texas Press, 1969.
U.S. Foreign Commerce Bureau. *Consular Reports,* 1879–1903.
Valadés, José C. "El 50 aniversario del Primer Congreso Obrero en América." *La Protesta,* 6 articles, January–April 1926, IISH.
———. "El hombre que derrumbó un régimen: Ricardo Flores Magón." *Todo,* March 5–August 6, 1942.
———. *Historia general de la revolución mexicana.* 3 vols. Mexico City: Manuel Quesada Brandi, Editor, 1963–1965.
———. "Noticia para la bibliografía anarquista en México." *La Protesta,* June 1927, IISH.
———. *El porfirismo: Historia de un régimen.* Vol. 1, *El nacimiento, 1876–1884.* Mexico City: Editorial Patria, 1941. Vol. 2, *El crecimiento.* Mexico City: Editorial Patria, n.d.
———. "Precursores del socialismo antiautoritario en México." *La Protesta,* May 22, 1928, IISH.
———. "Sobre los orígenes del movimiento obrero en México." *La Protesta,* June 1927, IISH.
———. *Topolobampo, la metropoli socialista del occidente.* Mexico City: Fondo de Cultura Económica, 1939.
Valverde y Téllez, Emeterio. *Crítica filosófica o estudio bibliográfico y crítico de las obras de filosofía.* Mexico City: Tip. de los Sucesores de Francisco Díaz de León, 1904.
Warman, Arturo. *. . . Y venimos a contradecir: Los campesinos de Morelos y el estado nacional.* Mexico City: Ediciones de la Casa Chata, 1976.
Wilkie, James. *The Mexican Revolution: Federal Expenditure and Social Change since 1910.* Berkeley: University of California Press, 1967.

Wolf, Eric R. *Peasant Wars of the Twentieth Century.* New York: Harper and Row, 1968.
Womack, John. *Zapata and the Mexican Revolution.* New York: Vintage, 1970.
Woodcock, George. *Anarchism: A History of Libertarian Ideas and Movements.* New York: World Publishing Co., 1962.
————. *Pierre Joseph Proudhon.* New York: Macmillan Co., 1956.
————, and Ivan Avakumovic. *The Anarchist Prince: A Biography of Peter Kropotkin.* London: Boardman, 1950.

Periodicals and Newspapers

Acción, Mexico City, 1919–1920.
Acción Mundial, Mexico City, 1916.
Afirmación, Buenos Aires, 1928.
Alba Roja, Mexico City, 1912.
Alba Roja, Zacatecas, 1918.
El Antireeleccionista, Mexico City, 1909–1910.
Ariete, Organo de la Casa del Obrero Mundial, Mexico City, 1915.
El Atalaya, Mexico City, 1923.
Aurora Social, Hermosillo, 1920.
Aurora Social, Monterrey, 1918.
¡Avante! Villa Cecilia, Tamaulipas, 1928–1930.
El Azote, Durango, 1917.
Bandera Roja, Mexico City, 1921.
El Colmillo Público, Mexico City, 1905–1906.
La Comuna, Mexico City, 1874.
La Convención Radical, Mexico City, 1886–1900.
El Craneoscopio, Periódico Frenológico y Científico, Mexico City, 1874.
CROM, Mexico City, 1930.
El Debate, Mexico City, 1910–1911.
La Democracia, Mexico City, 1872–1873.
El Demócrata, Mexico City, 1924.
Diario del Imperio, Mexico City, 1865.
Diario Oficial, Mexico City, 1906–1910.
El Dictamen, Veracruz, 1922.
Emancipación Obrera, Mexico City, 1914.
Evolución, Zacatecas, 1917.
Excelsiór, Mexico City, 1903 and 1907.
Fuerza y Cerebro, Tampico, 1918.
Germinal, Tampico, 1918.
Grito Rojo, Aguascalientes, 1918.
El Hijo del Ahuizote, Mexico City, 1890–1903.
El Hijo del Trabajo, Mexico City, 1876–1886.
La Huelga, Mexico City, 1875.
Ideas, Mexico City, 1914.
El Imparcial, Mexico City, 1900–1913.

La Internacional, Mexico City, 1878.
Lucha, Mexico City, 1913.
Lucha Social, Saltillo, 1918.
Luz, Mexico City, 1917–1920 and 1935.
Mexican Mining Journal, Mexico City, 1908–1916.
El Monitor Republicano, Mexico City, various years.
Nuestra Palabra, Organo de la CGT, Mexico City, 1922–1925.
Nuestros Ideales, Mexico City, 1922.
Nueva Era, Mexico City, 1912–1913.
Nueva Patria, Mexico City, 1914.
El Obrero Internacional, Mexico City, 1874.
El Obrero Liberal, Mexico City, 1913.
El País, Mexico City, 1900–1912.
La Paz, Chilpancingo, 1873.
El Pequeño Grande, Villa Cecilia, Tamaulipas, 1919–1921.
Pluma Roja, Periódico Anarquista, Los Angeles, 1915.
La Protesta, Buenos Aires, 1921–1929.
La Protesta, Lima, Peru, 1934.
Punto Rojo, Del Rio, Texas, 1909.
El Rebelde, Los Angeles, October 20, 1917.
Regeneración, Mexico City, Saint Louis, and Los Angeles, 1900–1911.
*Regeneración, Segunda Epoca, Organo de la Federación Anarquista Mexi-
    cana,* Mexico City, 1937–1962.
Rendención, Guadalajara, 1928–1929.
Resurgimiento, Puebla, 1921–1923.
La Revolución Social, Mexico City, 1922–1923.
La Revolución Social, Puebla, 1878–1879.
Siempre, Mexico City, 1972.
El Siglo XIX, Mexico City, various years.
El Sindicalista, Mexico City, 1913.
El Socialista, Mexico City, 1871–1886.
Supplemento de Siempre, Mexico City, 1972.
El Tiempo, Mexico City, 1911.
Tierra y Libertad, Mexico City, 1936 and 1958.
Tinta Roja, Mexico City, 1914.
El Tipógrafo Mexicano, Mexico City, 1911–1912.
Todo, Mexico City, 1934, 1942, 1945, 1953.
El Tornillo, Mexico City, 1937.
El Trabajador, Mexico City, 1921.
Trabajo, Mexico City, 1933.
Trabajo, Montevideo, 1923.
Trabajo Libre, Mexico City, 1919.
Tribuna Obrera, San Luis Potosí, 1934.
Tribuna Roja, San Luis Potosí, 1923.
Tribuna Roja, Tampico, 1916.
La Vanguardia, Orizaba, 1915.
Vida Libre, Tampico, 1918.
La Voz de México, Mexico City, various years.

Interviews

Bernal, Nicolas T. Mexico City, October 31, 1968.
Gasca, General Celestino. Mexico City, August 19, 1969.
Koniecki, Dieter. Mexico City, August 16, 1968.
Matta Reyes, Antonio. Tacubaya, Mexico City, July 8, 1975.
Salazar, Rosendo. Tlalnepantla, August 10, 1969.
Valadés, José C. Oaxtepec, November 6, 1969, and Mexico City, August 13, 1971.

Index

Abeja, La (factory): workers at, unionize, 46; site of CGT-CROM worker battles, 171–172
Acayucan (Ver.): 1906 uprising at, 93
acción directa: used by Lucha, 116–118; and Dr. Atl, 136; rejected by Calles regime, 116; advocated and used by CGT, 171–174; rejected, 175–177
ácratas: defined by Lucha, 119
Actopan (Hgo.): Chávez López defeated at, 40–41
Acuantla, San Francisco: and Chávez López, 33, 34; deportations from, 34–35
agrarianism: and anarchism, 15; at Río Verde, 62–72; suppression of, 77–78; mentioned, 37, 41, 52, 60, 82, 181
agraristas: of Casa join Zapata, 130–131, 171; mentioned, 69, 82
Aguascalientes (Ags.): railroad workers in, organize, 84; syndicates of, 127; Casa created at, 136; new anarchist groups in, 156; alternative to CROM urged in, 159
Aguirre, Rodolfo: signs Casa-Constitutionalist pact, 133; member of CSL, 161
Ahualulco (S.L.P.): versus Hacienda de las Bocas, 67–68
AIT. *See* International Association of Workers
Alameda Park: 141
alcabala: elimination of, 87
Aldana, Vicente: Monterrey Casa leader, 127
alhóndiga: during *tumulto* of 1692, 43
Allen, José: deported CGT member, 160
Almarás, Judge José María: and investigation of Cuéllar, 34–35
American anarchists: Knights of Labor, 80; in mining camps, 84; at Cananea, 91–92; and Tampico IWW, 157–160; CGT members deported, 160
American Federation of Labor: CROM attends convention of, 158–159; accused of manipulation, 160
Amsterdam: headquarters of AIT, 120
Anaconda Copper Company: part owner at Cananea, 91

anarchism: European background and development of, 3–12; in countryside, 15, 62–71; and urban working class, 17; and Rhodakanaty, 19–28; growth of, 48, 53, 57–59; in Círculo, 49; and cooperativism, 50; weakness of, 74–75; and Pan American Conference, 84–85; resurgence of, 85–87; of PLM, 89; of Ricardo Flores Magón, 88; of Enrique Flores Magón, 90; and Río Blanco, 93–99; as cause of Revolution, 103; of Amadeo Ferrés, 104–108; of López Dónez, 109; antipolitics of, 119–120; toward anarchosyndicalism, 120–121; in *El Sindicalista*, 123; defined, 123; goals of, 127; and Germinal, 157; as libertarian communism, 160–161; of CGT, 173; and FAM, 176–177; causation of, 178; summary on, 179–183; mentioned, 133
anarchist militias: ineffectiveness of, 10–11; of Casa, 127; in Revolution, 133–135
Anarchist Socialist Revolutionary Review (Boston): 79
anarchists: first urban *agraristas*, 15; impact of, on urban labor movement, 16; distinguished from "socialists," 16; as precursors of Revolution, 17; and Chávez López, 39–42; and urban workers, 44–46, 47, 103; of La Social, 46; form *sociedades de resistencia*, 49; and Sociedad, 50; and collectivism, 51–53; oppose 1876 civil war, 56; dominate Sucursal and Congreso, 57; oppose Díaz and García de la Cadena presidential bids, 57–58; weakness of, 74–75; rallies of, in Mexico City, 75; strength of, 76; repression of, 77–81; of PLM, 88–102; organize Confederación Tipográfico de México, 107; as *obreros intelectuales*, 107–111; create Luz and the Casa, 111–114; jailed, 114; disrupt Gran Liga, 116; beliefs of, 124; new groups of, surface, 156–157; form CGT, 159; support of agrarian movement by, 171; achievements of, 179–181; mentioned, 178
anarchosyndicalism: as mature indus-